A FIELD GUIDE TO LOTUS 1-2-3
Release 4 for Windows

Forrest Harlow
Angelo State University

boyd & fraser publishing company

I(T)P An International Thomson Publishing Company

Danvers • Albany • Bonn • Boston • Cincinnati • Detroit • London • Madrid • Melbourne
Mexico City • New York • Paris • San Francisco • Singapore • Tokyo • Toronto • Washington

Acquisitions Editor: Anne E. Hamilton
Production Editor: Patty Stephan
Composition: Rebecca Evans & Associates
Interior Design: Rebecca Evans & Associates
Cover Design: Rebecca Lemna/Lloyd Lemna Design
Manufacturing Coordinator: Tracy Megison
Marketing Manager: Daphne Meyers

bf ©1995 by boyd & fraser publishing company
A division of International Thomson Publishing Inc.

I(T)P The ITP™ logo is a trademark under license.

Printed in the United States of America

This book is printed on recycled, acid-free paper that meets Environmental Protection Agency standards.

For more information, contact boyd & fraser publishing company:

boyd & fraser publishing company
One Corporate Place • Ferncroft Village
Danvers, Massachusetts 01923, USA

International Thomson Editores
Campose Eliseos 385, Piso 7
Col. Polanco
11560 Mexico D.F. Mexico

International Thomson Publishing Europe
Berkshire House 168-173
High Holborn
London, WC1V 7AA, England

International Thomson Publishing GmbH
Konigswinterer Strasse 418
53227 Bonn, Germany

Thomas Nelson Australia
102 Dodds Street
South Melbourne 3205
Victoria, Australia

International Thomson Publishing Asia
221 Henderson Road
#05-10 Henderson Building
Singapore 0315

Nelson Canada
1120 Birchmont Road
Scarborough, Ontario
Canada M1K 5G4

International Thomson Publishing Japan
Hirakawacho Kyowa Building, 3F
2-2-1 Hirakawacho
Chiyoda-ku, Tokyo 102, Japan

1 2 3 4 5 6 7 8 9 10 BN 8 7 6 5 4

Library of Congress Cataloging-in-Publication Data

Harlow, Forrest.
  A field guide to Lotus 1-2-3 release 4 for Windows / Forrest
Harlow.
     p.   cm.
  Includes index.
  ISBN 0-87709-863-8
  1. 1-2-3 for Windows. 2. Business—Computer programs.
3. Electronic spreadsheets.   I. Title.
HF5548.4.L67H366   1995
005.369—dc20   94-39111
                                                    CIP

Text with 3.5" SMART disk: ISBN 0-87709-862-X

Contents

PART ONE   **BASIC LOTUS 1-2-3**

Chapter 3   **Basics of Functions, Formulas, and Formatting** **47**

PART TWO   **INTERMEDIATE LOTUS 1-2-3**

PART THREE   **ADVANCED LOTUS 1-2-3**

Chapter 13   **Macro Basics** **243**

Preface

A Field Guide to Lotus 1-2-3 Release 4 for Windows, is designed for use in a first course in spreadsheet applications. Most of the examples and problems relate to the world of business, but they do not assume a technical background on the part of the students.

TEXTBOOK APPROACH AND ORGANIZATION

1-2-3 for Windows is a very complex program. Most texts create "information overload" by introducing a broad range of terms, concepts, techniques, and commands before the student has developed any intellectual context for understanding and applying them.

This text follows a logical progression from simple to complex 1-2-3 applications. The introduction of 1-2-3 features follows the same plan—new features are introduced gradually, as the student's frame of reference expands.

This book is designed primarily for use in a classroom setting. It assumes that the student is using 1-2-3 in a microcomputer laboratory and that the instructor will orient the students to the necessary hardware. Consequently the book does not cover keyboard layout, diskette handling, computer innards, or the grubby details of installing Lotus 1-2-3 on the computer.

The text is broken into three parts. Part One covers topics that, in the author's opinion, even casual 1-2-3 users should understand. These chapters are designed to be covered in sequential order.

Part Two covers topics that, although widely useful, are not likely to be as universally applicable as those in Part One. The chapters in Part Two can be covered in any order.

Part Three covers macro programming. The details of macro programming are of most interest to those who aspire to be "power users." For a thorough introduction to macro programming, the chapters in Part Three should be covered in sequence. However, the final chapter can be used without the support of the earlier chapters in the section. It presents MACTOOLS, a unique macro application development system that takes most of the pain out of macro programming.

END-OF-CHAPTER EXERCISES

Some of the end-of-chapter exercises in this book are traditional, stated problems and cases. Others are disk-based, self-grading worksheets.

Standard Exercises

The traditional cases and problems require you to begin from a clear worksheet and type in all the requested labels and formulas. These exercises give you practice in setting up worksheets "from scratch." They reinforce the points made in the body of the chapter. Don't fail to do the exercises your instructor assigns you. You can learn a lot about Lotus 1-2-3 by listening to lectures and reading the text, but mastering the package definitely is not a spectator sport.

Self-Checking Exercises on Disk

The first twelve chapters have accompanying SMART exercises. SMART is an acronym for Self-Marking, Auto-Recording Templates. The disk in the back of this book contains 39 SMART exercises. To work with a SMART exercise, you have to open the file, read the instructions that will appear on your screen, and carry out the instructions.

The SMART exercises contain programs that will automatically check your work, assign a score, and maintain a log file of your progress. They also articulate with the instructor's monitoring software.

Complete details on how to use the SMART exercises can be found in Appendix A. Be sure to read Appendix A before using the SMART disk!

INSTRUCTOR'S RESOURCES

Available through the instructor's manual is a diskette that contains solved versions of all the SMART problems. The diskette also contains a macro-driven SMARTLOG worksheet for monitoring student performance on the SMART problems.

The SMARTLOG Worksheet

The instructor's SMARTLOG worksheet provides an automated method for recording and summarizing student performance on all assigned SMART problems. The instructor simply selects a computer for grade-recording and executes SMARTLOG. When the instructor places SMARTLOG in "log" mode, SMARTLOG automatically performs the following clerical duties:

1. Creates and updates an alphabetical class roster based on information inside student's SMART problems.
2. Records student scores on assigned SMART problems.
3. Sums total points achieved by each student.

In "log" mode, SMARTLOG runs in an endless loop which can be broken only by password. The instructor sets up SMARTLOG on any chosen computer, and students then are responsible for logging their grades. By using SMART-LOG, instructors can monitor student progress electronically. No manual grading, or manual grade-recording, is necessary.

SMART Problems as Testing Vehicles

Among their other virtues, the SMART problems are an excellent test bank. The instructor can assign some problems as homework and reserve others for use as hands-on tests. The test results can be logged with SMARTLOG, of course. The Instructor's Manual provides further details about the SMARTLOG worksheet.

A WORD TO STUDENTS: 1-2-3 AND THE REAL WORLD

Lotus 1-2-3 and similar programs are widely used in almost every profession from accounting to zoology. In many career fields, a thorough knowledge of spreadsheet software such as 1-2-3 can give you a competitive edge. If you are a business student, you are particularly likely to find yourself using 1-2-3 as an analytical and forecasting tool.

You probably will need about 100 hours of study and hands-on work to thoroughly master 1-2-3. Professionally speaking, they may be the most profitable 100 hours you ever spend. Mastering Lotus 1-2-3 is like equipping your mind with track cleats. Good luck.

Acknowledgments

Thank you to the following instructors who reviewed the manuscript and/or SMART disks. Your comments were helpful in shaping this text.

Peg Babcock
William Rainey Harper College

Tom Bankston
Angelo State University

Catherine J. Brotherton
Riverside Communicty College

Chris Cartes
Indiana Vocational Technical College

John Fender
Angelo State University

Thomas S. George
Housatonic Community College

Nettie F. Green
Shelby M. Jackson Memorial Technical Institute

Rose Laird
Northern Virginia Community College

Della Lee-Lien
Quinnipiac College

Philip Levinson
Jefferson College

Jerry Peters
Lambuth University

Sonny Stires
Palomar College

Linda Woolard
Southern Illinois University

Forrest Harlow
October 1994

PART ONE
BASIC LOTUS 1-2-3

The six chapters in this section cover
skills that all 1-2-3 users need to know.
After mastering this section, you will be
able to create, format, and print basic
1-2-3 worksheets and charts.

Getting Started

OBJECTIVES After studying this chapter, you should know how to:

- Define the basic Lotus 1-2-3 terminology and techniques.
- Use the mouse and keyboard to enter data.
- Save and retrieve files.
- Use the online Help facility.

A WORD ABOUT DOS AND WINDOWS When you first turn on your computer, a program called the Disk Operating System (DOS or MS-DOS) automatically takes control. DOS has been around for many years and probably is responsible for more ulcers than any other computer program. In its basic form, DOS simply checks out your computer's circuitry and then shows you a system prompt, like C>. DOS then waits for you to type a command it understands, such as DIR /W. If you do not know DOS commands, you are out of luck. DOS is not a very user-friendly operating system.

Fortunately your computer holds another more advanced operating system program called Windows. In the computer's memory, Windows sits on top of DOS, supplying a graphical user interface (GUI).

When Windows is running, you make the computer work by selecting icons or menu choices, rather than by typing DOS commands. In most cases, the icons are some sort of memory-jogging picture that suggests what they are for.

OF MICE AND WINDOWS In Windows applications, most users rely on a mouse to point to and select actions. However, if you do not have a mouse, take heart. You can operate 1-2-3 without one. In fact, many expert 1-2-3 users seldom touch their mice. Appendix E shows the keyboard equivalents of mouse actions.

If a mouse is attached to your computer, you will see an arrow on the screen. The arrow is called the **mouse pointer**. Grasp the mouse in your palm and scoot it in any direction. Notice that the onscreen mouse pointer moves in lockstep with the physical mouse movements.

A typical mouse has two buttons on top. By scooting the mouse pointer to an onscreen object and clicking the left mouse button, you can select the object. For some operations, you have to double-click the left mouse button. To **double-click** means to quickly press the left button twice while holding the mouse motionless.

LAUNCHING 1-2-3 FOR WINDOWS

This book assumes that the Windows operating system and the 1-2-3 program already have been installed on your computer's hard disk. Depending on how your computer is set up, starting Lotus 1-2-3 may be as simple as pointing to the Lotus icon and double-clicking on it. However, if you see only the bare system prompt, (like C:\> or C>), you will have to type these commands:

C:\>**CD\WINDOWS**↵   *(To make WINDOWS the default directory.)*

C:\WINDOWS>**WIN**↵   *(To launch the Windows system.)*

Assuming 1-2-3 for Windows is installed on your computer in a typical configuration, after you launch (start) Windows, you should see a screen like the one shown in Figure 1.1. To launch 1-2-3, double-click on the 1-2-3 icon. That is, move the mouse pointer onto the icon, hold the mouse still, and depress the left mouse button twice in rapid succession.

FIGURE 1.1
Starting 1-2-3

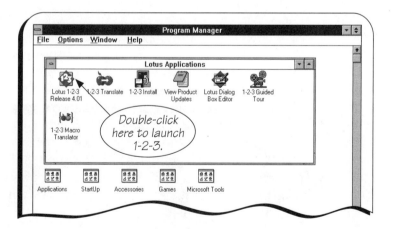

WORKSHEET LAYOUT AND TERMINOLOGY

When the 1-2-3 program is loaded into memory, you will see a display like Figure 1.2.

FIGURE 1.2
The Basic
1-2-3 Screen

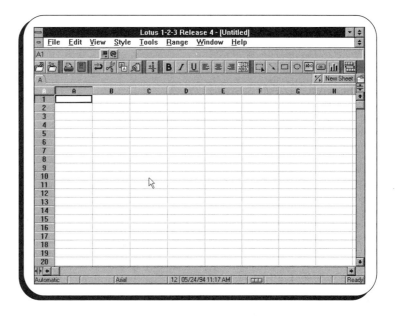

The 1-2-3 screen may look complex, but remember that you don't have to understand everything all at once. You can do useful work with 1-2-3 after mastering only a few basic elements. After you are comfortable with the basic elements, you can expand your horizons to include the fancier stuff.

The Control Panel

The **control panel** consists of three lines of information. The top line of the control panel (also the top line of the screen) is the **title bar**.

The Title Bar

Figure 1.3 shows the parts of the title bar.

FIGURE 1.3
Elements of
the Title Bar

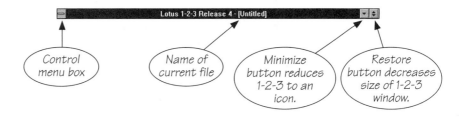

The title bar contains control boxes, the Lotus 1-2-3 name, and the name of the current worksheet file. Don't click on the control boxes yet; we are not ready to use them. An illustrated summary of control box uses appears later in this chapter.

The Main Menu

The **main menu** is the second line in the control panel. It contains a control box at either end, with the menu sandwiched between the boxes. Each menu item has an underlined letter called a **hot key**. Figure 1.4 shows the main menu elements.

FIGURE 1.4

The Main Menu

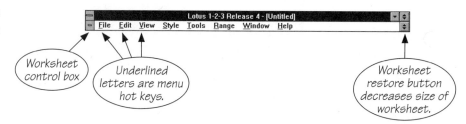

To select a menu item with the mouse, simply click on it. To select a menu item from the keyboard, hold down the ALT key while tapping the hot key of your choice.

When you select a menu item, a pull-down menu appears. For example, if you select File, your screen will look like Figure 1.5.

FIGURE 1.5

Selecting a
Menu Choice

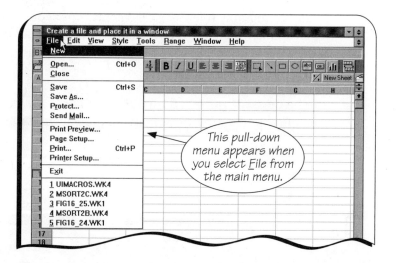

In the pull-down menu, you can click a choice with the mouse or press a hot key (an underlined letter). If you want to cancel a menu choice before completing it, move the mouse pointer into the worksheet grid and click, or hit the ESC key.

The 1-2-3 menu works just like the menu in a restaurant. The restaurant menu offers main menu choices such as meats, vegetables, desserts, and so forth. Each main category such as meat has subchoices and perhaps sub-subchoices, for example, meat/steak/well done. The payoff comes when you work your way to the end of your selected path. In our case, 1-2-3 is your attentive waiter; figuratively speaking, all you have to do is snap your fingers for a menu and point to the successive choices you want.

Some 1-2-3 menu choices show "super-shortcut" options to their right. For example, in Figure 1.5, the Open choice shows CTRL+O, which means to hold down the CTRL key and press the letter "oh." If you choose, you can use the super-shortcuts instead of going through the menu.

The Classic Menus

If you are familiar with DOS releases of 1-2-3, you may be feeling technologically challenged by now. Not to worry. The slash key and the colon key bring up "classic" 1-2-3 menus. Figure 1.6 shows how the classic slash menu looks in Release 4.

If you are upgrading from earlier versions of 1-2-3, you may want to use the classic menus to stay productive while you are learning the Release 4 menu system.

FIGURE 1.6

The Classic
1-2-3 Slash Menu

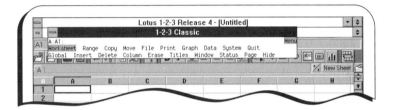

The Edit Line

The **edit line** is the third line of the control panel. Figure 1.7 shows the components of the edit line.

FIGURE 1.7

The Edit Line

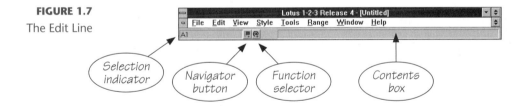

The leftmost box on the edit line is the **selection indicator**. It shows the address of the currently selected cell or the name of certain other items. Currently the selection indicator shows A1. There are two icons on the edit line: the **navigator** and the **function selector**. We will discuss their uses later. Notice the box to the right of the icons. It is called the **contents box**. When you enter data in the worksheet, the data appears in the contents box as you enter it.

The Icon Line

The **icon line** (Figure 1.8) is immediately below the control panel. Currently you see the default icon palette; there are several others. Each of the icons holds a shortcut for performing common 1-2-3 operations. Whether or not you use the icons is up to you. Anything you can do with an icon, you also can do using the menu. However, you must use a mouse to access the icons. You cannot invoke them from the keyboard.

Icons are selectable only by mouse.

At this point, you already know how to select an icon—put the mouse pointer on it and click. However, before you begin clicking at random on one icon and another, you should investigate what a particular icon does. To get a preview of an icon's purpose, put the mouse pointer on it and hold down the *right* mouse button. A brief description of the icon's purpose appears in the title bar of the control panel (the topmost line of the screen).

The Horizontal and Vertical Scroll Bars

The horizontal and vertical scroll bars contain scroll arrows and scroll boxes. By clicking on a scroll arrow or by dragging a scroll box, you can move the screen display without moving the cellpointer. Figure 1.9 shows the layout of the horizontal scroll bar.

The Status Bar

The bottom line on the screen is the **status bar**. It displays the current date and time, several clickable selector buttons, which we will discuss later, and assorted status indicators that tell you the condition of certain keys and system states. Figure 1.9 shows the layout of the status bar.

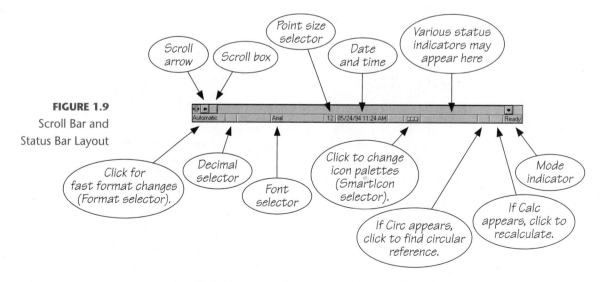

FIGURE 1.9

Scroll Bar and Status Bar Layout

Several status indicators may appear in the status bar's indicator area. The status indicators tell you the state of the keyboard and other system conditions. Table E.1 in Appendix E lists the status indicators.

Note the Mode indicator on the right end of the status bar. Unlike the status indicators, the Mode indicator always stays on the screen, but it does not always display the same message. The Mode indicator changes in response to your actions. Table E.2 in Appendix E lists the modes that can appear in the Mode indicator.

THE WORKSHEET WINDOW

The large gridded area is the heart of the **worksheet window**—a matrix of columns and rows. The letters across the top mark the columns. The numbers down the left side of the screen mark the rows. Figure 1.10 shows columns A through H and rows 1 through 20.

FIGURE 1.10
The Worksheet Window

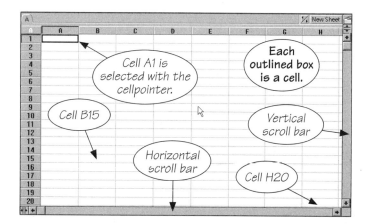

The Cellpointer

The hollow rectangle (currently positioned at A1) is called the **cellpointer**. The cellpointer is not fixed in place; it is movable.

Cells and Cell Selection

The intersection of a column and a row is called a **cell**. Cells are like pigeonholes where you can store information. Figure 1.10 displays 160 different cells. The intersection of column A and row 1 (referred to as A1, for short) is a cell; H20 is a cell; and so forth.

BASIC CELLPOINTER MOVEMENT

Think of the cellpointer as a portable door into the cells of the worksheet. To type text, numbers, or formulas into a cell, you have to **select** the cell by positioning the cellpointer—the "door"—on top of it. Any numbers or characters you type from the keyboard are routed into the cell you selected.

Arrow Keys versus the Mouse

The cellpointer can be moved around the worksheet in several ways. If you are a mouse enthusiast, simply roll the mouse. The mouse pointer, in the form of an arrow, moves as you roll; to select a cell, click the left mouse button while the arrow is inside the cell.

If you prefer the keyboard to the mouse, use the arrow keys to move the cellpointer. Many seasoned 1-2-3 users say the arrow keys are faster because they can be reached without removing a hand from the keyboard.

Try pushing the down arrow. Note that the cellpointer moves down one row, to cell A2. Also the selection indicator changes to indicate that the cellpointer now is sitting on cell A2, as shown in Figure 1.11.

FIGURE 1.11

Cellpointer Movement

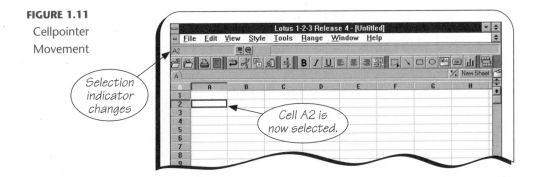

Now try pushing the left arrow. 1-2-3 beeps at you to indicate that you can't go left because you are already in the leftmost column of the worksheet. Spend a minute or two using the arrow keys (or rolling and clicking your mouse) to move the cellpointer around the part of your worksheet you can see on the screen. See if you can move the cellpointer in a stair-step pattern from A2 to H20.

Going HOME

Cell A1, the upper left corner of the worksheet, is called the **home location**. A1 is the natural starting point for building a worksheet.

After you get your cellpointer to H20, press the HOME key. Pressing HOME always sends your cellpointer "home" to cell A1, no matter where it was before.

There also is a HOME icon (on the sheet auditing palette). Unless your hand already is on the mouse, however, you probably will find it faster to press the HOME key than to find and click the icon.

For small 1-2-3 applications, you can move the cellpointer around quite nicely with just the arrow keys. As your applications grow larger, the fast-movement cellpointer keys become more important. For example, if you construct an integrated, multiperiod financial model with interlocking income statements and balance sheets, you easily could use 24 columns and a hundred rows. Under those circumstances, it pays to know how to use fast-movement techniques.

Using END to Find Boundaries

The combination of the END key and any arrow key sends the cellpointer from wherever it is to the boundary between blank and nonblank cells, or else to the worksheet perimeter in the direction indicated by the arrow key. Our empty worksheet has no nonblank/blank boundaries. *All* the cells are blank. Consequently pressing END and any arrow key sends the cellpointer around the perimeter of the sheet.

Select cell A1 (by moving your cellpointer to A1). Press the END key; then press the right arrow key. Your cellpointer instantly travels to cell IV1, the far upper right corner of the worksheet, 255 columns from A1. Note that you still are in row 1.

With your cellpointer on cell IV1, press END again, followed by the down arrow. The cellpointer pops down to cell IV8192, the lower right corner of the worksheet. Press END and the left arrow to get to the bottom left corner, cell A8192.

To get back to the HOME (A1) position, you can take your choice of cellpointer movement techniques:

1. Push the up arrow 8,191 times if you want to take the slow freight.
2. Press the END key, followed by the up arrow.
3. Press the HOME key.

Seven-League Boots: GOTO

The F5 key on the function keypad is called the GOTO key. There also is a GOTO icon. GOTO is used as a tool for making long jumps to specified locations in the worksheet. To use this tool, press the F5 key or click on the icon. Lotus displays a dialog box as shown in Figure 1.12.

FIGURE 1.12

The GOTO
Dialog Box

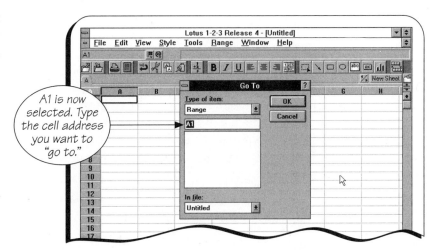

In the dialog box, type the cell address you want to send the cellpointer to. Then select OK or press ↵. Take a moment to practice sending your cellpointer to some exotic addresses such as AC2011 or IT517. Look carefully when you get there. Unless you develop some unusual 1-2-3 applications, this may be the last time you ever visit them!

When you get tired of jumping the cellpointer around the worksheet, send it back to A1, the HOME position. You can take your choice of any of the cellpointer-moving techniques we have discussed. Table 1.1 summarizes these techniques.

F5 is not the only function key used in 1-2-3; we will discuss the others in the appropriate context. Table E.3 of Appendix E lists all the function keys and their uses.

TABLE 1.1 **Basic Cellpointer Movement Methods**

Key	Effect
HOME	Moves the cellpointer to cell A1.
Arrow keys	Move the cellpointer up, down, right, or left one cell at a time.
PageUp, PageDown	Move the cellpointer up or down 20 rows.
Tab	Moves the cellpointer right one page.
Shift+Tab	Moves the cellpointer left one page.
END+arrow key	Moves the cellpointer to the boundary between blank and nonblank cells.
F5	Moves the cellpointer to far-distant cells in a single step.
Mouse	Click on the cell that you want to select. If the desired cell is off the screen, click on the scroll bar directional arrows or drag the scroll box to display the target area.

Worksheet Dimensions

As you saw in the previous section, the part of the worksheet you see when your cellpointer is in the HOME (A1) position is only a tiny part of the entire worksheet. There are actually 256 columns and 8192 rows within a worksheet.

1-2-3 also contains a third dimension. You can create up to 256 worksheets within a single file, much like putting additional tabs in a file folder. We begin exploring multiple worksheets in Chapter 3.

ENTERING LABELS AND NUMBERS

Label is 1-2-3 language for a text entry. Use the arrow keys (or mouse) to position your cellpointer on cell A2. Type the label Sales (but don't press the ⏎ key when you finish). As you type, the letters appear above the grid, in the contents box, and also in the current cell. Your worksheet now should look like Figure 1.13.

FIGURE 1.13
Entering Data

In the status bar, the Mode indicator has changed to Label. When you begin typing an entry, 1-2-3 examines the first character you type and judges whether you are typing labels or numeric data into a cell.

If the first key you press is an alphabetic character such as "S," 1-2-3 assumes that you are entering a label rather than numbers or formulas. Remember that "label" is the 1-2-3 term for a text entry.

Completing (or Canceling) an Entry

As you type, two more icons appear on the edit line—an X icon, and a Check icon. If you love the mouse, you can cancel an entry before completing it by clicking on the X icon, or you can confirm the entry by clicking on the Check icon. From the keyboard, you can cancel an entry before completing it by hitting the ESC key.

Instead of using the mouse, most users prefer to complete an entry by pressing the ⏎ key. When you press ⏎, the label Sales is placed in the current cell (the cell where the cellpointer is located). As Figure 1.14 indicates, the contents box also shows the contents of the current cell.

FIGURE 1.14

Completing an Entry

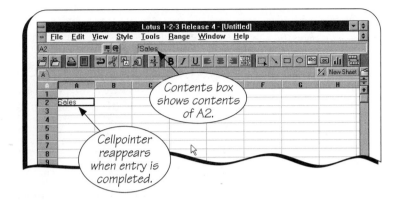

The label prefix (') in front of Sales in the contents box is just 1-2-3's way of remembering that cell A2 contains a text entry—a label—rather than a number or a formula. No label prefix shows up in the worksheet itself, but nevertheless 1-2-3 remembers cell B2 is a label whether your cellpointer is on the cell or not.

Move the cellpointer right to cell B2 (the simplest way is by pressing the right arrow). Notice that Sales disappears from the contents box because the cellpointer now is on a blank cell. The selection indicator always tells you what cell your cellpointer is sitting on, and the contents box always tells you the contents of the cell—that is, the word, number, or formula that is stored in the cell.

With your cellpointer on cell B2, type the number 245. Before you complete the entry, notice the Mode indicator. Previously, when you were typing a label into cell B2, the Mode indicator showed Label. Now 1-2-3 has sensed that you are typing a numeric entry because the first key you pressed was a numeric key. The Mode indicator displays Value. Your Lotus screen display should look like Figure 1.15.

FIGURE 1.15

Entering a Value

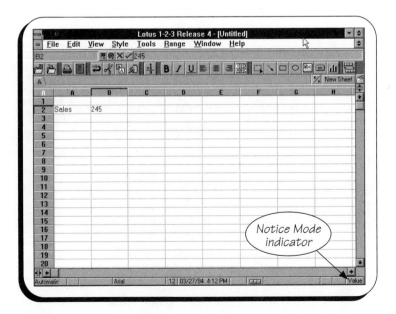

Now press ↵ (or select the Confirm icon with your mouse) to complete your entry into the worksheet at cell location B2. Look at the display of cells A2 and B2 in Figure 1.16.

FIGURE 1.16
Default Alignments

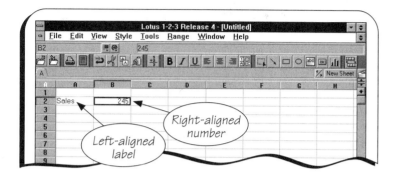

Alignment of Cell Contents

Notice that the label Sales in cell A2 is crowded against the left edge of cell A2, while the number 245 in cell B2 is crowded against the right edge of its cell. By default, labels go to the left and numbers go to the right. If we wanted, we could shift the label Sales or the number 245 to the middle or right side of their cells. The 1-2-3 term for how cell contents are positioned in a cell is **alignment**, or **justification**. Cell entries are said to be left-aligned if they look like A2; they are right-aligned if they look like B2.

Now enter the label Expenses in cell A3. Enter the number 121 in cell B3. Enter the label Profit in cell A4. Then move your cellpointer to cell B4. At this point your worksheet should look like Figure 1.17.

FIGURE 1.17
A Simple
Income Statement

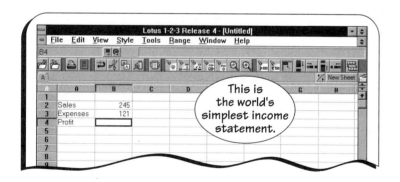

ENTERING FORMULAS: A FIRST TASTE OF 1-2-3 POWER

Let's assume that in cell B4 you want to compute profit (which is computed as the sales value minus the expenses value). With your cellpointer on cell B4, type **+B2–B3** and enter it in the cell. In cell B4, you will see 124, which is the result of subtracting 121 from 245. Your worksheet should look like Figure 1.18.

FIGURE 1.18

A Simple Formula

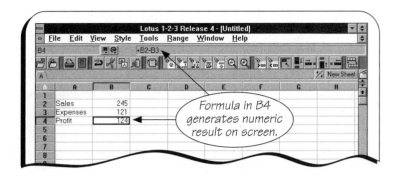

Formula in B4 generates numeric result on screen.

Now put the cellpointer on cell B2. With one eye on cell B4, enter the number 540 in B2. Cell B4 automatically changes its value to reflect the *new data* that you placed in cell B2.

You have just created a **formula.** We will have a great deal more to say about formulas, but this simple example shows the central idea: When you place a formula in a cell (as we did in B4), that formula constantly looks at other cells and recomputes its value when the values in the other cells change.

SAVING A WORKSHEET TO DISK

At this point, your worksheet file exists only in the computer's memory, also known as **random access memory**, or **RAM**. Think of RAM as the electronic equivalent of a cheap hotel room—it is only a temporary, and none too safe, place to keep data. We need to copy the file to a safer and permanent location. First, however, we need to make sure 1-2-3 knows where to store the copy of your file.

Key Concepts About Drives and Directories

Your computer has a number of file storage locations. It has at least one diskette drive (the A: drive), and at least one hard disk (the C: drive). The hard disk (C:) typically is subdivided into dozens of separate storage locations called **sub-directories**. Diskettes in the A: drive usually are not subdivided into subdirectories; they contain only a single directory.

As you can see, there are lots of separate storage locations where 1-2-3 could place your file. Before you actually save your file, you should specify the worksheet directory (the standard drive and directory or subdirectory for files). Once you specify that worksheet directory, then 1-2-3 will remember to use it for saving (and retrieving) files until you change it again.

Changing the Worksheet Directory

To change the worksheet directory to the A drive, select Tools User Setup. The User Setup dialog box appears. In the Worksheet directory box, delete the existing text and type A:\, as shown in Figure 1.19.

FIGURE 1.19
Using Tools User
Setup to Specify the
Worksheet Directory

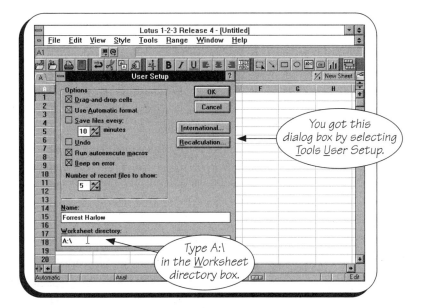

Click on the OK button to complete the job. We assume that you want to save your files to a diskette in the A: drive.

You also can specify the drive and directory during the actual file-saving process, but some classic menu file operations (such as those used in SMART problem-checking code) may not work as expected.

First-time Save

Before saving, be sure your floppy disk is in the diskette drive. Then click on the File Save icon or select File Save from the menu. Your screen should look like Figure 1.20.

FIGURE 1.20

Anatomy of the
File Save Dialog Box

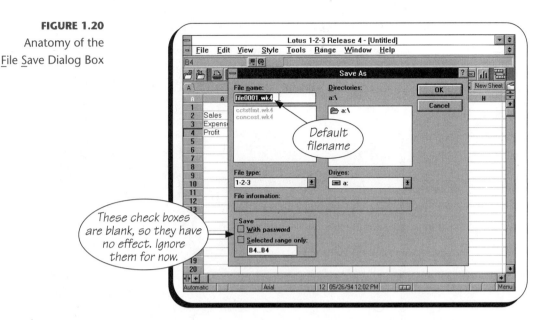

Specifying a Filename

The dialog box also contains a default (preselected) filename, file0001.wk4. You seldom if ever will want to use the default filename. Type MYFIRST into the filename box (uppercase or lowercase doesn't matter).

Then click on OK or press ↵ to complete the file save. The file is saved to the root directory of the A: drive, and the title bar changes to "Lotus 1-2-3 Release 4 – [MYFIRST.WK4]." 1-2-3 automatically supplies the default filename extension, .WK4.

1-2-3 Release 4 can use files created by earlier releases. However, earlier releases of 1-2-3 will not be able to use Release 4 files if you save them with the .WK4 extension.

Subsequent Saves

After you have saved a file the first time, 1-2-3 does not bother you with unnecessary questions when you save again. For example, if you now click on the File Save icon with your mouse, or select File Save, 1-2-3 immediately saves the latest version of MYFIRST.WK4 to disk, no questions asked.

A Word About Dialog Boxes

Dialog boxes are a standard feature of the menu system, including the File Save menu. We already have used them, but let's take a minute to look in more detail at how they work.

The dialog box title bar contains a control box for displaying the dialog box menu, the name of the dialog box, and a question mark button. If you are using a mouse, you do not need the menu. The question mark button brings up onscreen help about the dialog box. You can click on the title bar and drag the dialog box in case it is covering a part of the screen you need to see.

Many dialog boxes have check boxes and option buttons, which you click to enable or disable. To enter data in a text box, click on it and type your entry. To complete a dialog box action, click on the OK button or hit ENTER. To make the control box go away without doing anything, select the Cancel button or press the ESC key.

CORRECTING TYPOS

Correction by Type-over

A crude but effective way to correct a typo is simply to type over it. For example, if you accidentally typed Sules in cell A2, instead of Sales, you could move the cellpointer to A2 and type the correct label, Sales. The new, correct entry would wipe out the previous entry. The same technique works for numbers, of course.

Correction by Editing

If the bad entry is long and complex, it is usually easier to edit the entry than to retype it. To edit a cell, move the cellpointer to it and press the F2 key. Use the left arrow to move the edit cursor to the bad part; hit the DEL key to delete the bad characters; and type the corrections. Then hit ENTER.

ERASING A CELL'S CONTENTS

The Right Way

If you want to wipe out the contents of a cell and leave it totally empty, make the cell current (by putting the cellpointer on it) and hit the DEL key. To try this technique, enter your first name in cell E1. After entering it, hit the DEL key. Your name will disappear from the cell; E1 now is as clean as if you had never placed anything in it.

The Wrong Way

If you place the cellpointer on a cell, hit the spacebar, and hit ↵, the cell may *look* empty to a human eye, but it is not empty in the eye of the computer. The spacebar writes a space character (ASCII character #32) into the cell. The space character looks like nothing to human beings, but to the computer it is just as real as the character "A" or "Z."

Whatever else you do, do *not* use the spacebar to "erase" a cell's contents. Cells that look empty but contain space characters can cause faulty results when they are included in some computations.

**WHERE THE
MOUSE EXCELS:
WORKING
WITH RANGES**

A **range** is a block of adjacent cells. Many 1-2-3 operations involve ranges.

Marking a Range with the Mouse

We are still working with the file called MYFIRST. For your first experiment with ranges, let's goof up and then recover our goof by erasing it.

1. Enter the label Jones in cell D3, Smith in D4, and Baker in E5.
2. Move the mouse pointer to cell D3.
3. Holding down the left mouse button, drag the mouse down and to the right until the selected (highlighted) area looks like Figure 1.21.

When you release the mouse button, 1-2-3 assumes you are finished marking the range.

FIGURE 1.21

Beginning a
Range Selection

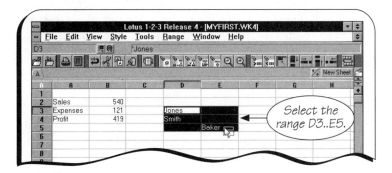

The Mouse Quick Menu

With your mouse pointer inside the highlighted range, press the *right* mouse button. The mouse *quick menu* appears, as shown in Figure 1.22.

FIGURE 1.22

The Mouse
Quick Menu

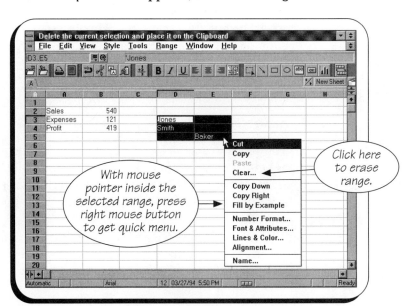

To erase all data from the selected range, click on Clear in the quick menu and click on OK in the dialog box that appears. As you can see in Figure 1.22, the mouse quick menu contains other choices; we will discuss them in their appropriate context.

Erasing a Range with the Keyboard

To erase a range with the keyboard, move the cellpointer to the top left corner of the range; press F4; use the arrow keys to mark the range; hit ↵. The range is now highlighted. To erase all data in the highlighted range, press the DEL key.

The idea of ranges is used in many 1-2-3 operations. A selected range can be used for many operations besides erasing.

GETTING OUT OF 1-2-3

At some point you will be ready to get out of 1-2-3 and return to the Windows Program Manager. This section tells you how to quit 1-2-3 gracefully. Never simply turn off the computer to get out of 1-2-3!

1-2-3's Built-in Safeguard

If you have not changed your file's contents since your last File Save, 1-2-3 quits working and returns you to Windows. However, if you have made changes since saving, 1-2-3 displays a dialog box reminding you that you need to save your work before quitting.

Quitting by Mouse or Keyboard

To quit by mouse, double-click on the 1-2-3 control box (the control box is on the title line in the upper left corner of the screen). To quit by using keyboard keys, use ALT+FX. That is, while holding down ALT, hit F and then X. Whether you use the mouse or the keyboard does not matter. In either case, you will see the screen in Figure 1.23.

FIGURE 1.23

Quitting 1-2-3

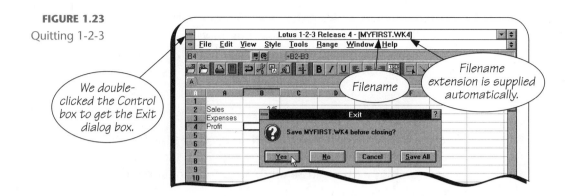

We already saved this file once, but afterward we made some changes, as when we entered and then erased data. 1-2-3 knows that something in the worksheet has changed since the last save. The dialog box gives us a chance to save the changes before exiting.

Click on the Yes button or press ALT+Y to save and exit. If we selected the No button, 1-2-3 would shut down without saving the latest version of the file. If we selected Cancel, 1-2-3 would return us to Ready mode. The Save All option applies if you have multiple files open (we don't).

LEARN HOW TO USE 1-2-3's ONLINE HELP

As a beginning Lotus 1-2-3 guru, the biggest favor you can do for yourself is to learn to use the built-in Help facility. Help calls up an electronic encyclopedia of information on how to use 1-2-3, and unlike a book, you cannot forget it or misplace it. There are several ways to get Help.

Help from the Menu

The menu has a Help choice. If you select it, you get a menu that thoroughly covers use of the Help facility.

The F1 (Help) Key

The F1 key has only one purpose in 1-2-3: It calls up Help. If you hit F1 from Ready mode, you can select from its index, but Help is also context sensitive. In other words, if you begin some operation and then hit F1, you automatically get helpful information on the current operation.

Dialog Box Help

All dialog boxes contain a Question-mark button. Click on it to get instant Help on the particular task you are doing.

MORE ABOUT CONTROL MENUS AND CONTROL BUTTONS

The 1-2-3 Control menu box is at the left end of the title bar. Figure 1.24 shows the Control menu, which appears if you click the Control menu box.

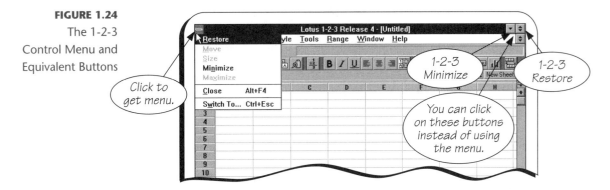

In Figure 1.24, Move, Size, and Maximize are dimmed, meaning they are not available at this time. Currently the 1-2-3 window is maximized, meaning it occupies the whole screen; there is no room for moving, sizing, or maximizing the window.

If you select Restore, the 1-2-3 window shrinks to a smaller size. If you select Minimize, 1-2-3 becomes a small icon (double-click on the icon to restore).

Restore and Minimize have mouse equivalents in the form of the arrowhead and double arrowhead buttons at the right end of the title bar. Click on the down arrowhead to Minimize the 1-2-3 window, or click on the double arrowhead to Restore the window.

The Close menu choice exits 1-2-3. However, 1-2-3 prompts you to save your worksheet if you have any unsaved changes. The Switch To menu choice lets you switch to other active applications.

The Worksheet Control menu box is below the 1-2-3 Control menu and works in a similar fashion, except that Worksheet Control affects only the worksheet window. To activate the menu, click on the Worksheet control button or press ALT+hyphen. The Worksheet Control menu's Restore option also has a mouse button equivalent, as shown in Figure 1.25.

Figure 1.26 shows the effect of the Worksheet Control menu's Restore option. You can get the same effect by clicking on the worksheet's Restore button without using the menu.

FIGURE 1.26
Decreasing
Worksheet Size
with Restore

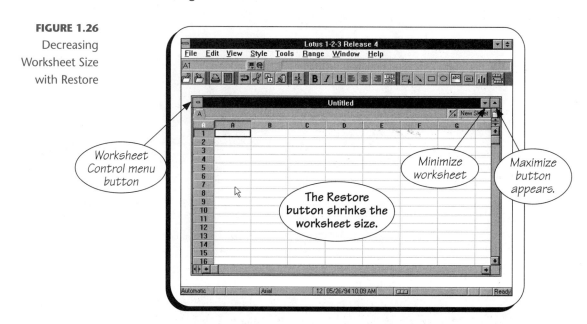

In Figure 1.27, the mouse has been used to click on and drag the worksheet to a smaller size. Notice that the mouse pointer at the lower right corner of the worksheet is a double-headed arrow. The same thing works on any other corner.

FIGURE 1.27
Resizing a
Worksheet with
the Mouse

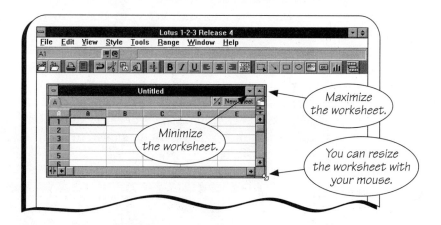

In Figure 1.28, the worksheet's Minimize button has been clicked to reduce the worksheet window to an icon. Double-clicking on the icon restores the worksheet.

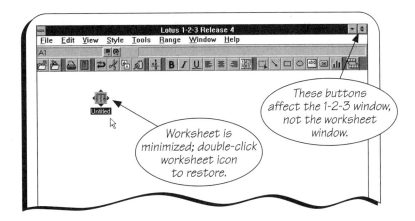

FIGURE 1.28
Minimizing a
Worksheet

**ABOUT THE
END-OF-CHAPTER
PROBLEMS**

At this point, you already know a respectable amount about 1-2-3. Before we begin building more complex worksheets, make sure you have a firm grasp of these principles by working through the following exercises.

Joe Bob LeBouef I

Joe Bob LeBouef, Head Football Coach at Sasquatch University, has a problem. The President and the Board of Regents want to terminate Sasquatch U's football program on the grounds that it is a money-loser. Joe Bob considers this to be a very bad idea—worse than abolishing motherhood and apple pie. He wants to evaluate his football program himself before giving in to the barbarians who want to kill it.

Joe Bob wants someone to set up a 1-2-3 template to help him crunch the football program's numbers. He knows 1-2-3 is good for this kind of job, but he is clueless about how to use it.

Joe Bob has heard that you are a 1-2-3 guru. As fate would have it, you are taking his Phys Ed class (Bowling 101). He offered you a deal you couldn't refuse: Set up the template and maybe get an A, or don't set up the template and get an F.

Joe Bob drew the following proposed template on the back of a football helmet. As you can see, he is beginning very modestly. However, if your first template works, he has big plans for adding more sophisticated details.

Your job is to:

1. Enter the labels.
2. Enter the necessary formula where you see the box.
3. Punch in various numbers for TICKETS and COSTS to verify that the template works correctly.

When you complete Joe Bob's template, save it to disk (by selecting File Save). Use JOEBOB1 for the filename.

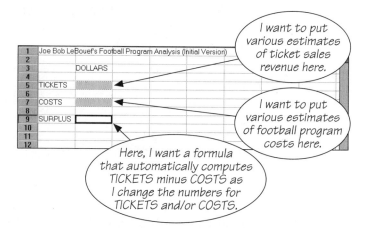

Set up the following worksheet:

----A----	----B----	----C----	----D----	----E----	----F----
1	999	333	999			
2	333	999	333			
3	999	333	999			
4						

1. Move your cellpointer to cell A1. Now press the END key; then press the right arrow. Where does your cellpointer go? Now press END again, followed by the down arrow. Why does the cellpointer stop in cell C3?

2. Now select and erase *only* the cells that have 333 in them.

3. Erase all the remaining occupied cells, in one fell swoop.

4. Use the F5 function key (GOTO) to send the cellpointer to cell A152. Enter the word MOJO in the cell by typing the word and pressing the down arrow. Enter the word JOJO in A153 by typing the word and pressing the up arrow. Send the cellpointer to cell A1. Now press END followed by the down arrow. Why does the cellpointer stop in cell A152? Press END and the down arrow again. Why does the cellpointer stop in cell A153? Now one last time, press END followed by the down arrow. Where does the cellpointer end up?

5. Enter your first name in cell A100. Enter your last name in B100. Now select the range A100..B100. Try using the Delete key to erase the contents of the range.

The SMART exercises for this chapter are:

1. **SID.wk1**   SID is an automated worksheet that stores your personal identification on your SMART diskette. You only have to use SID once; it is not necessary to use it again unless your identification is somehow erased from your SMART diskette.

2. **01AU03.wk1**   01AU03 is an exercise in cellpointer movement and data entry. Retrieve it after you have retrieved and completed the SID worksheet. The on-disk SMART exercises require that you retrieve files from disk and save files to disk. We will discuss those topics in detail in Chapter 2. For now, simply follow these instructions to get started on your SMART exercises:

    a. Launch Lotus 1-2-3.
    b. Place the diskette with your SMART exercises in the floppy disk drive (which we assume to be the A: drive).
    c. Select Tools User Setup (specify the A: drive).
    d. Select File Open and select filename SID.
    e. The SMART system's SID worksheet asks you to type your Student IDentification—last name, first name, and class designation. Your instructor will tell you what to use for the class designation. If you are not in an organized class, type None for the class. After you fill out the SID worksheet, you are ready to begin your first real SMART exercise, 01AU03.
    f. Select File Open 01AU03.

    The SMART problem 01AU03 loads into memory. Read the instructions and follow them. When you are ready to quit working on 01AU03, select File Save to save the changes you made to disk.

    Quit Lotus 1-2-3. You are finished with the first set of SMART exercises.

Worksheet Setup

After studying this chapter, you should know how to:

- Design worksheets for reusability.
- Create formulas.
- Sum ranges.
- Build filenames.
- Save and retrieve files.
- Edit cell contents.
- Close files.

Let's set up the core of a useful 1-2-3 worksheet: a construction cost estimator. First we need to cover some rules about data entry. The rules are important to review if you know how to type but are not very familiar with computational software. You may have some habits that are all right when you are using a word processor, but not when you are using 1-2-3.

DO NOT USE LETTERS IN PLACE OF NUMBERS In 1-2-3, when you are typing numbers that contain a zero, don't try to use the upper- or lowercase "oh." Use the numeric "0." The same thing goes for trying to use the letter "l" for the number "1." Also, do not hit the spacebar before typing a number. If you mix these (or any other) alphabetic characters with digits, the result is a label—not a number.

1-2-3 enters the label, but it has no status at all as a number, no more than "U2" or "Napoleon" would. This can lead to befuddling results when you try to do arithmetic with that particular cell.

WORKSHEET CREATION: DESIGNING FOR REUSABILITY

In the professional world, 1-2-3 worksheets normally are used over and over again, not just once with one set of input data. In a reusable worksheet, some cells contain changeable data, and other cells contain formulas that constantly "look at" the data cells. When you change a data cell, the formula cells automatically recompute their values based on the new data.

This idea of reusability is a key feature of 1-2-3 and of spreadsheets in general. The following example shows how to apply it.

Creating a Reusable Construction Cost Estimator

Reproduce the information shown in Figure 2.1, beginning from a clear 1-2-3 worksheet. Put your cellpointer on cell A1; type CONSTRUCTION COST ESTIMATOR and press the down arrow to get to A3. Type ITEM in cell A3. Press the right arrow to move your cellpointer to cell B3. Type NUMBER and press the right arrow. In cell C3, enter UNITCOST. In cell D3, enter TOTAL. Continue until you have entered all the cell contents shown in Figure 2.1.

FIGURE 2.1

Beginning a Construction Cost Estimator

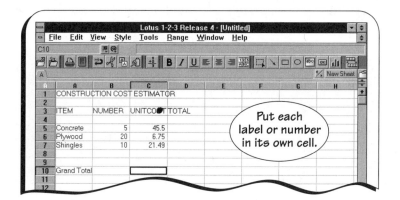

Our construction project currently uses only three kinds of materials—some project! Later you can expand it to realistic size; for now we will work with this midget. The 1-2-3 principles are the same whether there are three items, or 300, or 3000.

We want 1-2-3 to compute the TOTAL cost of each item—concrete, plywood, and shingles—in the appropriate cells in column D. We also want 1-2-3 to compute (in cell D10) the grand total of all the items. To coax 1-2-3 to do this for us, we need to create formulas.

Using Formulas

A formula creates arithmetic relationships among cells. We want cell D5 to display the product of cell B5 times cell C5; cell D6 should display the product of cell B6 times cell C6; cell D7 should display the product of cell B7 times cell C7; and cell D10 should display the sum of cells D5, D6, and D7.

A good part of the power of 1-2-3 comes from its ability to link cells through formulas. Once we set up our relationships, we can change the numbers in columns B and/or C, and 1-2-3 will instantly recompute the formula values in column D.

Put your cellpointer on cell D5. The sign for multiplication in 1-2-3 is the asterisk (*). Type exactly this, with no spaces between any of the characters: +B5*C5 (don't press ↵ yet). Your screen should look like Figure 2.2.

FIGURE 2.2

Creating a Formula

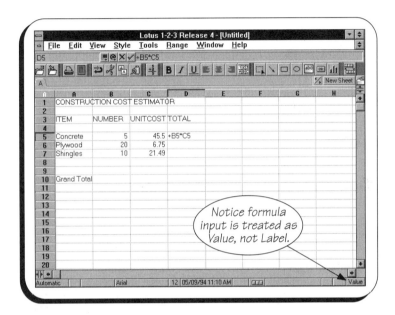

Look in Figure 2.2 at the lower right corner of the status bar (the Mode indicator). 1-2-3 has sensed that you are entering a numeric value rule into cell D5; the Mode indicator says Value. If you had not started the entry with a plus sign, or some other nonlabel, 1-2-3 would have taken the entry as a label—a somewhat strange label, but a label nevertheless. Remember that "label" is 1-2-3 lingo for "word."

Initial Indicators for Formulas

Any time you begin a cell entry with an equal sign, a plus, a minus, a left parenthesis, a @, a $ sign, a period, or a number, 1-2-3 knows you want to use the cell for numbers or formulas rather than for labels. If you had not started your formula with a valid numeric sign, 1-2-3 would have assumed you wanted the label B5*C5 in the cell. Before you scoff at 1-2-3 for being dumb enough to assume that B5*C5 could possibly be a label, remember this: 1-2-3 cannot possibly know your motivations; maybe B5*C5 is what you call your dog and you are trying to type in your dog's name. So, 1-2-3 has to take things literally.

The literal rules are:

1. If a cell entry starts with an alphabetic character, the entry must be a label rather than a numeric entry.
2. If a cell entry starts with one of the special characters shown in Table 2.1, it must be a number or formula entry rather than a label.

For formulas you usually will use the plus sign rather than one of the other special numeric signs, just as we did in this example.

TABLE 2.1 Initial Characters for Formula Entries

Character	Example of Use
=	=A1–A2
+	+A1–A2
–	–A2+A1
$	$A$1–A2
.	.5*A2
(	(A1–A2)
1234567890	2+A2
@	@SUM(A1..E1)

Good enough. The plus sign tells 1-2-3 you are entering a formula. Now press ↵. Figure 2.3 shows what you should see.

FIGURE 2.3

The Formula in Place

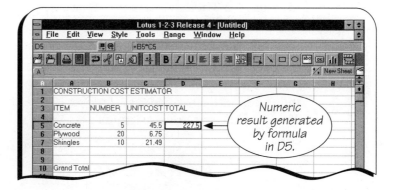

Formulas: The Power Behind the Throne

In Figure 2.3, the contents box shows the *formula* that you put in D5, however, cell D5 in the worksheet shows the *numeric result* of the formula. How can this be? It can be because 1-2-3 actually stores the formula itself in the cell and uses the formula to compute the number you see on the screen. The cellpointer uncovers the deep-down value rule—the formula—for the current cell and displays it in the contents box.

Now move your cellpointer to D6, and enter the appropriate formula to compute the number of sheets of plywood times the unitcost per sheet, +B6*C6. In cell D7, do the same for Shingles, +B7*C7. By the way, don't leave spaces in formulas. If you try to enter something like +B7 * C7, 1-2-3 beeps at you, puts you in Edit mode, and waits for you to remove the spaces.

Summing Cells by Formula

To total the cost of the individual items, put your cellpointer on cell D10. Enter the formula +D5+D6+D7 in D10. Your worksheet now should look like Figure 2.4.

FIGURE 2.4
Totalling
the Column
by Formula

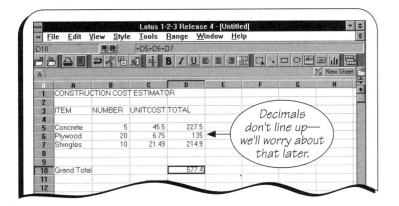

A Shorthand Way to Sum Ranges

In Figure 2.4, we calculated the grand total cost in cell D10 by using the formula +D5+D6+D7. For summing only a small range of cells, such a formula works fine. However, if we had had to sum a long column, typing the address of every cell in the column would have become cumbersome.

Summing rows and columns is one of the most common worksheet jobs, and 1-2-3 has a special tool that makes it easy: the SUM icon. If you select cell D10 and click on the SUM icon, @SUM(D5..D7) appears in cell D10. Of course, you could have gotten the same result without using the icon by entering @SUM(D5..D7) instead of +D5+D6+D7.

We will explore several other function shortcuts in Chapter 3. In the meantime, remember the SUM icon. It will be useful as you do the SMART exercises for this chapter.

Don't worry that the figures in column D do not line up neatly. We will get into formatting the worksheet in Chapter 3.

**KEY IDEA:
WORKSHEET
REUSABILITY**

So there is our complete estimate of what our "construction job" will cost. Of course, if this were the only computation you intended to do, you could have done it more quickly with a paper, pencil, and pocket calculator! However, the underlying idea behind a 1-2-3 worksheet is *reusability* with different data sets. That idea depends on formulas that compute their values by looking at the changeable data areas of the worksheet. In our example, the range B5..C7 is the data area.

Advantages of Reusable Worksheets

The advantage of the worksheet over any hand calculation becomes apparent when you want to change something. Maybe you actually need 7.5 units of concrete, 33 plywood units, and 57 bundles of shingles; or maybe the unit cost of some of the items has changed. With your formula-based, reusable worksheet, you can simply put your cellpointer on the items to be changed in column B or C and type in the new data. 1-2-3 instantly recalculates the affected formulas in column D.

The formulas in column D give you a painless tool for computing the costs of different jobs simply by changing the figures in columns B and C. Without formulas in column D, you would be using Lotus 1-2-3 as nothing more than a glorified typewriter.

A formula such as +B5*C5 is a universal calculator; it automatically gives the answer no matter what specific numbers a user enters in cells B5 and C5.

Beginning with the on-disk SMART exercises for this chapter, the SMART checker changes the values in data cells as a way to check whether you grasp the idea of formulas and worksheet reusability. If your answers are not formula-based, SMART will not give you credit because your answers will not be correct for the new data set.

**SAVING AN
EXISTING FILE:
WHEN AND WHY**

In the uncertain world of computers, you need to save your files, and save them, and save them again, as you work. This section discusses the "when and why" of periodic file-saving operations.

When to Save

Save early and often. Most experienced 1-2-3 users save their work every five or ten minutes.

Why to Save

RAM is fickle. If the electric power goes off, or if the computer locks up for some reason, everything in RAM goes away. For example, if a power failure comes right now as you sit at your computer staring at the construction cost worksheet file, you will lose everything you have done.

If you have been following instructions, you haven't saved the file yet. So, a power outage or brownout at this moment would wipe all the information from the computer's memory chips—and all your work on CONCOST is in the chips. You would be left with nothing to show for your efforts.

Disk storage is much more reliable; on disk, information is stored as tiny magnetic **bits**. The bits will last for decades if you take good care of the disk.

Before going further, save your file. Select File Save. Use the name CONCOST.

Saving Automatically

It is easy to become absorbed in a project and forget to save on schedule. If you have trouble remembering to save often, select Tools User Setup. You should see a dialog box like the one shown in Figure 2.5.

FIGURE 2.5
Using Tools
User Setup for
Auto-Saving

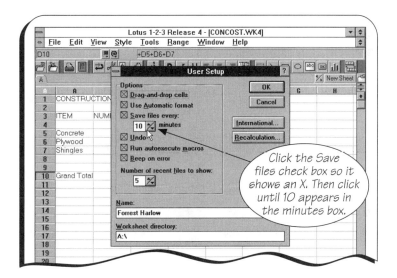

Set the Auto-save feature to 10 minutes. That way, 1-2-3 will watch the clock for you and automatically offer the File Save dialog box every 10 minutes.

Notes on Choosing Filenames

1. Start with a letter or digit such as A, B, C, 1, 5, or 9.

2. Use only letters and digits unless you are familiar with the DOS file-naming rules—some special characters work, but others, such as spaces and colons, do not.

3. Total length of the filename cannot be more than eight letters/digits taken together.

4. When possible, use a memory-jogging name for a file. "CONCOST" is better than "XK456T7" because it helps you remember what the file contains.

RETRIEVING A SAVED WORKSHEET FROM DISK

In the previous section we discussed how to save your CONCOST worksheet to disk. Now we are going to pretend that you want to get out of 1-2-3 and go home. Click the Control menu box and select Close. Simulate going home.

Now pretend you just returned to your computer; you want to work on your CONCOST file again. Launch Lotus 1-2-3. Select Tools User Setup and make the diskette drive (A:) the default. Refer to Figure 1.19 if you need a refresher on the User Setup dialog box. Your CONCOST worksheet does not appear on screen; all you get is the bare 1-2-3 grid. Don't panic. CONCOST is sitting safely on disk in the form of magnetic blips; all you have to do is load it back into the computer's memory chips.

To retrieve the file, select File Open. In response to your File Open command, 1-2-3 checks the default drive and displays the worksheet files in the list box. At this point, you should be looking at the screen display shown in Figure 2.6.

FIGURE 2.6

Opening a File

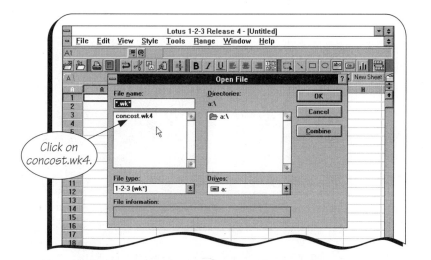

You may see many filenames instead of just CONCOST—it depends on what files are on the diskette you are using. If more than one worksheet file is on disk, 1-2-3 displays them all in the list box. You can click on the list box scroll bar to move up and down the list, and then double-click on CONCOST, the file you want to retrieve. For simplicity, the list box in Figure 2.6 shows only CONCOST.

When you select CONCOST, 1-2-3 transfers a copy of the CONCOST file from your diskette into your computer's memory. Note that the CONCOST file is *still on your disk* after this operation. 1-2-3 merely read and copied the file from disk into memory, just as you might read this page and copy it down with a pencil and paper as you read. You would then have two copies of this page: one in the book, and one on your notepad. 1-2-3 works the same way. After a File Open operation, you have a copy of the file in the computer's memory chips, *and* you still have the file on disk. The two copies are identical *until* you begin changing the worksheet in memory by typing entries from the keyboard.

Thus your permanent copy of CONCOST is still snugly on disk; a working copy of CONCOST is in main memory. You should see the display shown in Figure 2.7.

FIGURE 2.7
Copy of
CONCOST
in RAM

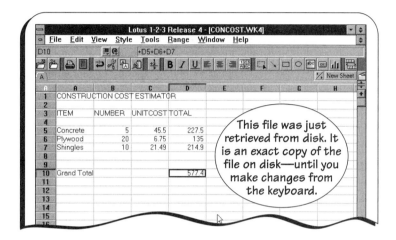

Your cellpointer is sitting on whatever cell it was in when you saved the file. That is why you see the reference to D10 on the status line; your cellpointer was on D10 when you saved the file.

ADDING AN ITEM TO CONCOST

Let's make some additions to CONCOST. Type in the new information, as Figure 2.8 shows in row 8.

FIGURE 2.8
Adding an Item
to CONCOST

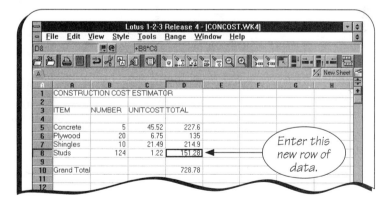

After you type the new formula in cell D8, the total cost in cell D10 does not automatically change—the total cost formula in cell D10 is still +D5+D6+D7. Put your cellpointer on cell D10 and enter the new formula +D5+D6+D7+D8.

This process of summing up a column by typing a reference to every cell could easily get cumbersome. If you wanted to add up 500 cells, it would be impossible. Note that you could use the @SUM function in D10, instead of the cell-adding formula discussed earlier.

Editing the Contents of a Cell

In the CONCOST worksheet we didn't specify any units of measure in column A, so let's modify the label Concrete to show that the worksheet is measuring concrete in terms of cubic yards.

We could make our modifications in either of two ways. The hard way would be to put the cellpointer on the cell to be modified and retype the entire entry with whatever modifications we wanted. If you are a glutton for punishment or a fast typist, you may prefer that method. The other way is to edit the cell to be changed.

Put the cellpointer on cell A5—the cell with the word "Concrete" in it. Now look at the function keys. Press the F2 function key. Figure 2.9 shows what you should see.

FIGURE 2.9

Editing a Cell

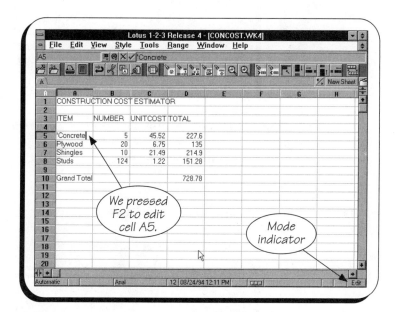

In Figure 2.9, look at the Mode indicator (lower right corner of your screen, in the status bar). It informs you you are in Edit mode. Your worksheet cellpointer is frozen any time you are in Edit mode, so the right and left arrows will operate on your edit cursor. The **edit cursor** is the blinking vertical bar at the end of the label.

If you wanted to change the entry to Reinforced Concrete, you could use the left arrow to move the edit cursor to the "C" in "Concrete," and type the word "Reinforced." If you just want to add something at the end of the Concrete entry, as we do, leave the edit cursor where it is (at the end of the word "Concrete"). Next modify the Concrete entry by adding , Cu/Yd and then press ⏎. You should see the display shown in Figure 2.10.

FIGURE 2.10

Label Display
Truncated

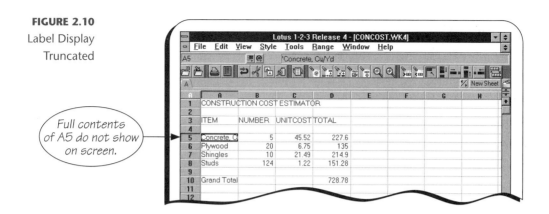

Full contents
of A5 do not show
on screen.

Changing Column Widths

Wait a minute. Something looks wrong! All you see in cell A5 is "Concrete, C" even though you went to the trouble to change the cell contents to Concrete, Cu/Yd. To add to the mystery, look at the contents box in the control panel. It says cell A5 contains Concrete, Cu/Yd, just like you thought it did.

Our display problem is only cosmetic; we can corrrect it by changing the width of the column. The standard 1-2-3 screen display gives each column a width of 9 characters. However, in the computer's memory chips, you can store as many as 512 characters in any cell.

The entry we put in cell A5 was Concrete, Cu/Yd, which has 15 characters (instead of the 14 you probably just counted because the space after the comma counts as a character). When we tried to display the 15 characters, an onscreen traffic jam resulted because cell B5, to the right of cell A5, contains something—namely, the number 5. A number always takes up the whole cell where it is, even if it is a little number like 5.

1-2-3 only has two choices: Blot out the 5 on the screen or show only the part of A5's contents that will fit in the standard 9 spaces. The only reasonable choice is to leave the screen display of the neighboring cell alone and truncate the screen display of cell A5's contents. That is what 1-2-3 did, and that is why the screen display of A5 doesn't agree with the full contents of A5.

If cell B5 had been totally blank, with no contents, 1-2-3 would have wrapped the screen display of A5 over into B5.

Wrapping into adjacent empty cells only applies to text entries—labels. If a number has too many digits to display in the onscreen cell width, 1-2-3 either changes it to scientific notation or fills the cell with *************, depending on the cell's formatting mask (discussed in Chapter 3). For numbers, it does not matter whether the rightward cell is occupied or not. 1-2-3 never allows numbers to wrap over into adjacent columns. To provide display room for big numbers, widen the column as explained next.

For our labels, we can eliminate these electronic quarrels for screen display rights by widening column A. Let's set column A to a width of 20. To do this, be sure your cellpointer is in column A. Select Style Column Width from the menu. You should see a dialog box like the one in Figure 2.11.

FIGURE 2.11

The Style Column Width Dialog Box

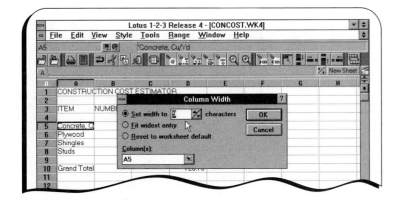

Enter 20 in the Set width to box, or click on the box arrows until 20 appears. Select OK. Now your screen should look like Figure 2.12.

FIGURE 2.12

Column A Widened

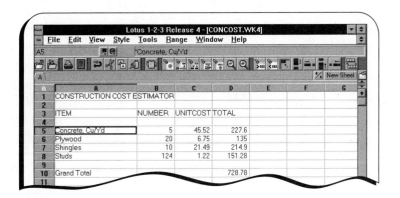

Style Column Width Fit Widest Entry automatically changes the width of the current column to contain the widest label. You also can change a column width by clicking and dragging the junction between two column headers.

THE METAPHYSICS OF CLOSING AND OPENING FILES

1-2-3 allows you to open additional files without closing the current one. In other words, several worksheet files can be in memory at the same time, but each file uses up some of your RAM.

At this point in your 1-2-3 career, you have created and saved two files: MYFIRST.WK4 and CONCOST.WK4. Right now, a modified copy of CONCOST is in memory, and the original version is on disk. MYFIRST is not in memory; it exists only as magnetic blips on disk.

If you now click the File Open icon (or select File Open) and select MYFIRST, 1-2-3 loads a copy of MYFIRST from disk into memory, in addition to the already-open CONCOST file. By selecting Window Tile, you could see them both at once, in reduced-size windows. By selecting Window Cascade, you could see them with one partially behind the other.

However, there is no reason to load two (or more) files into memory unless you need to flip quickly back and forth between them. Keeping multiple files in memory uses up RAM. For most purposes it is better to keep only one file open at a time. We will discuss the details of tiling and cascading multiple files in Chapter 9.

Using File Close to Conserve Memory

If you wanted to *remove CONCOST from memory* and begin working only on MYFIRST, you would select File Close. If you have modified CONCOST since last saving it, 1-2-3 displays a dialog box asking you if you want to save the current file before closing.

Unless you are just doodling, you would select Yes. 1-2-3 then wipes CONCOST out of memory. 1-2-3's worksheet settings such as column widths are returned to their default states. The disk version of your file is *not* erased, of course. If you then open another file such as MYFIRST, the newly opened file has RAM all to itself.

Using File Close to Get a Clean Slate

Saving a file updates it on disk and leaves the file in memory for further changes. Closing a file wipes it from memory, without necessarily saving any changes.

Sometimes you will want to wipe out a file from the computer's memory and start over from scratch, without saving your work and without retrieving another file from disk. For example, if you are experimenting with various commands and data formats, you may want to "throw away" your work and simply get a clear worksheet to continue doodling on. This book often asks you to do just that.

MORE ON EDIT MODE The F2 key has only one use in 1-2-3: It puts you in Edit mode. Once you are in Edit mode, the worksheet cellpointer is frozen. As you already know, the left and right arrows move the little edit cursor rather than the main worksheet cellpointer when you are editing the contents of a cell. When you are in Edit mode, you also can use the keys shown in Table 2.2.

TABLE 2.2　Editing Keys in Edit Mode

Key	Function
BACKSPACE	Moves the edit cursor one space to the left each time it is pressed and destroys whatever character was there. That is, it works as a destructive backspace.
DELETE	Deletes the character above the edit cursor and closes up the gap by shifting all rightward characters leftward.
END	Moves the edit cursor past the rightmost character. The effect is the same as if you had pressed the right arrow repeatedly to move to the end of the edited data.
ESC	Abandons the edit and returns you to Ready mode. No changes are made to the cell formerly being edited.
HOME	Moves the edit cursor to the first character. If you are editing a label, the first character will be the label-prefix sign.
Spacebar	Inserts a blank character at the edit cursor position and pushes the rest of the entry rightward.

Now let's pause and regroup. Use the following end-of-chapter exercises to consolidate your grip on the chapter concepts.

CASE

Joe Bob LeBouef II

Joe Bob LeBouef, whom you met in Chapter 1, was very impressed with your initial template. Now he wants you to add some detail. For REVENUE, he wants subcategories for tickets, food, and so on. He also wants subcategories for EXPENSES.

Joe Bob drew you a second picture on the back of a football helmet. Your job is to

1. Set up the labels and any necessary formulas or functions.
2. Punch in enough numbers to be sure the template works correctly.

Save the file under the filename JOEBOB2. Remember that you do not have to complete the worksheet before saving—save it every 5 minutes or so as you work, and also save it when you finish.

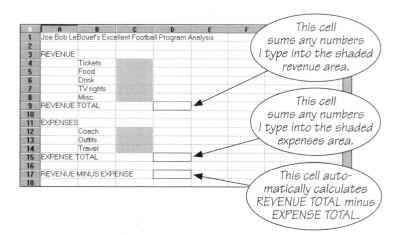

Joe Bob LeBouef III

Joe Bob LeBouef, Head Football Coach at Sasquatch University, really is beginning to like your work. He says you definitely look like a candidate for an "A" in his Phys Ed class. Now Joe Bob wants you to create another, more sophisticated worksheet, like the following one.

Once again, Joe Bob offered you a deal you couldn't refuse: If you set up the template to his satisfaction, you get both an A and a full athletic scholarship; if you don't set up the template, you get an F in his Phys Ed course and he will have your transcript flagged for noncompletion of required Phys Ed.

Joe Bob drew you the following picture.

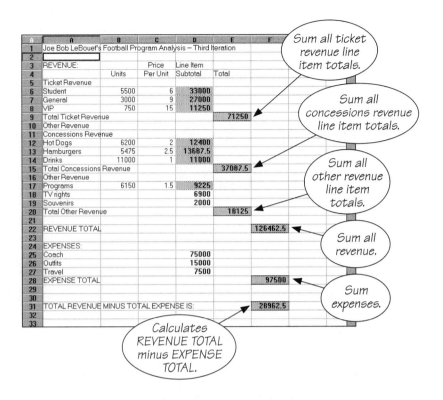

The figures you see in Joe Bob's worksheet are examples that Joe Bob penciled in on the back of an old football jersey. The numbers in columns B and C are only examples. Joe Bob wants to be able to change any of those numbers. In your template, the shaded cells should contain formulas or functions. For lines containing data for units and unit price, the formula for line item totals will be units*price per unit. Outlined cells in the Total column should contain formulas or functions to sum the totals in their respective category, except the final box, which is total revenue minus total expense.

Save the file under the filename JOEBOB3. Remember that you do not have to complete the worksheet before saving—save it every 5 minutes or so as you work, and also save it when you finish.

1. Put your cellpointer on cell T50. Type 231, that is, two, three, and the letter "ell" rather than the number one. Notice that 1-2-3 makes no objection until you try to enter the hybrid number label. Change the "ell" to a one and enter it.

2. If you are an experienced typewriter user you may need more convincing that 1-2-3 doesn't like alphabetic characters in a cell that starts off with a legitimate number like 1 or 5 or 4. Try to enter this: 3oo. When that doesn't work, ESC and try to enter this: 3OO, where the last two digits are the capital letter "oh." Of course, that won't work either. So resign yourself to using numeric digits.

3. With your cellpointer in cell A1, enter this: Hi423. Does 1-2-3 think this combination of characters and numbers is a word or a number? How can you tell?

4. Move your cellpointer to cell A2. Try to enter this: 1 23. What happens when you press ↵? Why won't 1-2-3 accept the entry? *Tip:* Use the ESC key to abandon the attempt to enter it.

5. Now try to enter this: 775J. Why does 1-2-3 reject this entry? Use the DEL key to kill the letters; press ↵ to see what happens now. Does 1-2-3 buy it this time?

6. Move your cellpointer to cell W25. Type 1236, press the spacebar, and ENTER. Hmmm. What do you suppose is giving 1-2-3 indigestion? Fix the problem and make the entry.

7. Put this word in cell C7: FLOTBALL. Oops. "FLOTBALL" should be "FOOTBALL." Use F2 to edit; use the left arrow to move the edit cursor; position the cursor on the wrong letter; type an O; now you see "FOLOTBALL." Press the DEL key to kill the bad "ell"; press ↵ to get the corrected word into cell C7.

8. Enter XZ in cell A2. Edit, and insert a Y between X and Z.

9. Put the cellpointer on cell A10. Before you type anything else, press the spacebar. What shows in the Mode indicator? Now type 787 and press ↵. Is it a "word" or is it a number? *The moral:* A space is a character, the same as "a," or "b," or "C" so far as 1-2-3 is concerned.

10. Erase the range A1..F15. Then, in the range A1..C3, enter these numbers:

    | 2 | 8 | 3 |
    | 4 | 10 | 5 |
    | 6 | 107 | 9 |

11. Put the cellpointer on D1. Enter a formula to sum up whatever is in cells A1, B1, and C1.

12. Put the cellpointer on A5. Enter a formula to sum up whatever is in cells A1, A2, and A3.

13. Put the cellpointer on G18. Enter a formula or function to find the sum of *all* the 9 cells in the range A1..C3.

14. Put your cellpointer on D10. Enter a formula to find the product of cell B2 times cell C3.

15. Set column A to a width of 3. Reset column A to 65. Then reset A to the default width of 9.

Retrieve, complete, and save the following SMART exercises.

1. **02AU06** requires you to help out a friend who is putting himself through school by painting houses. He needs a worksheet that calculates how many gallons of paint will be required to do any given job. You get to provide it.

2. **02AU08** is a simple formula-based exercise. It requires you to type in formulas such as +B6*C6. This problem alters the data cells, to bring home the idea that formulas should be *cell references*, not dead numbers. If you build your formulas like +23*5, you will not get much credit when SMART alters the data cells! The most important idea of this problem is that worksheet formulas should be set up so that the worksheet is a universal calculator for whatever data is placed in the data cells.

3. **02AU15** is a simple payroll worksheet. However, the worksheet is not set up in the home area. Find it. Once again, set up your formulas using cell references, not dead numbers.

Basics of Functions, Formulas, and Formatting

OBJECTIVES After studying this chapter, you should know how to:

- Use common @ functions.
- Create complex formulas.
- Control formula evaluation order.
- Change the format of labels and numbers.
- Use basic fancy formatting techniques.

You already know how to build simple formulas and how to use the @SUM function. This chapter rounds out your knowledge of these basic worksheet-building tools and introduces you to techniques for improving the appearance of your worksheets.

FUNCTIONS Functions are built-in shortcuts for making complex computations. Scores of functions are built into 1-2-3. Most of them are for specialized jobs. We will introduce only a few widely used ones here, but if you understand how to use the common functions, you easily can figure out how to use the more esoteric ones.

Function Parts

Most functions have three elements: the **function sign**, the **function name**, and the **function argument**. The general structure of most functions is:

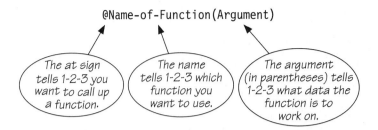

Some Common Functions—And Some Common Traps

The most widely useful functions generate sums, counts, averages, maximums, and minimums. 1-2-3 has an old set and a new set of functions for doing these jobs. We are going to look at both and try to steer you clear of the dangers that lurk in some members of the old set.

If you currently have a file in memory, select File Close. Save your work to disk. Your worksheet clears; no files are now in memory. Set up the new worksheet shown in Figure 3.1.

FIGURE 3.1

Widely Used, But Tricky, Functions

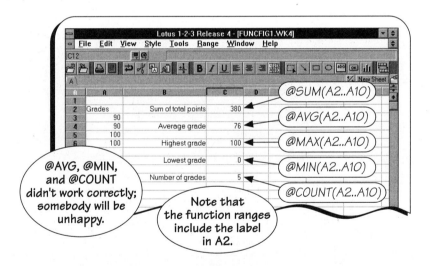

The function in cell C2, currently showing the value 380, is your old buddy @SUM from Chapter 1. The range extends from A2 through A10, which includes the label in A2 and also the currently empty cells from A7 to A10. The empty cells have no effect on the @SUM function or any other function, so long as they are truly empty. If we add more grades to the bottom of the list in column A, the function automatically includes them, and the result changes.

The @SUM function is fairly foolproof; it gives correct results even if you include label cells as well as numeric cells. All labels, such as the one in A2, have a numeric value of zilch—zero. With @SUM it doesn't matter if you include labels in the range to be summed.

However, the function in C4, @AVG(A2..A10), shows a value of 76, which is *not* correct. The average is wrong because the range (A2..A10) includes the label in A2. Since labels are treated like a numeric zero, the label messes up the average.

The @MAX function in C6 works correctly, giving a value of 100 in this case because 100 is the largest value in the specified range. However, if all the numbers were negative, @MAX would give a wrong result of 0 because of the label in A2.

The @MIN function incorrectly shows 0; it should show the lowest grade, 90. Once again, the label in A2 has caused the problem.

The @COUNT function informs us that there are five nonblank cells in the range A2..A10. This is true, but the count includes the label in A2 as well as the numeric cells.

Foolproofing the Functions

Normally you do *not* want your functions to factor labels into their computations. Accidentally including labels in the argument range is a common cause of hard-to-find computational errors in averages, minimums, maximums, and counts. The "foolproof" version of the functions will give the correct answer, even if there are labels inside their ranges.

Select File Close and at the prompt specify FUNCFIG1 as the filename. Now set up the worksheet shown in Figure 3.2.

FIGURE 3.2
Foolproof Functions

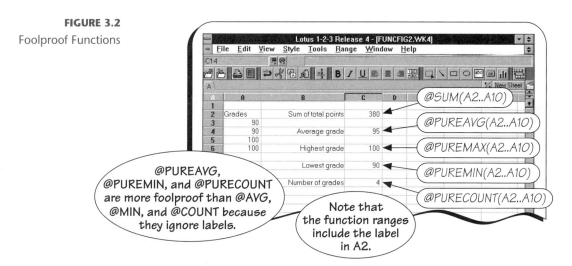

The PURE function forms give correct results, even though A2 is included in the range for each function. Unless you actually need to include labels in your averages, maximums, minimums, and counts, use the PURE forms.

Online Help for Functions

1-2-3 provides lots of function help. Click on the @ box on the edit line; then click on List All. You will see a dialog box with a scrollable list of functions.

Scroll down to AVG and click on it. A brief description of the function appears. To get a thorough explanation of how the function works, press F1 or click on the ? button at the upper right corner of the dialog box. You should see a display like Figure 3.3.

FIGURE 3.3
Getting Help
on Functions

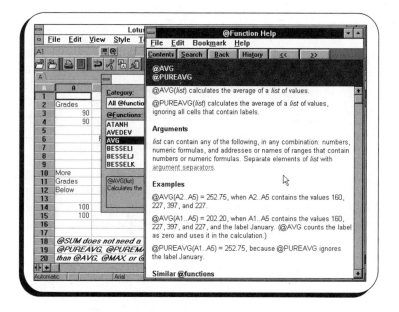

Close your file. Name it FUNCFIG2.

FORMULAS REVISITED

We already have used some simple formulas, but it is time for a more thorough treatment of the subject. A formula is an instruction to 1-2-3 to calculate a cell value from a more complex set of numbers and/or cell references.

Think of a formula as the right side of an equation. The left side of the equation is not written out; it is simply the cellpointer location. If you position the cellpointer on cell D5 and type +B5*C5, you really are saying: CELL D5 = +B5*C5. Remember that the only purpose of the leading + sign is to signal 1-2-3 that the subsequent characters are elements of a formula rather than plain text.

Arithmetic Operators in Formulas

The separate elements of a formula are always tied together by one or more of the arithmetic operators. Table 3.1 shows the operators in a tabular format.

TABLE 3.1   Arithmetic Operators

Operator	Symbol	Examples of Use in Formulas		
Addition	+	3+2	+A1+B1	4+B2
Subtraction	–	3-2	+A1-B1	+B2-5
Multiplication	*	3*2	+A1*B1	+B2*6
Division	/	3/2	+A1/B1	+B2/3
Exponentiation	^	3^2	+A1^B1	+B2^4

As the examples in Table 3.1 indicate, you can use the operators on either plain numbers—constants—or cell references, or you can mix and match. Any of the examples theoretically could be placed in any cell of the worksheet. If you wished to, you could move your cellpointer to cell Z85, far distant from the home area, and base its value on A1 times B1 by entering +A1*B1 in Z85.

Also, you are not restricted to having only a single arithmetic operator in a formula. This is a perfectly valid formula:

+A1/B1*B2-C2

Or this:

+A1+B1+C1+A2+B2+C2+A3/B3+C3*R17

So is this:

+A1/B1*(1+B2)-C2^5+Z100-@SUM(A10..B30)

Note the use of a function inside a formula.

The maximum length of a formula is 240 characters. However, it is doubtful that you will build many formulas longer than 30 or 40 characters. The great majority of your formulas will be only a few characters long.

Precedence: What Gets Done First

The ability to enter complex formulas in 1-2-3 cells gives you a great deal of computing power, but complex formulas can cause problems for the unwary. Problems can arise because 1-2-3 has to have some rules for deciding which part of a complex formula gets computed first, which gets computed second, and so forth. If you don't know 1-2-3's rules, mass confusion can result.

For example, consider this formula:

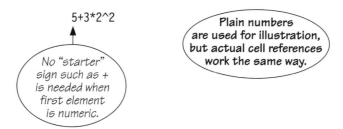

5+3*2^2

No "starter" sign such as + is needed when first element is numeric.

Plain numbers are used for illustration, but actual cell references work the same way.

Should the formula be evaluated left to right, right to left, or by starting with some particular operator, regardless of position? When there is a mixture of operators, it can make a big difference what gets done first, what gets done second, and so forth.

Now figure out the answer to the formula 5+3*2^2. If you agree that the answer is 17, you are thinking like 1-2-3. Lotus first raises 2 to the second power (2^2) to get 4; then it multiplies 3 by 4; finally it adds the 5 to the 12. Left to its own devices, 1-2-3 always works out exponents first. Next it handles multiplication and division. The last steps in computing the value of a formula are plain addition and subtraction.

However, you can interfere with 1-2-3's usual order of evaluation. The default order does not yield the result you want in many common situations. To control the order of evaluation, *put the things you want evaluated first in parentheses*. Table 3.2 shows the operators and their order of evaluation.

TABLE 3.2   **The Hierarchy of Arithmetic Operators**

Operator	Description
( )	Any elements in ( ) are computed first, regardless of their natural level of precedence. If one set of ( ) is nested inside another, the inmost set gets evaluated first, then the outer set gets evaluated. ((this first))

If you do not use ( ) to change the order of evaluation:

Operator	Description
^	Exponentiation is done first, left to right.
* /	Multiplication and division are next, left to right.
+ –	Addition and subtraction are last, left to right.

With this hierarchy in mind, once again consider the formula:

5+3*2^2

If you wanted 1-2-3 first to multiply 3 times 2, then raise the result to the third power, and then add in the 5, you could use parentheses like this:

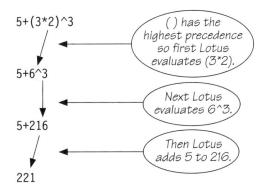

If you wanted 1-2-3 first to multiply 3 by 2, add the five, and lastly raise the whole lump to the third power:

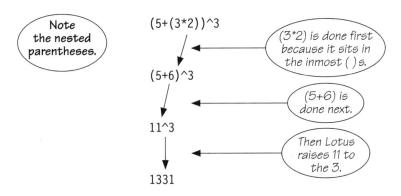

If all the operators in a formula have the same precedence, for example, if there are only pluses and minuses with no parentheses, 1-2-3 evaluates from left to right:

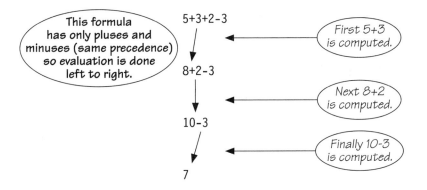

These examples used literal numbers—constants—but the order of evaluation is the same when you use cell references in formulas.

THE LAYER-CAKE STRUCTURE OF WORKSHEET CELLS

At this point, let's pause and take another look at the nature of worksheet cells. In effect, each cell in the worksheet is a tiny computer capable of

- Accepting input from the keyboard or from other cells.
- Processing the input.
- Changing the appearance of the processed input.
- Producing formatted values as output.

Think of every worksheet cell as having four layers, like Figure 3.4.

FIGURE 3.4
Anatomy of a Cell

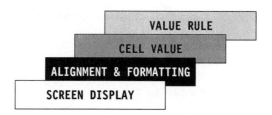

VALUE RULES, VALUES, ALIGNMENT, AND FORMATTING

When you make a cell entry, you are providing a rule for determining the cell's value. This **value rule** is the lowest, most fundamental layer of the cell. The cell entry determines the cell's value directly if you enter a simple number or a label. If you type in a formula such as +B1*C1, the cell value is created when the worksheet works out the arithmetic of the formula. The **cell value** is one layer above the value rule.

The cell values are "squeezed" through **alignment and formatting masks** to yield a **screen display**. These masks are one layer above the cell value, and they are strictly cosmetic. Make a mental note that neither alignment nor formatting has any effect on the value rule or the value in a cell.

Keep the exploded diagram in mind as you work through this book. Remember that the cell entry—the value rule—determines cell value, and that the cell value is filtered through a formatting mask to produce the screen display. This concept will help you to understand formulas, functions, and formatting options.

ALIGNING LABELS ON ENTRY

If you choose, you can specify the alignment of labels at the time of entry by supplying one of these label prefixes:

Label Prefix	Alignment
'	Left aligned
^	Center aligned
"	Right aligned

By default, labels are left aligned. Unless you begin your label entries with some other label prefix, 1-2-3 automatically supplies the left-alignment label prefix ('). If you begin an entry with a carat (^), 1-2-3 centers the label in its cell. If you begin with a double-quote ("), 1-2-3 aligns the label to the right boundary of the cell.

Do not use label prefixes to change the alignment of numbers. For example, if you attempt to left align the number 100 by typing '100, the entry will be a label rather than a number.

CHANGING ALIGNMENT OF EXISTING CELL CONTENTS

1-2-3 Release 4 allows you to right, center, or left align numeric cells as well as label cells. To change the alignment of a range after you have entered data, mark the range with the mouse and then click on one of the alignment icons. You can accomplish the same alignment tasks from the keyboard by following these steps:

1. Anchor the cellpointer by pressing ALT+F4 (function key 4).
2. Highlight the range with the direction keys.
3. Press ↵ to select the range.
4. From the menu, select Style Alignment Left, Center, or Right.

ALIGNING COLUMNAR DATA

Changing the alignment of data helps make your worksheets look more professional and frequently improves the clarity of the worksheet. As a rule, you will want to set your alignment so that labels and numbers line up in any given column.

You can align labels with the numbers beneath them in several ways. The simplest way is to right align the label by selecting cell B1 and then using the Right align icon.

To practice alignment, open the CONCOST file (click on the File Open icon or select File Open from the menu). 1-2-3 copies the CONCOST file from disk into the worksheet. It should look like Figure 3.5.

FIGURE 3.5
CONCOST Revisited

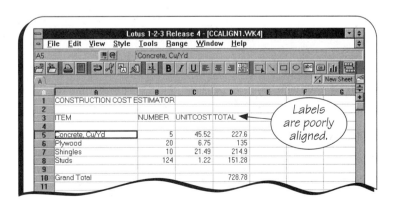

Aligning Column Headings

The column heading labels do not line up with the numbers in columns B and D. The UNITCOST heading in C3 lines up by accident because it almost fills the width of column C.

We can achieve alignment most easily by selecting the B3..D3 range and clicking on the Right-align icon or pressing ALT+R. After right aligning the B3..D3 range, the worksheet should look like Figure 3.6.

FIGURE 3.6

Changing Column
Header Alignment

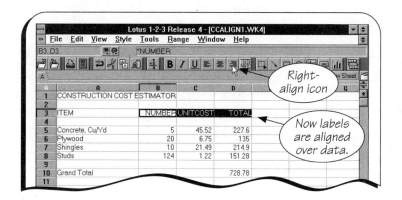

Now issue a <u>F</u>ile <u>S</u>ave command and save your file to disk. Remember to get in the habit of saving your work every five or ten minutes.

FORMATTING NUMERIC CELLS

As you have just seen, you can change the alignment of labels, numbers, or both. However, simply aligning labels and numbers is not enough to give a worksheet a finished look.

Changing the Default Format and Style

You can change the default format (and other defaults) by selecting <u>S</u>tyle <u>W</u>orksheet Defaults. In the business world, many users set the default format to Comma with 2 decimal places so that columns of financial figures will line up neatly.

Automatic Format

By default, 1-2-3 uses the Automatic format setting. Under the Automatic setting, 1-2-3 examines the data you type and automatically classifies it label or numeric. If 1-2-3 detects a label, no special format is applied, but the label is left justified.

By default, numbers are right justified. However, under Automatic format, 1-2-3 goes one step further. The program examines the way in which you enter the number and, in some cases, changes the cell from Automatic format to some format that matches your entry.

Once a cell changes from Automatic format, 1-2-3 no longer tries to apply new formats if you change the cell's data. For example, if you type $125.00 into a cell currently showing Automatic format, the format changes from Automatic to Currency,2. Then 1-2-3 washes its hands of the cell's format, which will remain C2 until you manually change it.

Beware of $\underline{S}$tyle $\underline{N}$umber Format $\underline{F}$ormat Label

If you select a range and use $\underline{S}$tyle $\underline{N}$umber Format $\underline{F}$ormat Label, any numbers you enter afterwards in the range will *not* really be numbers; they will be labels. The purpose of $\underline{S}$tyle $\underline{N}$umber Format $\underline{F}$ormat Label is to allow easy entry of mixed digit-and-alphabetic data such as street addresses. If you prepare a range this way, you can enter such data as 145 Oak Street without the trouble of manually typing an initial label prefix.

However, for actual numbers, $\underline{S}$tyle $\underline{N}$umber Format $\underline{F}$ormat Label is the electronic equivalent of a draught of hemlock; numbers entered into the range turn into labels and cannot be used in computations.

Do not confuse $\underline{S}$tyle $\underline{N}$umber Format $\underline{F}$ormat Label with $\underline{S}$tyle $\underline{A}$lignment. The $\underline{S}$tyle $\underline{A}$lignment command does not turn numeric entries into labels; it merely shifts their alignment. In contrast, $\underline{S}$tyle $\underline{N}$umber Format $\underline{F}$ormat Label turns numbers into labels—which you usually do not want to do.

Comma Format

At this point, the column head labels and numbers in CONCOST line up, but the numbers look rather ragged. The decimal places do not line up. We can easily dress up the numbers by selecting an appropriate format. Comma format is perhaps the most widely used of all numeric formats. It presents a specified number of decimal places and also shows commas in large numbers.

We are going to use Comma format on CONCOST. First, enter 95 in cell B5 so that we have some larger numbers in the worksheet. Next select the range B5..G10. Then select $\underline{S}$tyle $\underline{N}$umber Format. Move the highlight up and down the $\underline{F}$ormat choices in the list box. The Sample box changes to show you how the highlighted choice would affect your data. In Figure 3.7, the highlight is on Comma, so the Sample box shows what the current cell would look like if we select Comma format.

FIGURE 3.7

The Style Number Format Dialog Box

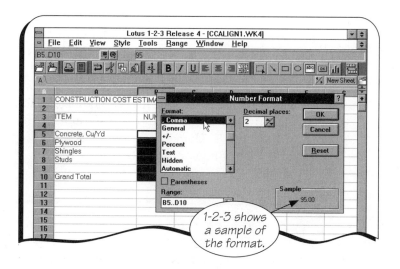

Select Comma. All numbers in the selected range B5..G10 now should look as shown in Figure 3.8.

FIGURE 3.8

Comma Format

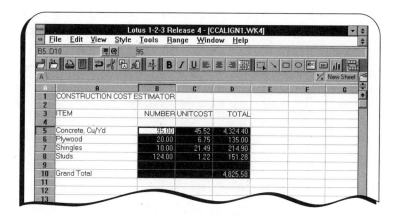

That looks much more professional; each number shows two decimal places, and thousands are separated by commas. But it still isn't quite right. The topmost numbers in columns C and D and the TOTAL COST number really should be shown with leading dollar signs.

Currency Format

Currency format, like Comma format, is widely used. We are going to apply Currency format to some of the cells in CONCOST.

Select the range C5..D5. Then select Style Number Format. From the Format list box, select Currency. The default number of Decimal places is 2; that is what we want. Select OK to complete the process. Next, format cell D10 the same way. If you do not drop the ball, your construction cost estimator now should look like Figure 3.9. As you can see, Currency format is like Comma format except for the leading dollar sign.

FIGURE 3.9

Applying
Currency Format

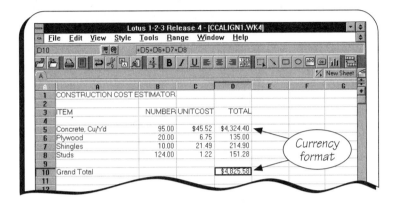

NUMERIC FORMATS: APPEARANCE VERSUS REALITY

Remember that the format applied to a cell does not affect the value rule or the value of the cell. To see this principle in action, change cell B5 of CONCOST to 95.7. Your worksheet should look like Figure 3.10.

FIGURE 3.10

Screen Display versus
Computed Value

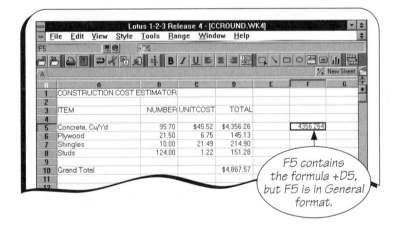

In cell F5, we entered the formula +D5; however, F5 is in General format; it is not limited to showing two decimal places as D5 is. F5 shows the computed value 4356.264, which is what D5 actually computes. This difference between computed values and formatted displays can cause a column of numbers to show small disparities between the screen display and the total. The @ROUND function, discussed in Chapter 12, can fix the problem.

If a cell's value is too big to display in the selected format, you will see ************ in the cell. For example, if you entered 100000 in cell B5 of CONCOST, the worksheet would suddenly take on the appearance of Figure 3.11.

FIGURE 3.11
Data Too Wide
for Format

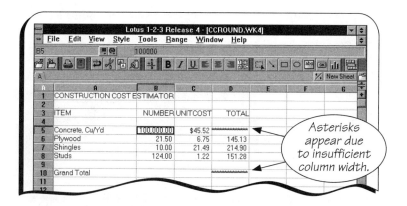

All your value rules and values are still there; but the columns are not wide enough to display the values in your selected format. To fix the problem, widen the affected columns (using Style Column Width).

USING TEXT FORMAT TO UNCOVER FORMULAS

It is easier to understand a worksheet if you can actually see the formulas in their cells, all at once. The Style Number Format command contains a Text choice that lets you peer down into the bottom layer of each cell in a range. Anywhere that formulas are the bottom layer, you can see them. This command is like stripping the masks off people at a costume ball. Computational results and fancy format disappear, and you can see how the formulas tie cells together.

To see how this works, first save your file—we are about to temporarily reformat all the active area and respecifying the various current formats would be tedious. Then select the range A1..D10 of your CONCOST file. Next select Style Number Format Text. You will find yourself looking into the lowest layer, the value rule layer, of all cells in the range. Cells that contain labels or plain numbers as value rules still show the label or number, but cells whose value rules are formulas show the formula itself. Figure 3.12 shows the results.

FIGURE 3.12
Using Text Format
to Look at
Value Rules

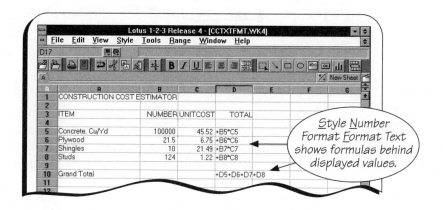

As your worksheets get more complex, there will be times when you make mistakes in setting up formulas. When the numbers look wrong, it is tedious to examine formulas by moving the cellpointer from cell to cell. Style Number Format Text is a much faster, easier "debugging" tool.

If you want to save the file with the Text format, use File Save As and call it CONCTEXT. That way, you will not overwrite the nicely formatted CONCOST with the grubby text format.

FORMATTING FROM THE STATUS BAR

You also can select a format by clicking on the leftmost box in the status bar, which in the following example shows Automatic. However, the status bar format selector is not as flexible as the Style Number Format command, and it is not much faster.

HELP! THE COMPUTER ATE MY DATA!

Remember that when you see *********s in a numeric cell, it only means that the column width is too narrow to display the number in the format you have chosen. Don't panic—the number is still there. Recall the idea of format masks—you are trying to squeeze the number through a mask that won't fit in the existing column width. The solution is to widen the column with Style Column Width.

EXPANDING THE CONCOST WORKSHEET

Now, let's add a bid-generating section to CONCOST. We used 1-2-3 to compute the cost of the job; we might as well make 1-2-3 compute the markup over cost. While we are at it, we will make 1-2-3 write a bid letter to our potential customer. Make the additions to your CONCOST file that are shown in Figure 3.13.

FIGURE 3.13
Additions to CONCOST

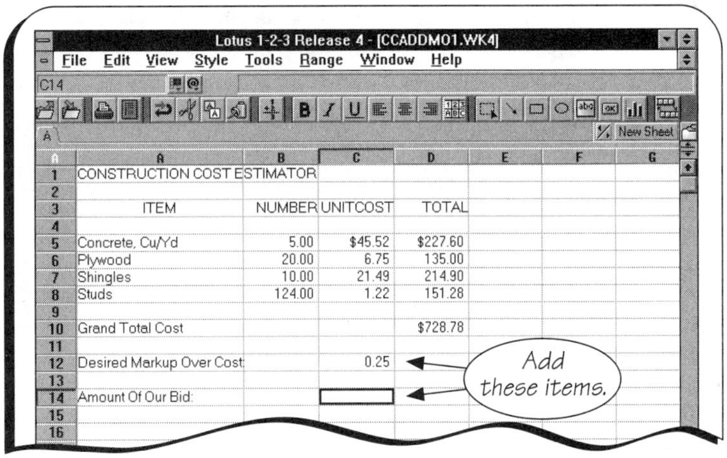

In cell C14, we need a formula that adds a profit of 25% of cost to the calculated cost. Put this formula in C14: +C12*D10+D10.

The first part of the formula—the "+C12*D10" part—computes the value of cell C12, where the markup fraction is, times the value of cell D10, where the computed cost is. The markup is then added to the value of cell D10. Instead of using this roundabout method, you could simply have entered the formula +.25*D10+D10; that would have been all right if you didn't want to play around with different markup computations. By using a separate cell to hold the markup, however, we can play "what-if" by changing the value in C12. If we had used a literal .25, it would have been necessary to change the formula itself to .15, or .1223, or whatever markup we wanted to try out. Your worksheet now will look like Figure 3.14.

FIGURE 3.14

Bid-generating
Formula

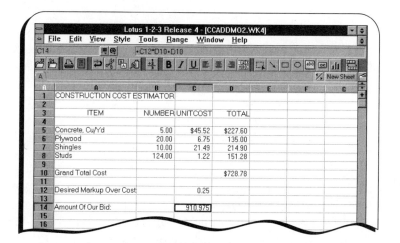

Play some "what-if" by changing the value of cell C12. Notice that our bid in cell C14 automatically recalculates itself every time you change the markup value in cell C12.

Finally, let's make 1-2-3 prepare a form letter. We could set up the form letter below or to the right of the existing data, but there is a better way. We can put the form letter on its own separate worksheet inside the CONCOST file.

Creating Multiple Sheets

To add a new worksheet (or "sheet" for short) to CONCOST, click on the New Sheet button on the right side of the control panel. A new file folder tab labeled "B" appears, and your cellpointer is at A1 in the new sheet. In sheet B, reproduce the form letter shown in Figure 3.15.

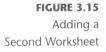

FIGURE 3.15
Adding a
Second Worksheet

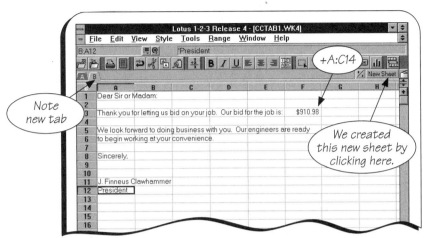

With the form letter in its own sheet, we can change it without worrying about any effect on sheet A (unless Group is on, which is discussed later).

A Formula That References Another Worksheet

Our form letter is in sheet B, but it needs to get bid information from worksheet A. To refer to a cell in another worksheet, start your formula with the appropriate tab identifier. For example, cell F3 in the preceding example needs to get its value by looking at the bid figure in worksheet A. Enter the formula +A:C14 in cell F3. The formula tells 1-2-3 that cell F3 is to determine its value by looking at cell C14 *of sheet A*. If the value in cell C14 of worksheet A changes, so will the value in cell F3 of worksheet B.

Naming Worksheet Tabs

1-2-3's default tab names (like A and B) are not very descriptive. Let's change the name of the form letter tab. Double-click on tab B, type Form Letter, and press ↵. The tab now says "Form Letter" instead of "B." While we are changing tab names, we might as well give worksheet A a better tab name. Double-click on tab A and type Estimator. Then click on the Form Letter tab. Your tabs now should look like those in Figure 3.16.

FIGURE 3.16
Naming a
Worksheet Tab

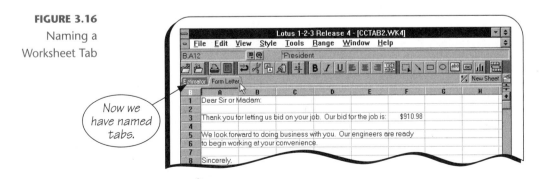

Save your worksheet now (by clicking on the File Save icon or by selecting File Save).

FONTS AND FANCY FEATURES

1-2-3 has many features for enhancing the appearance of a worksheet. You can access these features by selecting Style Font & Attributes. We are going to use the menu, but you can accomplish the same jobs with the icons. If you click on the icon selector in the status bar and select the Formatting palette, 1-2-3 displays the appropriate icons.

Using Style Font & Attributes

We are going to alter the appearance of the entire form letter. Select the range A1..F12. Then select Style Font & Attributes. You should see a dialog box like Figure 3.17.

FIGURE 3.17

Using the Style Fonts & Attributes Dialog Box

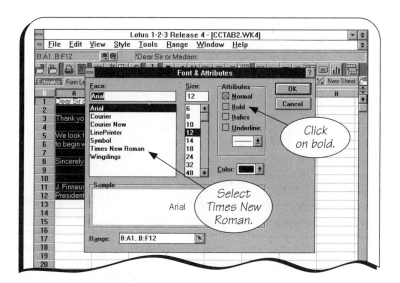

Click on the boldface check box. Then select Times New Roman, 12 point.

Using Style Lines & Color

Style Lines & Color is handy for adding special effects to the selected range. Let's use it to add an attention-getting frame around our bid price. Select A3..F3. Then select Style Lines & Color. From the dialog box, select Designer Frame. Your form letter now should look like Figure 3.18.

FIGURE 3.18
Adding a
Designer Frame

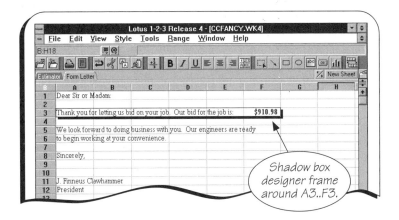

CANNED STYLES   Instead of designing your own fancy layout, you can use the Style Gallery command to apply any one of fourteen predesigned style templates to the current range. If your data layout happens to fit one of the templates, you can get fancy formatting on the cheap. Figure 3.19 shows the Style Gallery dialog box.

FIGURE 3.19
The Style Gallery
Dialog Box

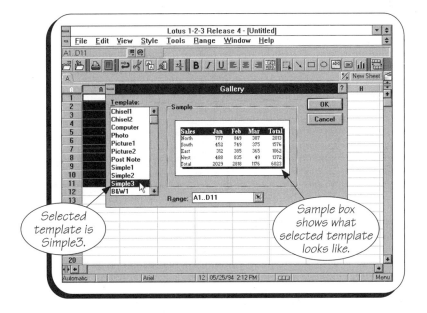

Notice the Sample box. It gives you a preview of the currently selected style template. In Figure 3.19, we have selected the Simple3 template. If you click on OK, any currently selected range would be formatted like the Simple3 sample.

Joe Bob LeBouef IV

Joe Bob LeBouef, Head Football Coach at Sasquatch University, thinks you are a wonderful person and a spreadsheet guru. He has been very pleased with your previous worksheets. Now he wants some formatting improvements. Once again, Joe Bob offered you a deal you couldn't refuse. You agreed to make any changes he wants. Joe Bob drew you this picture.

Don't set up an entirely new worksheet; open your JOEBOB3 file from Chapter 2, and immediately File Save as JOEBOB3F. Then make modifications to JOEBOB3F.

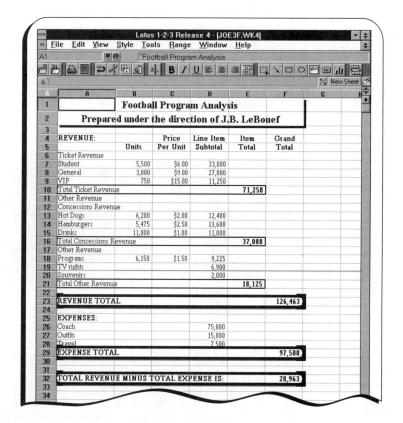

Joe Bob wants these formats, fonts, and effects:

- Heading centered across the range A1..F2; bold; Times New Roman font in 18-point size.
- Shadow box around the heading.
- Column B in Comma format, zero decimal places.
- Column C in Currency format, two decimal places.
- Columns D, E, and F in Comma format, zero decimals.

- Boldface in other ranges, as shown.
- Medium-weight outline around rows 10, 16, and 21.
- Designer frame around rows 23, 29, and 32.

Remember to save your file every few minutes as you work. Use the filename JOEBOB3F.

E. S. Cargot

Monsieur E. S. Cargot, a chef at Trimalchio's Restuarant, is a great cook, but he has absolutely no head for numbers. In the past that was not a problem, but Trimalchio's has decided to start a catering operation. It will work like this: A client calls Trimalchio's and requests a dinner for 40, or 400, or whatever, to be laid on at location x, on date y.

Mr. Cargot is going to be the chief chef for the catering operation. He needs a fast, reliable way to convert recipes for 1 into recipes for any specified number of people.

Cargot wants you to set up a system for him. On the bottom of a copper cauldron he sketched out his idea for you.

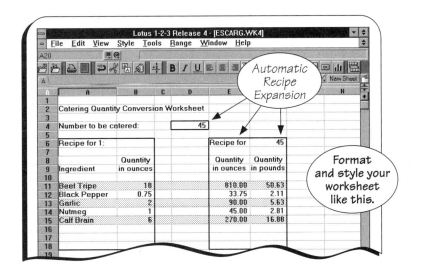

Basically, Mr. Cargot wants to enter the Number to be catered, the ingredients, and the Quantity in Ounces (for 1 serving); your job is to provide any necessary formulas to convert his one-serving data into x-serving data, in both ounces and pounds. If you do well, Cargot will give you a year's free pass to Trimalchio's Wednesday Noon Buffet. When you finish, save the file using the filename ESCARGOT.

There is a way to copy the formulas instead of entering each one, but we haven't covered that yet, so do it the hard way.

The Mileage Log Case

J. J. Aardvark, a friend of yours, has a part-time job selling encyclopedias. Often he drives considerable distances, making calls on prospects. For tax purposes he needs to keep a complete log of business mileage driven. He can deduct (total business mileage*per-mile allowance) as a business expense. He also wants to compute minimum, maximum, and average trip lengths. J.J. has a notebook computer and Lotus 1-2-3. He wants you to set up a worksheet for him, in such a way that he can punch in starting and ending odometer readings for each sales call and automatically get a current report. He sketched this example of what he wants.

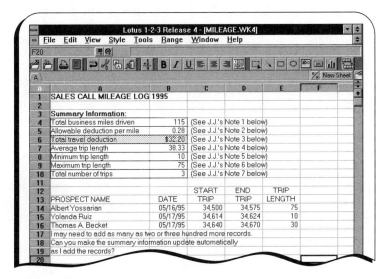

(1) Sum the TRIP LENGTH column. Automatically pick up any records I add to the bottom of the list.

(2) Here I enter this year's allowable rate, such as 0.28 per mile.

(3) Multiplies the two cells above, to get total deduction.

(4) Computes the average of the values in the TRIP LENGTH column, as far down the column as I enter values.

(5) Automatically picks the shortest value in the TRIP LENGTH column.

(6) Automatically picks the largest value in the TRIP LENGTH column.

(7) Automatically counts the number of trips made.

1. Select File Close to clear your worksheet if it is not clear. Enter this number in cell D10: 123456. Format D10 as Text. Does cell D10 look any different? Why or why not?

2. Format D10 so that it looks like this: 123,456.

3. Format D10 so that it looks like this: $123,456.00. *Tip:* widen the column when you get *********.

4. Format D10 so that it looks like this: 123456.0000.

5. Enter 123456 in D11 and D12. Format the range D10..D12 for Currency format, no decimal places.

6. In cell D12, enter the value rule +D10/5. Observe the resulting value. Now format D12 as text. In cell D14, enter the formula +D12*2. Does the text screen format of cell D12 affect the value of cell D14?

7. Set this up and plug in the necessary figures and formulas.

   J. Alfred Prufrock, a friend of yours, operates a concrete contracting firm. Recently you mentioned to him, very modestly, that you were a whiz-bang Lotus 1-2-3 expert who could set up *any* number-crunching problem.

   > "Zat right?" he replied gruffly. "Then set me up a computerized bid sheet system, so I don't have to stay up half the night figuring and refiguring job bids. Can you do that? Eh? Eh?"

   > You looked at him cooly and nonchalantly. "Is that all?" you said. "No problem. When do you want to see it?"

   > J. Alfred chewed his cigar a moment, and said, "Right now."

   > You shrugged and responded, "O.K. Write down the way you want it set up, and give me 20 minutes."

   Fortunately you had a computer at hand, so you sat down and went to work. Here is the setup J. Alfred gave you:

```
CONCRETE JOB-COST CALCULATOR

                              NUMBER        UNIT      TOTAL
        ITEM                  OF UNITS      COST      COST

        Ready-mix, Cu/yd
        Rebar, 1/2", feet
        Rebar, 1/4", feet
        Mesh, 6x6, rolls
        Forms, square feet
        Bulldozer, hours
        Backhoe, hours
        Labor:
          Placer, hours
          Screeder, hours
          Finisher, hours
          Foreman, hours
        Estimated # trips to job
        Miles from hq to job
        Total miles travel        p.s. this is est.trips * miles
        Rate per mile, dollars
        Total travel expense      J.A. wants this summed in total col.


        Total Job Cost:

        Markup:
        Total Bid:
```

Remember to save your file every few minutes as you work.

The following exercises are on your SMART disk. Retrieve, complete, and save them back to disk.

1. **03AU08** is a straightforward exercise in using various numeric and label formats.

2. **03AU10** is a large, SMART version of the construction cost estimator problem in Chapter 3. It requires both simple formulas and formatting.

3. **03AU15** reinforces the earlier ideas of cell references in formulas, and it also requires specific formats for selected cells. The problem introduces the idea of referencing a cell by using its address as the formula, for example, +G31.

Copying, Moving, and Worksheet Management

OBJECTIVES   After studying this chapter, you should know how to:

- Copy labels and numbers from one range to another.
- Copy formulas from one range to another, using relative and absolute references.
- Create sequences by copying.
- Move ranges to different locations.
- Insert and delete rows and columns.
- Create named ranges.
- Freeze rows and columns.
- Split worksheets into panes.

COPYING CELLS AND RANGES   Copying is a time-saving technique for "cloning" cell value rules. If you need to reproduce the value rule of a cell, copying is much faster and more accurate than manually retyping the contents over and over.

     Copying does not change the source range (what you copied). However, copying does change the target range (where you copied to). Everything in the target range is obliterated and replaced with a copy of the source range.

If you have a worksheet in memory, select File Close and save it before closing. Now you have a totally blank worksheet in memory. We are going to use it as a "doodle pad."

Copying Techniques

There are several ways to copy cell value rules. The same techniques work for labels, plain non-formula-based numbers, and formulas, but copying formulas has certain quirks, which we will discuss later. For now, let's copy some labels and numbers.

Copying by Dragging

The simplest, quickest copying technique is called **dragging**. To explore this technique, enter the label Sales in cell A1. To copy the label by dragging, first select the range to be copied (A1, in our example). Then move the mouse pointer toward the edge of the selected range until the mouse pointer changes to a hand, as shown in Figure 4.1.

FIGURE 4.1

Preparing to Copy

To make the copy, hold down CTRL and press the left mouse button. The open hand changes to a closed fist with a plus sign on it. Drag to the range where you want the copy to appear. In Figure 4.2, we have dragged to cell D2.

FIGURE 4.2

Dragging a Copy

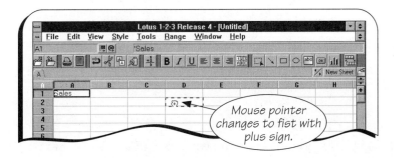

When you release the CTRL key and the mouse button, the copy appears in the selected cell. Dragging also works for copying a multicell range; everything works the same way, except that you select more than a single cell in the first stage.

The dragging technique is fast, but it has limitations. If you want to make multiple copies of a range, or if you want to copy data to other worksheets, you need the following techniques.

Using Edit Copy and Edit Paste

Edit Copy transfers a copy of the range you select to a storage area in RAM called the **clipboard**. The clipboard is not a part of any file, and data copied to the clipboard stays there until you replace it.

Let's copy the label in A1 to the clipboard. With your cellpointer in A1, select Edit Copy. The clipboard now contains a copy of the label.

Move the cellpointer to B1. Instead of copying to a single cell, select the range B1..C6; then select Edit Paste. 1-2-3 looks on the clipboard and "pastes" a copy of the contents into the selected range, as Figure 4.3 shows.

FIGURE 4.3
Edit Copy Followed
by Edit Paste

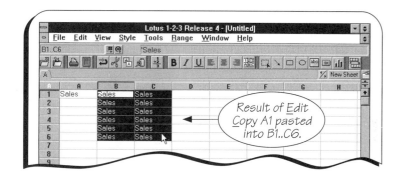

Using Edit Copy Right and Edit Copy Down

To make rightwards multiple copies of a single cell, first select the cell to be copied and any desired number of cells to its right. Then select Edit Copy Right. To make copies of a single cell down a column, select a downward range and select Edit Copy Down.

Copying with the Mouse Quick Menu

The quick menu offers still another way to copy. You can mark the range to be copied with your mouse, and then press the *right* mouse button with the mouse pointer inside the range. The quick menu appears. Select the Copy quick menu choice. Then select the destination for the copy and again invoke the mouse quick menu, selecting the Paste option. The mouse quick menu also has copy-right and copy-down choices.

A Pitfall in Copying Ranges

1-2-3 gets confused by partial overlaps. If you partially overlap the source and target ranges in a copy operation, you usually will get strange results. Do not ever use a partial overlap in a COPY operation.

Select File Close to get a clear worksheet; you need not save your work. Set up the following worksheet; then select the range A1..A5 as shown in Figure 4.4.

FIGURE 4.4

Marking a
Range to Copy

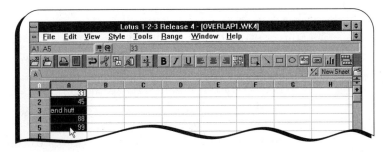

Select Edit Copy. Then select cell A2. Next select Edit Paste to copy A1..A6 from the clipboard to A2..A7. You will get the highly undesirable results shown in Figure 4.5.

FIGURE 4.5

Effect of
Overlapping
Ranges

The partial overlap royally confused 1-2-3; it forgot what was where and ended up reproducing A1 into A2..A6. Select File Close without saving and set up the data in the range A1..A5 again.

If the TO range completely overlaps the FROM range, no problem occurs. It would be perfectly all right to copy the range A1..A6 to the range A1..C1. If you did that, everything would function as it should.

Copying Formulas

The mechanical side of copying formulas works just like copying text or simple numbers. You use exactly the same techniques. However, the results may seem a little surprising until you get the hang of it. In the preceding examples of copying simple numbers and labels, the cells' value rules made no references to other cells. Formulas *do* refer to other cells. When a formula is copied, there must be some protocol for deciding how to treat the copied cell references.

Let's approach formula copying by stepping through an example. Clear the worksheet with File Close and set up a worksheet like Figure 4.6.

FIGURE 4.6

Preparing to
Copy a Formula

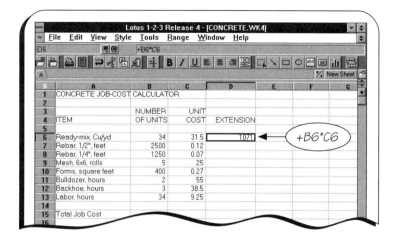

In terms of worksheet geography, the formula in D6, +B6*C6, means "multiply the cell two columns to the left, by the cell one column to the left." What we want is a way to reproduce the formula in the range D7..D13. No one except a masochist would want to do this manually, by physically moving the cellpointer and entering the formula seven more times. So, let's copy it.

One-to-One Formula Copy

The cellpointer is on cell D6—D6 is "selected." We want to copy the value rule in D6 into D7..D13, but let's start small and just copy the value rule of D6 into D7. After copying, place your cellpointer on D7. Your worksheet should look like Figure 4.7.

FIGURE 4.7

One-to-One
Formula Copy

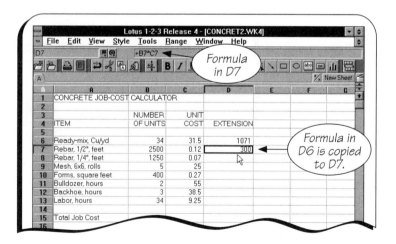

1-2-3 seems to be guilty of insubordination. You asked it to copy the value rule in D6 into D7, but 1-2-3 did not literally do that. If 1-2-3 had taken your order literally, cell D7 would show a value of 1071, just like cell D6 does, because the formula in D7 would have been +B6*C6.

1-2-3 assumed that you wanted the value rule in D7 adjusted relative to the value rule in D6. 1-2-3 always makes this adjustment unless you explicitly prevent it. Normally the adjustment is exactly what you want. In most cases, you do *not* want a literal copy of some cell's formula value rule; you want a formula that is adjusted for position in the worksheet.

Relative Addressing in Formula Copies

By default, then, 1-2-3 adjusts a copied formula rather than making a literal copy. This automatic adjustment of formula-based value rules in a copy operation is called **relative addressing**.

One-to-Many Formula Copying—Relative Addressing

To finish our column of formulas:

1. Put the cellpointer back on D6.
2. Copy D6 into the range D6..D13.

Your cellpointer is in D6 after the copy. Now move your cellpointer to D13 by pressing END+down arrow.

Your cellpointer pops down to cell D13. The cellpointer stops when it gets to the boundary between occupied and unoccupied cells. Your worksheet now should look like Figure 4.8.

FIGURE 4.8

One-to-Many
Formula Copy

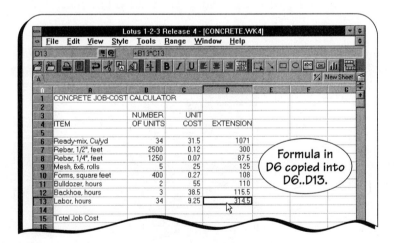

Look at the formula in D13. Sure enough, it has been adjusted relative to the cell you copied from; it will read +B13*C13.

Save the concrete job-cost calculator using the filename CONCRETE. Then clear the worksheet with File Close. Let's create a new worksheet to further explore copying formulas.

One-to-Many Formula Copying—Absolute Addressing

Beginning from your clear worksheet, widen column A to a width of 20 with Style Column Width. Set up the worksheet shown in Figure 4.9.

FIGURE 4.9

Pro Forma
Worksheet

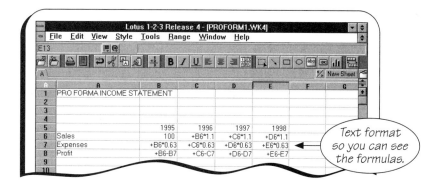

The formulas shown inside the worksheet will not actually show up when you type them, of course—I am putting them there so you can see the web of relationships tying the cells together. The model assumes that sales in 1995 are 100 and that sales will grow 10% per year in 1996, a further 10% in 1997, and still a further 10% in 1998. Annual expenses are assumed to be 63% of sales each year. Profit is computed by subtracting each year's expenses from that year's sales.

After you enter the labels, the year headings, and the initial sales figure in cell B6, enter the formula in C6 and copy C6 into D6..E6. Enter the formula shown in B7; then copy to C7..E7. Finally, enter the formula shown in B8 and copy it to C8..E8. All these copying operations use relative addressing because you want the target cells adjusted relative to the position of the source cell.

What you have now is the kernel of a 1-2-3 financial modeling system. As it stands, however, it is too simple to be of any real-world use, but it illustrates the web of cell relationships in a "what-if" model. The model is somewhat like an electronic house of cards; if you change the sales figure in cell B6, every other cell in the matrix recalculates itself according to its value rule. All the value rules depend directly or indirectly on the initial sales cell, B6. Play a little "what-if" by changing cell B6 to a number other than 100. When you get tired of watching the ripple effects, put 100 back in B6.

It would be nice to be able to play "what-if" with the sales growth rate. One way to check the effects of a different sales growth rate is to edit cell C6, change 1.1 to 1.07, or 1.22, or whatever growth rate you want, and then copy the edited cell into D6 and E6. But this is a great deal of trouble. There is a better way. Make the additions shown in Figure 4.10 to your model.

FIGURE 4.10
Relative Reference
Won't Work

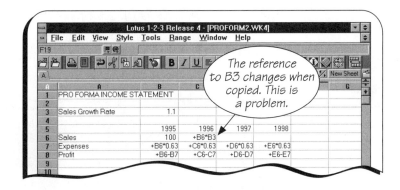

Notice the alteration in the formula in cell C6 to pick up the value of cell B3, instead of multiplying by a fixed 1.1. By using the formula +B6*B3, the value of cell C6 will be tied both to the sales figure in cell B6 and to the growth rate in cell B3. There is only one fly in the ointment. If you copy the formula in C6 into D6..E6, the formulas will look like this:

    +B6*B3   +C6*C3   +D6*D3

Can you see the problem? 1-2-3 would adjust the references to B3 because of relative addressing. It is fine for 1-2-3 to adjust B6 to C6 to D6, but the second cell reference should *not* be adjusted. The growth rate is always in cell B3, so the second part of the three formulas should reference cell B3. To make 1-2-3 "freeze" the reference to B3, we have to use a copy-freezing technique called **absolute addressing.**

Absolute Addressing

To tell 1-2-3 not to adjust the cell references in a formula during a copy operation, put dollar signs in front of the column and row designators. In our model, edit cell C6 and change the formula to +B6*$B$3. Then copy C6 into D6..E6. Your worksheet should look like Figure 4.11.

FIGURE 4.11
Absolute Reference
to Input Cell

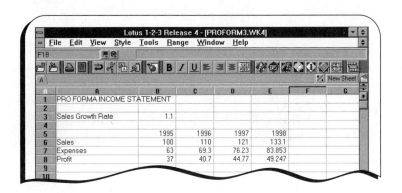

To see the formulas inside the worksheet, mark the range B6..E8 and select Style Number Format Text, followed by Style Alignment Right. You should see a screen like Figure 4.12.

FIGURE 4.12
Effect of Copying
Absolute Reference

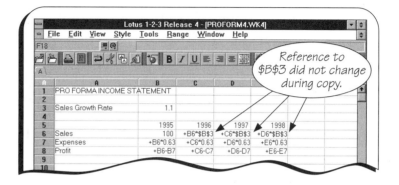

The leading $ signs prevented any alteration to the "$B$3" component of the formula. But notice that the "B6" in cell C6 changed as the formula in cell C6 copied across columns D and E.

Now reformat the range B6..E6 in Currency,2 format; reformat B7..E8 in Comma,2 format; and proceed to play "what-if." Change the sales growth rate in cell B3 to 1.25, or 1.06, or whatever you please, and watch the change ripple through the model. For example, if you change the sales growth rate to 1.30, your screen should look like Figure 4.13. Save this worksheet; you will need it again shortly. Call it PROFORMA.

FIGURE 4.13
Effects of Changing
Input Cell

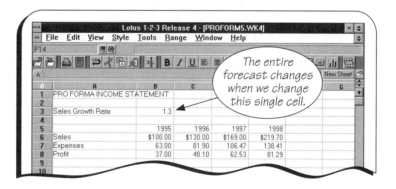

Multiple Copies of a Range: Formulas

Rather than copying cells one at a time, we could have made a mass copy of the range C6..C8 into D6..E6. For such a small worksheet this technique saves little time, but it would save a great deal of time if our model had 20 rows of financial data instead of three. For practice, erase the range D6..E8 and then copy C6..C8 into D6..E6.

Mixed Addressing—Freezing Rows or Columns

Rather than freezing both the row and column references in a formula, you can freeze only one or the other. For example, if you wanted the rows to adjust when the cell was copied, you could use the general form $COLUMN ROW. If you wanted the columns but not the rows to adjust, you could use the form COLUMN $ROW. To explore this wrinkle, clear your worksheet with File Close and set up the worksheet shown in Figure 4.14.

FIGURE 4.14
Mixed Addressing
Formulas

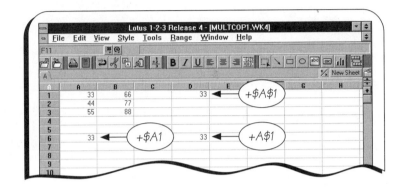

Now, copy A6 into A6..C8. Then copy D1 into D1..F3. Finally copy D6 into D6..F8. After completing the three copy operations, your screen should look like Figure 4.15.

FIGURE 4.15
Effects of Mixed
Addressing

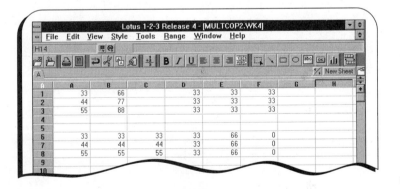

The D1..F3 range shows the value 33 throughout because the formula in the copy-from cell was $A$1—a full absolute reference that prevented either columns or rows from adjusting during the copy. The D6..F8 range had a relative reference to the *column*, but not the *row*, because the formula in D6 was +A$1. Thus the column was free to adjust as D6 copied into columns E and F. However, the row reference was frozen. The A6..C8 range adjusted for row, but not for column due to the $A1 formula, which permitted the row to change during a copy, but not the column. The formulas that underlie these values are shown in Figure 4.16.

FIGURE 4.16
Mixed Addresses
in Text Format

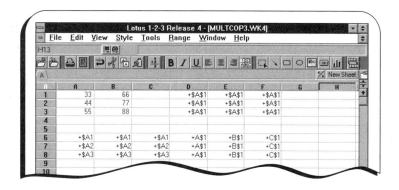

Using the F4 Key For Absolute or Mixed Addressing

Rather than typing dollar signs ahead of column/row references you can use Point mode in conjunction with the function key F4. For example, you could have entered the formula in D1 above by:

1. Putting your cellpointer on cell D1.
2. Typing a + to indicate a formula.
3. Using the left arrow to move the cellpointer to cell A1. 1-2-3 automatically goes into Point mode when you move the cellpointer while entering a formula.
4. With the cellpointer on cell A1, press the F4 key. The entry/edit line would show +$A$1.
5. Press ⏎ to complete the entry of the absolute reference.

If you had pressed F4 twice, the entry/edit line would have changed to A$1; a third press would yield $A1. You would have generated a mixed reference.

If this material on mixed references seems unusually confusing, don't worry. Mixed references are not used all that frequently. The bread and butter operations are relative addressing and absolute addressing.

Completing a Sequence by Copying

There is a particularly smart icon for reproducing a sequence of data from a single-cell sample. For example, if you entered 1995 in cell A1, selected the range A1..A10, and then clicked on the icon, 1-2-3 would look at your example in A1 and increment it to 1996, 1997, and so forth downwards through A10. If you entered the label January in C3, selected the range C3..G3, and then clicked on the icon, 1-2-3 would understand that you wanted a sequence of month labels in the range. The icon also builds sequences of days of the week or times of day, beginning from your example. Figure 4.17 shows the effect of some of these supersmart icon tricks.

FIGURE 4.17

Automatic
Sequencing

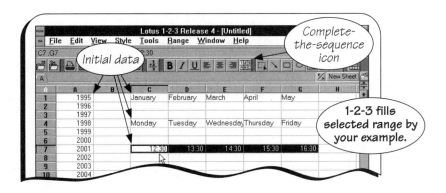

 The <u>R</u>ange Fill by <u>E</u>xample command does the same job as the icon. The
menu command is more flexible, if you need fine control.

**MOVING CELL
VALUE RULES**

Moving allows you to rearrange the placement of the elements in your worksheet. Formula cells with relative addresses are adjusted in the same way they
are in a Copy command. However, the Move command also adjusts absolute
references in the moved range. 1-2-3 assumes that when you Move a range,
you want to preserve all the cell relationships within that range—a reasonable
assumption.

Moving by Clicking and Dragging a Range

This technique works just like drag-copying, except you do not hold down the
CTRL key. Simply select the range to be moved, click on a range boundary, and
hold down the mouse button while you move the mouse.

Moving via the Clipboard

To explore moving by clipboard, retrieve your PROFORMA file and then use
Style <u>N</u>umber Format Text to display the range A1..E8 in text format. You
should see the display shown in Figure 4.18.

FIGURE 4.18
Pro Forma
Worksheet
Prior to Move

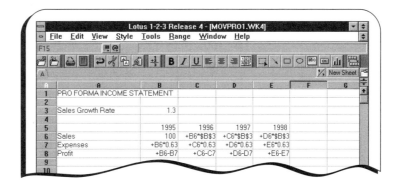

Let's move the range A3..B3 to C3. To do so, simply select A3..B3, select Edit Cut; select cell C3; and then select Edit Paste. Alternatively, you can use the mouse quick menu. After the move operation, your worksheet should look like Figure 4.19.

FIGURE 4.19
Pro Forma
Worksheet After
Move by Clipboard

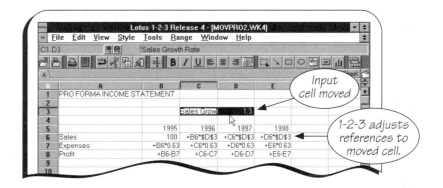

Notice the changes to the value rules; they have automatically adjusted for the shifted location of the sales growth rate. After you have meditated on the effects of the Move command, do a File Close. We do not want to save these modifications to disk.

INSERTING AND DELETING ROWS, COLUMNS, AND WORKSHEETS

1-2-3 allows you to insert and delete rows, columns, and worksheets. However, if you need to rearrange your worksheet, moving is safer than inserting or deleting, for reasons discussed later.

How to Insert and Delete

To insert, select Edit Insert. To delete, select Edit Delete. The dialog boxes are very similar for either selection. The dialog box for Edit Insert looks like Figure 4.20.

FIGURE 4.20

The <u>E</u>dit <u>I</u>nsert Dialog Box

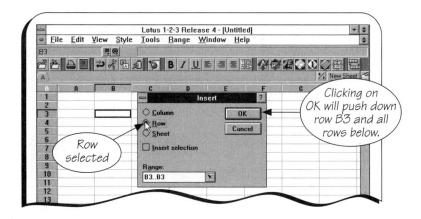

When you insert a row, the current row and all rows below it move down. When you insert a column, the current column and all columns to the right move rightward. However, the worksheet never can be larger than 8192 rows and 256 columns. Thus, you cannot insert rows or columns if the result would push any nonblank cells outside the boundaries. If Group mode is active, insertions or deletions affect all sheets in the file.

When you insert inside a named range, the named range automatically expands to include the inserted rows or columns. When you delete inside a named range, the named range automatically shrinks.

Moving versus Inserting or Deleting

As we have said, it is safer to rearrange a worksheet by moving selected ranges than by inserting or deleting rows or columns. These are the reasons why moving is safer:

1. If you delete a row or column to which a formula refers, the formula shows ERR. Any formulas that reference that formula then show ERR. The result can cascade through your worksheet.

2. Inserting and deleting affects not only the visible area, but the entire worksheet. For example, if you are looking at the home area and delete rows three and four, the effect goes all the way to column IV. If you are working on a worksheet in cooperation with others, you may unintentionally destroy some of their work. By the same token, inserting rows may disrupt macros that lie outside the visible area.

 Be sure not to insert or delete rows in your SMART worksheets or you will get a real-world example of the dangers. SMART contains macro code that references specific cell addresses. If you alter the addresses by inserting or deleting, the SMART checker will not work correctly.

USING RANGE NAMES IN PLACE OF CELL REFERENCES

1-2-3 has a command that lets you attach names to ranges of cells. The named range can be as small as one cell or as big as the whole worksheet. Once the name is attached, you can use the range name in place of cell addresses.

Naming a cell or a range of cells has advantages:

1. The range name you pick can serve as a memory-jogger about what the range contains. For example, it is easier to remember that a cell named "Sales" contains sales data than it is to remember that some abstract address contains sales data.

2. You can move the cellpointer around the worksheet by clicking on the navigator box and selecting a range name to "go to."

3. Range names are "sticky." You can insert rows or columns, above or below the named range, and the name still will be attached to the contents of the originally named cells, wherever they go.

Follow these guidelines for range names.

- Range names can be up to 15 characters in length and can contain characters, digits, or underscore characters. Some other characters work, but some don't.
- Start all range names with a character (like A or Z).
- Don't use key names (such as HOME) or function names (such as SUM) as range names.
- Don't use cell addresses (e.g., Q3 or AB54) as range names.
- You can enter range names in uppercase, lowercase, or mixed case.
- You can create as many range names as you need.
- When you insert or delete columns or rows within a named range, 1-2-3 automatically expands or shrinks the named range.
- If you move data into the first or last cell of a named range, 1-2-3 automatically deletes the range name. Any formulas that refer to the range name then will result in ERR.
- In a given file, you cannot use the same range name more than once, even on different sheets. For example, in a two-worksheet file, you cannot name cell A1 TOP in worksheet A and also in worksheet B.
- In a multisheet file, if you use the Navigator button (discussed later) to move the cellpointer to a range name, 1-2-3 automatically selects whatever worksheet contains the range name. For example, if you have a cell named DOG in sheet B, but sheet A is current, if you select DOG, sheet B becomes current.

To see how range names work, retrieve the PROFORMA file. Select cell B3. Select Range Name to get the Name dialog box. Enter GRORATE in the Name box. Your screen should look like Figure 4.21.

FIGURE 4.21

Creating a Range Name

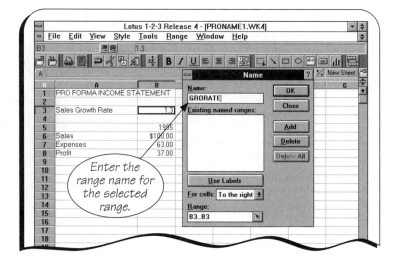

Any cell containing a formula that refers to the named range now will show the range name, rather than the cell address, in the contents box when you select the cell. For example, if you select cell C6, your contents box should look like Figure 4.22.

FIGURE 4.22

Range Name References in Formulas

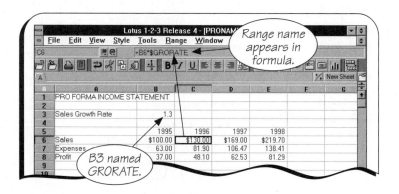

Naming Multicell Ranges

Up to this point we have named only single cells. Let's expand our horizons. Select the range A1..E8. Next select Range Name and enter PAGE1. Then entire range A1..E8 now bears the range name PAGE1. You now can substitute PAGE1 for any command that you want to apply to the range A1..E8.

Navigating With Range Names

Range names are a handy cellpointer-movement crutch. To see how this works, click on the Navigator button in the edit line of the control panel. You should see a range name list like the one in Figure 4.23.

FIGURE 4.23
The Navigator
Button

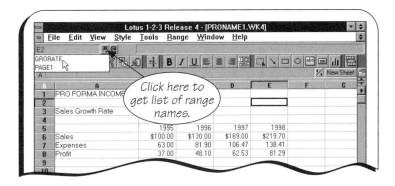

If you click GRORATE, 1-2-3 instantly selects cell B3 (because B3 is named GRORATE). The Navigator button is a very handy technique for moving around in large worksheets.

Range-Naming Cells From Existing Labels

1-2-3 offers a way to create range names automatically by using labels in cells next to the cells you want to name. For example, if we wanted to name the cell B6..B8 with the labels in A6..A8, we could select A6..A8 and then select Range Name Use Labels.

Deleting Range Names

To delete only selected range names, select the range name and click on the Delete button in the Name dialog box. If you want to get rid of all your range names at once, use the Range Name Delete All button in the Name dialog box. If you click Delete All, 1-2-3 wipes out all range names in the file.

DEALING WITH LARGE WORKSHEETS The ability to copy formulas makes it easy to create large worksheets. Once your worksheet expands beyond a single "screenful," you cannot see all the worksheet cells on the screen at once. Since your identifying labels are usually at the top and the left side of the worksheet, some or all the identifiers scroll off the screen as you move your cellpointer downward or rightward.

In a large worksheet, it is hard to remember what a given cell represents without seeing the row and column labels that identify it. This section discusses several techniques for dealing with large worksheets.

By selecting View Zoom Out, you can squeeze more cells onto your display (View Zoom In restores your display size).

If you still cannot see enough of the worksheet, you either can split your screen or select View Freeze Titles. Open the file BIGPRINT and we will experiment with these techniques.

FREEZING TITLES IN LARGE WORKSHEETS

In BIGPRINT, select cell B8 and begin moving rightwards. Notice that the labels in column A move off the screen as your cellpointer moves past column C. To keep the column A labels from scrolling off the screen, press HOME, and then move your cellpointer back to cell B8. Select View Freeze Titles and click the Both option button as shown in Figure 4.24.

FIGURE 4.24

Freezing a Screen Area

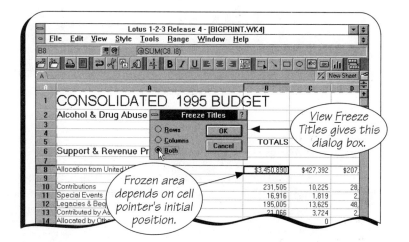

The Both option freezes all rows above the cellpointer and all columns to the left of the cellpointer. The Rows option freezes all rows above the cellpointer without freezing any columns. The Columns option freezes columns to the left of the cellpointer, without freezing any rows. We want to freeze both rows and columns so we can see both the column headers and row labels, no matter where we move the cellpointer.

Select OK. Then move the cellpointer downward and rightward to cell I56. Your screen now should look like Figure 4.25.

FIGURE 4.25
Effect of Freeze
Titles Both

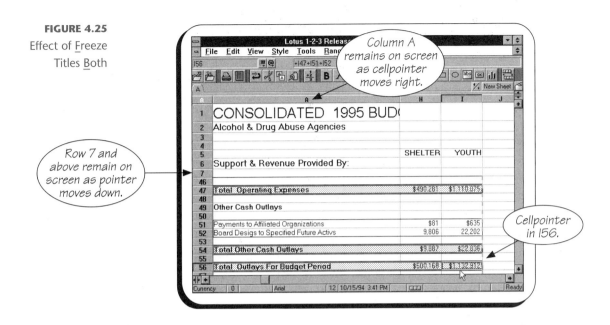

Creating A Second Pane in A Worksheet

Now let's experiment with another technique for managing large worksheets. Select View Clear Titles to unfreeze your screen. Press HOME.

Let's assume we need to see both the upper and lower section of BIGPRINT at the same time. Move your cellpointer from A1 to A9. Then select View Split. In the Split dialog box, click on Horizontal and deselect the Synchronize scrolling box. Your screen should look like Figure 4.26.

FIGURE 4.26
The View Split
Dialog Box

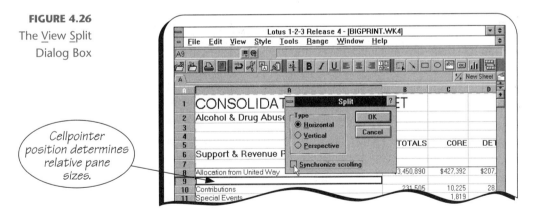

Select OK. Your worksheet now is split into two horizontal panes. You can select either pane by clicking inside it or by pressing F6. Select the lower pane and move your cellpointer to A60. Your screen now should look like Figure 4.27. Notice that the lower pane shows rows 53 through 60, while the upper pane shows rows 1 through 8.

FIGURE 4.27

Screen Split into Two Panes

Upper pane still shows HOME area.

Lower pane selected; cellpointer in Row 60.

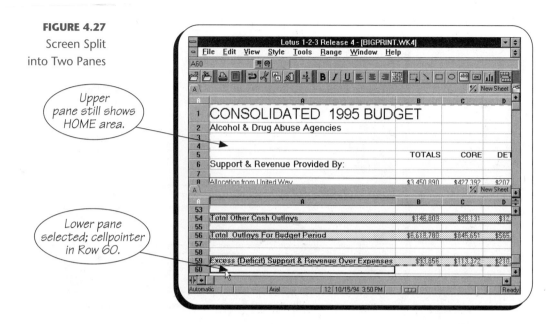

Since we clicked on the Unsynchronize scrolling box, we also could move the cellpointer sideways in either pane, without altering the view in the other pane. We also could have selected a vertical split if we had wanted to see widely separated columns on the screen simultaneously. To unsplit the screen, select View Clear Split.

The Future Cost of Burgers and Fries

In our economy, the price of goods and services tends to rise over time. Assume the staff of life (burger, fries, and drink) rises in price at the general inflation rate of x% per year. Set up a template that computes, year by year, the cost of such a meal over the next 40 years, given the parameters in D17..D19. If the parameters are changed, your future burger cost computations should reflect the changes. Use the following template design and provide the fancy formatting.

The meal cost the first projected year (1996 in the example) can be computed as (current cost+(current cost*annual inflation rate)). The meal cost in subsequent years will be (prior year cost+(prior year cost*annual inflation rate)). Enjoy your fast food during your retirement period...

Set up the formula in the top cell for each column, and copy; don't even think about reentering the same formula forty times!

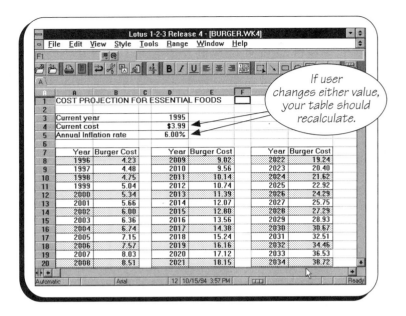

Begin these exercises with a clear worksheet.

1. Enter 5 in cell A7. Copy A7 to H20.

2. Enter 556 in A1. Copy A1 to the range A2..A15.

3. Copy A3 to the range B3..H3.

4. Erase the range A1..H20. Enter 111 in A2. Copy A2 into the range A3..H18.

5. Erase the range A1..H20. Enter a 1 in A1. Enter the formula +A1+1 in A2. Now copy the formula in A2 into the range A3..A15. To see what is going on underneath the numbers, select the range A1..A15 and put it in text format. After you finish looking, use Style Number Format to return the range to default format.

7. Erase the range A3..A15. Now copy A2 into A3..B15, that is, into the original area of column A and the adjacent area of column B.

8. Clear your worksheet with File Close. Put a 1 in cell A1. In the range A1..F3, set up a table so that:

   • Each cell in B1..F1 is 1 greater than the leftward cell.

   • Cell A2 is equal to cell F1.

   • Cells B2..F2 are 1 less than the leftward cell.

   • Cell A3 is equal to F2.

   • Cells B3..F3 are twice as great as the leftward cell.

Don't type numbers in every cell. Use formulas and copy them.

When everything works right, enter a 2 in cell A1. What happens?

9. Move the range A1..F3 to H10..M13.

Retrieve, complete, and save these exercises:

1. **04AU09** is designed to give practice in copying simple formulas. It also asks you to use the Help key (F1) to look up two functions, @SUM and @AVG, and use them in the problem. However, the problem also can be done without using the functions. Using the functions is optional. Once again, this problem alters the data cells to see if you are using cell references instead of plain numbers. When you run the checker, you will notice that the entire block of data cells is wiped out and replaced.

2. **04AU10** reinforces skills at copying formulas and introduces relative versus absolute formulas. The problem cannot be solved for full credit without creating absolute references—unless you are willing to type formulas into each cell. Once again, SMART alters values in the data part of the worksheet to see if you grasp the idea of cell-based formula construction.

3. **04AU11** covers formula copying with relative and absolute references.

4. **04AU12** is slightly different from your other SMART problems. When you retrieve the file, you will see none of the usual question marks, and the identifying labels are not provided. You have to type in the labels (shown in column A) as well as the formulas in column D. It does not matter whether you actually type the numbers shown in columns B and C. The checker enters its own numbers under QUANTITY and UNITCOST.

Set up 04AU12 like this:

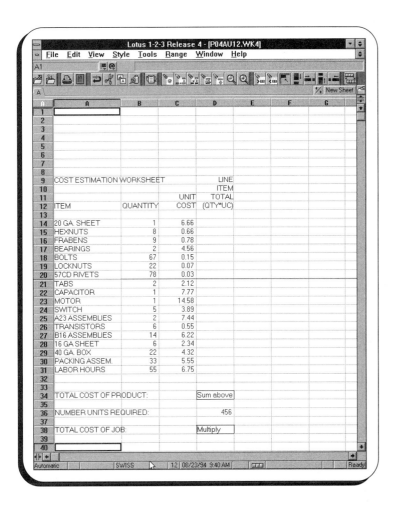

5. **04AU15** is a simple problem involving multiplication and division, copying the formulas to large ranges, and formatting.

6. **04BU20** is a fairly complex problem. It covers large-scale formula copying, both relative and absolute. The fact situation is also more complex than any earlier problems. The most common student error is to fail to extend the formula copying to the full 12 months. This problem has many formula cells. To keep checking time reasonable, SMART does not check all the formula cells in 04BU20; it selectively jumps around.

Charts and Graphics

OBJECTIVES   After studying this chapter, you should know how to:

- Create charts.
- Move charts.
- Delete charts.
- Select and change chart types.
- Add notes to charts.
- Add graphic elements to charts.

Any numeric data you create in a Lotus 1-2-3 worksheet can be displayed as a **chart** (a graphic representation). Often a chart is easier to understand than a bare table of data. If a picture is worth a thousand words, a chart is worth a thousand numbers.

CHART ELEMENTS   Charts are made up of standard elements. The main part of a chart is called the **plot**. The plot contains the representation of your data.

All plots except those for pie charts have a horizontal axis called the **x-axis** and a vertical axis called the **y-axis**. The intersection of the two axes is called the **origin**. 1-2-3 automatically scales the y-axis to fit your data and marks the scale with tick marks at regular intervals.

The chart's title and subtitle appear in a box above the plot. The chart's legend appears to the right of the plot. The **legend** identifies the different data series in the plot. A **data series** is a separate category of data in the plot.

Figure 5.1 shows a simple bar chart (1-2-3's default chart type) with only a single data series. The chart's plot is of the data series in the range A1..A3. There are three bars along the x-axis because there are three numbers in the data series. The y-axis automatically scales itself to show the smallest and largest numbers in the data series, with a bit of headroom left over.

FIGURE 5.1
Chart Parts

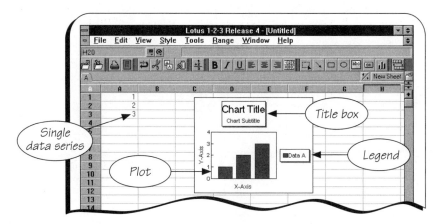

SELECTING A CHART TYPE

1-2-3 offers eight basic chart types. Some of the types have a 3-D variant. The bar, line, area, and pie charts are widely used in many disciplines, particularly in the business world. The XY type is most widely used in scientific and engineering applications. The HLCO, Mixed, and Radar types have specialized applications and find less general use. Table 5.1 shows the chart types with tips on usage.

TABLE 5.1   Chart Types and Uses

Chart Type	Typical Use
Line	Shows data trends over time. Can be used with single or multiple data series. 3-D variant available.
Area	Shows data trends over time but emphasizes the area beneath the plotted points. Can be used with single or multiple data series. 3-D variant available.
Bar	Shows data trend over time with single data series; emphasizes relationships among data items with multiple series. 3-D variant available.
Pie	Shows proportion of each item to the total. Only used for a single data series. 3-D variant available.
XY	Shows relationship between independent and dependent variables. Requires at least two data series. Widely used in engineering and scientific applications.
HLCO	Shows relationships between high, low, close, and open values. Used with a single data series. Used almost exclusively for charting price variations in securities.
Mixed	Shows a bar chart for the first three ranges; then switches to a line chart for the next three. Uses multiple data series.
Radar	Shows divergence from a central point. Single data series.

**SETTING UP
FOR AUTOMATIC
CHART CREATION**

Creating charts is almost ridiculously simple. To begin exploring the world of charts, set up the worksheet shown in Figure 5.2. It contains projected first-quarter sales data for Blatz Pickle, Incorporated, a small pickle-packing firm.

FIGURE 5.2

Blatz Pickle Sales
Projection

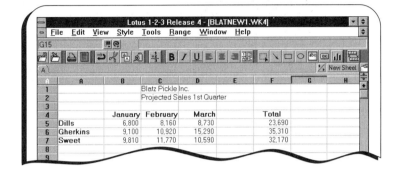

We have placed title information above the body of the sales data, row labels to the left of the data, and column headers above the monthly data. The placement of information on the worksheet is important if you want to take advantage of 1-2-3's built-in chart-labeling system.

After you set up the worksheet, save it under the filename BLATZ. You will need it for the end-of-chapter exercises, as well as for immediate use.

Creating a Bar Chart

Bar charts are perhaps the most commonly used tool for presenting data graphically. In this section we will use bar charting as an avenue to examine the basic charting techniques.

First we are going to do a simple bar graph of Dill sales for January through March. Select the range A1..D5. The range includes the title information, the month labels, and the row label "Dills" as well as the monthly sales data for Dills.

After selecting the range A1..D5, select Tools Chart or click on the Bar-chart icon. Your screen should look like Figure 5.3.

FIGURE 5.3

Selecting a
Chart Range

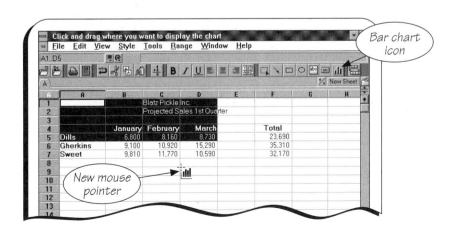

Notice that the mouse pointer changes to a chart symbol. You can move it at will. 1-2-3 is waiting for you to select the range where you want the chart to appear. Click and drag the mouse pointer (the chart symbol) down into row 19 and over into column H. When you release the mouse button, your screen should look like Figure 5.4.

FIGURE 5.4

Single Data Series Bar Chart

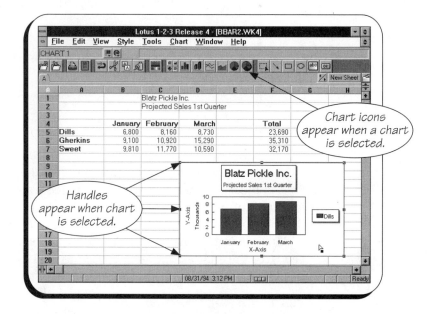

Anatomy of the Chart

Chart titles and subtitles appear automatically if you include them in the chart range. The legend automatically shows whatever label you include to the left of the data ("Dills," in our case).

The graphics themselves (the *plot*) reflect the numeric data; monthly dill pickle sales, in our example. 1-2-3 gets the labels on the x-axis (January, February, March) by looking above the numeric data. The scaling on the y-axis is automatic. 1-2-3 scales the y-axis to accommodate the smallest and largest value in the numeric data.

Notice the **handles** (little boxes) around the edge of the chart. Handles appear whenever a chart is selected. If you click outside the chart area, they go away. If you then click inside the chart area, they reappear. You can click and drag any handle to change the size of the chart.

The Chart SmartIcon Set

Any time you create or select a chart, the Chart SmartIcon set appears automatically. It contains clickable tools for selecting chart types and drawing tools. Figure 5.5 shows the chart SmartIcons and their uses.

FIGURE 5.5
The Chart
SmartIcon Palette

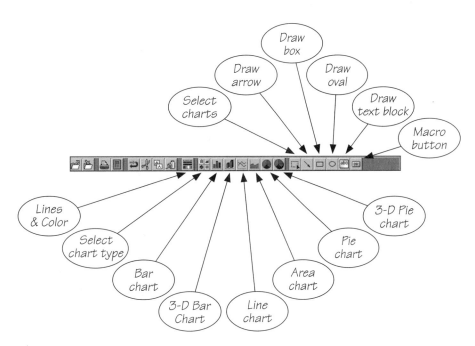

Creating a Multirange Chart

Now let's expand the graph to include all three pickle types. We could get rid of the current graph by clicking inside it and then pressing DEL, but let's leave it on the screen while we create another.

Select the range A1..D7. Then select Tools Chart or click on the Bar-chart icon. This time, let's change the size and placement of the chart. Click and drag from A9 to about D19. Figure 5.6 shows what your new chart should look like.

FIGURE 5.6
Multiple Data
Series Bar Chart

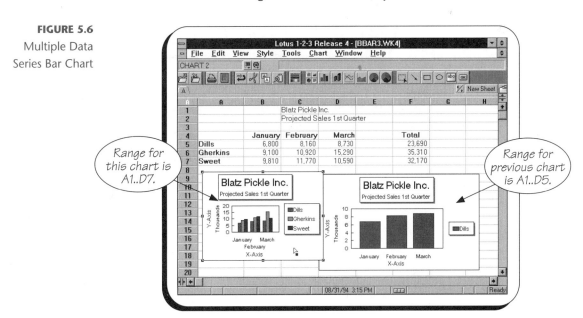

Resizing a Chart

Notice that we overlaid the new chart slightly over the old one. We could have sized the new chart so that it overlaid even more, or none, of the other chart. For that matter, we could have placed the new chart in some other part of the worksheet or laid it over the numeric data.

Also notice that the original chart no longer has any handles because it is not selected. The new chart does have handles because it *is* selected.

Let's shrink the size of the original chart. Click anywhere inside it, click on the lower left handle, and drag the handle into column E. Then click on the new chart to select it. Drag the lower right handle into column E and downward slightly. Try to duplicate what you see in Figure 5.7.

FIGURE 5.7
Resizing a Chart
by Dragging

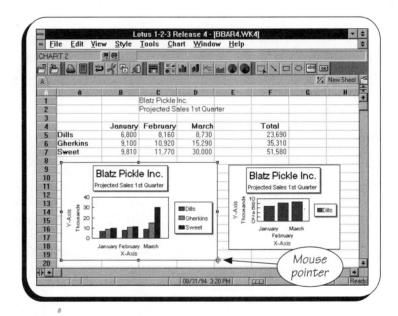

SOME MAGIC: AUTOMATIC REDRAW When any of the numbers in your charted data ranges change, your charts redraw themselves automatically. To see this feature in action, change January Dill sales to 20,000, and change March Sweet sales to 40,000. Both charts quickly redraw themselves to reflect the changed data, as Figure 5.8 shows.

FIGURE 5.8
Automatic
Redraw of Data

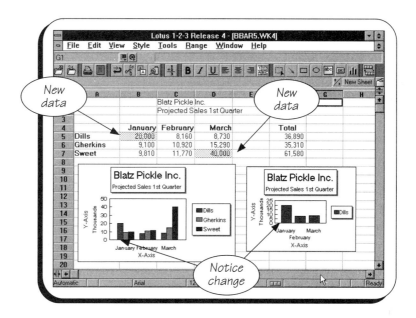

Notice that the charts in Figure 5.8 now show a different scale, as well as different bar heights. 1-2-3 changes the scaling values as necessary to fit the largest and smallest data items. There is a way to override this auto-scaling feature, but normally it is exactly what you want.

Now change January Dill sales to 6,800, and change March Sweet sales to 10,590 (the original values). Once again, the charts redraw themselves to reflect the altered data series.

MOVING A CHART

To move a chart, click anywhere *inside* the chart (not on the handles). Then begin dragging. The mouse pointer turns into a clenched fist as you drag the chart. Release the mouse button when the chart is relocated to your satisfaction.

You can move a chart over other worksheet elements without losing them. Although not visible, the other elements are not destroyed; they reappear if you move or delete the chart.

DELETING A CHART

To delete a chart, select it by clicking anywhere inside it; then press DEL. For example, if we wanted to delete the simple bar chart but leave the multirange chart, we could click inside the simple bar chart, and then press DEL. What could be simpler?

MANUALLY ADDING TITLES TO A CHART

Your data may not always be set up in the predefined format for automatic title and legend generation. In that case, you have to add titles and legends manually.

Before we examine this topic, let's unclutter the home area of the screen. Select each of the two bar charts in turn, and drag them out of the home screen area.

Now let's graph only the Total data in the range F4..F7. Select F4..F7 and click on the Graph icon. Size the graph as shown in Figure 5.9. Notice that we are overlaying all the data except the Total column. Not to worry—it's still there, behind the chart.

FIGURE 5.9
Chart Without Predefined Titles

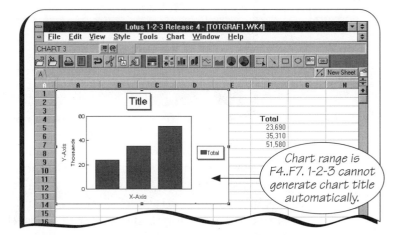

To add headings, double-click inside the chart's title box or select Chart Headings. The Headings dialog box appears, as Figure 5.10 shows. Within the dialog box, you can either type the headings into the text boxes or you can click on the Cell check box and specify a cell that contains the desired heading. In Figure 5.10, we have simply typed the headings we want.

FIGURE 5.10
The Chart Headings Dialog Box

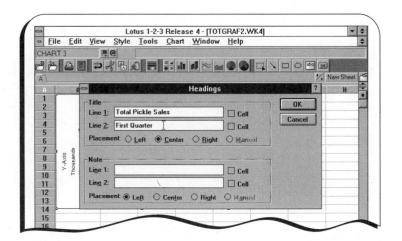

After you select OK, your new headings appear in the chart's title box. Figure 5.11 shows the result.

FIGURE 5.11
Manually Entered
Chart Headings

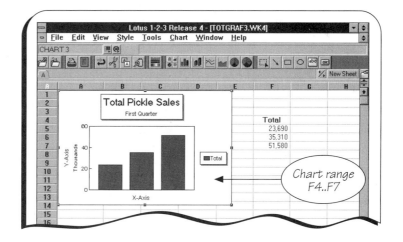

SELECTING AND CHANGING CHART TYPES

You easily can preview the effects of various chart types and change from one to another. Click on the Select-chart-type icon or select Chart Type. You should see the dialog box shown in Figure 5.12. Notice that we have clicked on 3D Bar.

FIGURE 5.12
The Chart Type
Dialog Box

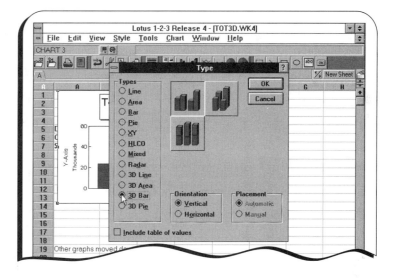

If we select OK, our graph changes to a 3-D effect, as Figure 5.13 shows.

FIGURE 5.13

A 3-D Bar Chart

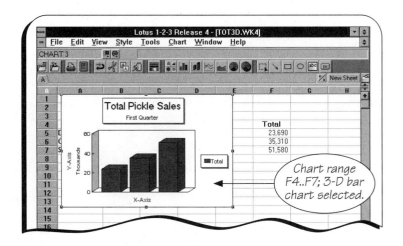

FIGURE 5.13

A 3-D Bar Chart

Line Charts

Select the range A1..D7. Click on the Chart icon or select Tools Chart; select the range A21..E33; and select Chart Type. Click on 3D Line. Your line chart should look like Figure 5.14.

FIGURE 5.14

A 3-D Line Chart

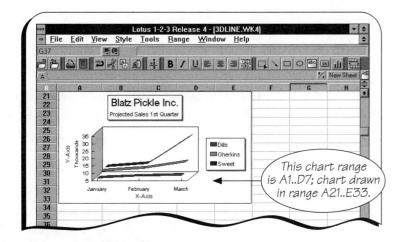

FIGURE 5.14

A 3-D Line Chart

Now select the chart by clicking inside it. Select Chart Type and change to 3-D area. Your chart now should look like Figure 5.15.

FIGURE 5.15
A 3-D Area Chart

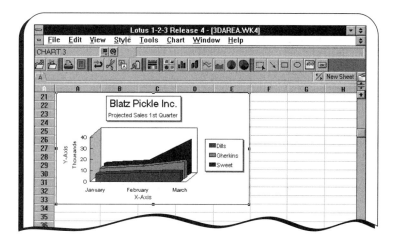

Now select File Close. Save your file as PICKLE. We will need it again shortly.

Creating A Pie Chart

Pie charts are used to show proportions of parts to the whole, at a single point in time. For this purpose, pie charts are much better than other chart types. To experiment with pie charts, create a worksheet like the one shown in Figure 5.16.

FIGURE 5.16
Typical Pie
Chart Data

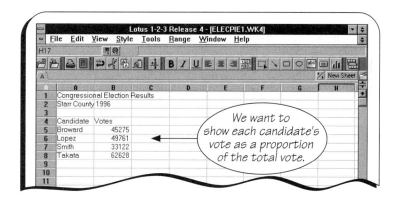

Select the range A1..B8. Click on the chart icon or select Tools Chart. From the Chart dialog box select 3D Pie. Your pie chart of the election results should look like Figure 5.17.

FIGURE 5.17
A Pie Chart of
Range A1..B8

FIGURE 5.17

A Pie Chart of
Range A1..B8

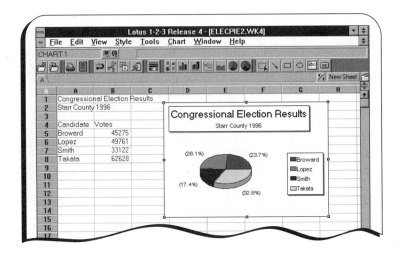

Exploding a Pie Chart

You can pull one pie slice away from the others by clicking on the slice and dragging it slightly outward. To explode all the slices, select Chart Data Labels, click on the All by option box, and specify the desired percentage in the percentage box. In Figure 5.18 we have specified a 20 percent explosion factor.

FIGURE 5.18

The Chart Data
Labels Dialog Box

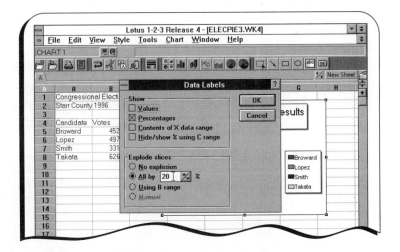

Your chart should look like Figure 5.19. Note the pie slices have been exploded outward; each slice is separated from its neighbors by a small gap. Also, each candidate's share of the total vote appears in parenthesis. Each candidate's slice of the pie is proportional to the percentage.

FIGURE 5.19
An Exploded
Pie Chart

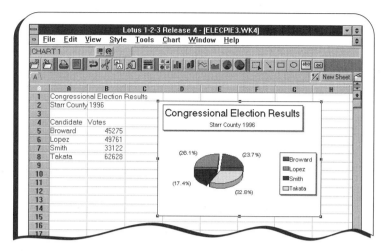

Now select <u>F</u>ile <u>C</u>lose. Save your worksheet at the prompt. Name it ELECPIE.

XY Graphs

Now let's do an XY graph. The XY type is used for graphing dependent/independent mathematical relationships. The dependent variable goes on the y (vertical) axis; the independent variable goes on the x (horizontal) axis. XY graphs are the only kind in which you actually need the X range as an active part of the graph itself.

Your SMART disk has a file called RAINFALL. RAINFALL is a table of historical data showing rainfall and the associated corn yield in Kernel County, Iowa. We want to plot rainfall against corn yield to see if there is any relationship (not surprisingly, there is). If you do not have the SMART disk handy, set up the data as shown in Figure 5.20.

FIGURE 5.20
Typical Data for
an XY Chart

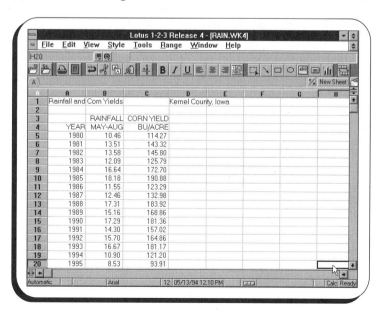

Only an XY chart accurately shows the exact relationship between the two variables. An area, bar, or line chart could show the two variables over time, but we are not really concerned with time progression; we want to know how each corn yield is associated with its rainfall value. Rainfall is the independent variable—it affects corn yield, not the other way around!

Select the range B5..C20. Then select Tools Chart. Set the type as XY. Then click on the large type box without connecting lines, as shown in Figure 5.21. Clicking on this box prevents 1-2-3 from connecting the data points with lines. When you view your graph, you will have 16 data points representing the relationship between rainfall and corn yield.

FIGURE 5.21

Selecting an XY Scatter Plot

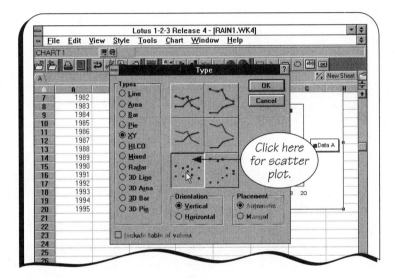

Your XY graph should look like Figure 5.22. Note that the points on the graph do not fall exactly in a straight line. That means that rainfall is not the only variable that affects corn yields.

FIGURE 5.22
Scatter Plot of Corn
Yield Against Rainfall

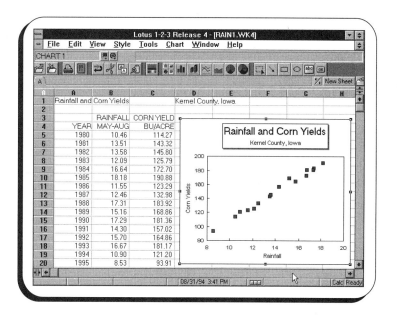

ADDING NOTES TO CHARTS

To add explanatory notes to charts, select Chart Headings. In the dialog box shown in Figure 5.23, we have added two notes indicating the data sources for the chart. The notes appear in your chart, as shown in Figure 5.24.

FIGURE 5.23
Adding Explanatory
Notes to a Chart

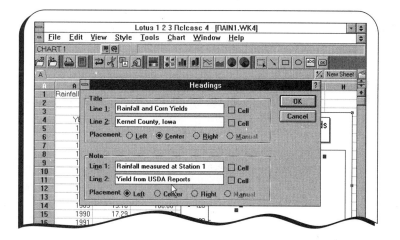

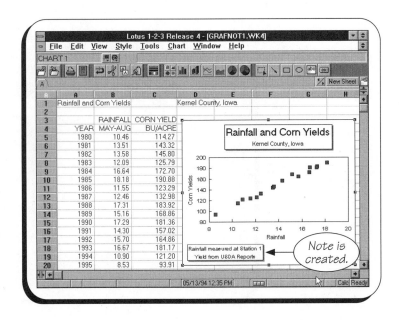

Select File Close; save your worksheet; call it RAINFALL. You may need it again.

CHANGING CHART ORIENTATION

Bar, Line, Area, XY, and HLCO charts can be flipped from the standard vertical to a horizontal orientation. To change orientation, click the large style button in the Chart Type dialog box that corresponds to your desired orientation.

ADDING GRAPHICS

1-2-3 has a graphic "draw layer" that sits on top of the worksheet. The draw layer can be used to enhance your worksheet data and call attention to important items. In your more frivolous moments, it also makes an excellent doodling tool!

Objects (such as lines you create) in the draw layer can be moved around and laid on top of any other worksheet component, including charts. Once created, the objects can be selected, moved, and deleted just like any other worksheet element.

Let's use the draw layer to dress up the PICKLE file. Close your current worksheet and open PICKLE. Move and resize the 3-D area chart, as shown in Figure 5.25.

FIGURE 5.25
PICKLE with
Graph Resized

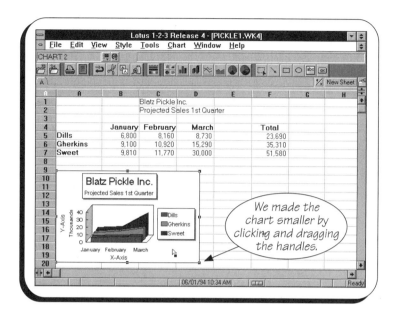

Assume that you are the CEO of Blatz Pickle, and you are not pleased with projected dill pickle sales. You want to send Smedley, the Dill sales manager, an attention-getting message. Being a 1-2-3 guru, you decide to add a graphic message to the existing worksheet and send Smedley a copy.

Using Tools Draw

From the Tools Draw menu, you can create lines, arrows, arcs, rectangles, ovals, freehand drawings, text boxes, and macro buttons (discussed in Chapter 13). To get Smedley's attention, let's create a text box and put a message inside it.

Select Tools Draw Text. The mouse pointer becomes a set of crosshairs. Put the crosshairs inside the chart, then click and drag until you have a box like the one shown in Figure 5.26. In the newly created text box, enter the message shown in Figure 5.26.

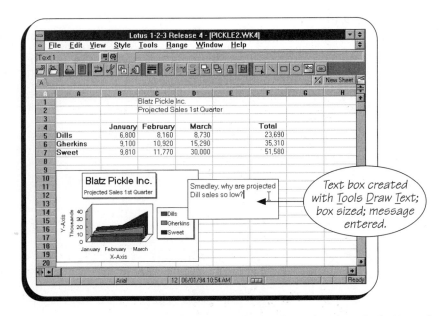

Let's boldface the message. With the text box selected, select $\underline{S}$tyle $\underline{F}$ont & Attributes. Click the Bold check box and select OK. Now let's make the text box frame heavy. Select $\underline{S}$tyle $\underline{L}$ines & Color. Click on the Line Style arrow. From the dropdown list click on the fourth line width and select OK. A bold border appears around the text box.

Now let's draw an arrow from the text box to the total dill sales figure in cell F5. Select $\underline{T}$ools $\underline{D}$raw $\underline{A}$rrow. Move the mouse crosshairs to the top center of the text box; click and drag to cell F3. The arrow is selected. Now make the arrow a heavy line, using the $\underline{S}$tyle $\underline{L}$ines & Color menu.

Repeat the arrow-drawing process, placing an arrow from the text box to dill sales in the chart. Your screen should look like Figure 5.27.

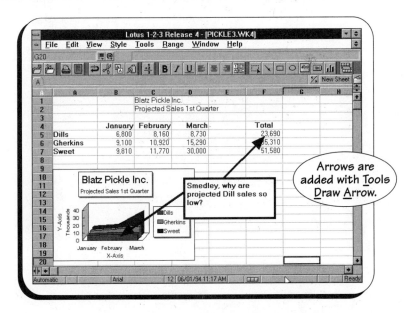

Our enhanced worksheet should get Smedley's attention. In Chapter 6 we discuss how to print worksheets like this. Save your file. Name it SMEDLEY.

Lone Star Methane

Congratulations. Due to your outstanding proficiency with 1-2-3, you have just landed a job with the consulting department of Adams, Adams, and Adams (AAA), a large consulting firm. Your first job assignment is with Lone Star Methane (LSM), a large natural gas distribution company. LSM is interested in:

1. Developing a long-range projection of total consumption in its principal marketing areas, CityA, CityB, and CityC.
2. Developing an estimate of when additional pipelines will have to be constructed.
3. Developing an estimate of when existing gas supplies from the source of supply—the Ogalalla Field—will be inadequate to meet usage (based on existing prices and growth patterns).

LSM has given you the data on diskette. The filename is LONESTAR.WK4. The file contains two sets of data. The top set shows consumption by city. Beneath the city data you will find production trends in the Ogalalla field. The data sets in LONESTAR. WK4 look like this:

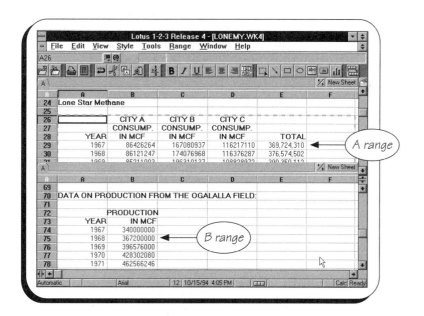

Your report will be presented to LSM's Board of Directors, most of whom are not number oriented. LSM wants your findings in the form of an easily understandable graph.

Create a line chart of total consumption and total production. Then draw arrows showing trends. Your finished graph should be similar to the following example.

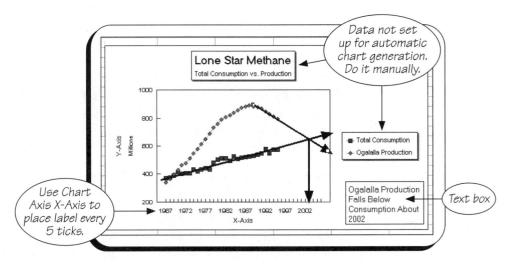

Use LONESTAR.WK4 (on your student disk) for these exercises.

1. Create a 3-D pie chart of 1967 consumption for City A, City B, and City C.
2. Create a 3-D pie chart of 1995 consumption for City A, City B, and City C.
3. Sum the consumption data for each city for the entire period 1967–1995. Do a plain pie chart of total consumption by city.

SMART DISK EXERCISES

1. **05AU22** is similar to previous problems, except it asks you to prepare a bar graph of certain data ranges. Retrieve it, complete it, and save it back to disk.

Printing

OBJECTIVES After studying this chapter, you should know how to:

- Preview your work before printing.
- Print reports of any length.
- Compress a report.
- Print in portrait or landscape mode.
- Specify the titles, headers, and footers that will appear on every page of a report.
- Set margins

BASICS OF PRINTING The basics of printing are very simple. In 1-2-3 for Windows, the elements of a printed page looks almost exactly as they do on the screen. If you have used such features as different font sizes, graphs, and drawn objects inside the selected print range, they automatically appear in your print job.

To generate a basic, no-frills printout, either click on the Print icon or select File Print to get the Print dialog box. Then click on OK in the Print dialog box. 1-2-3 automatically prints the entire active area (the area where you have made cell entries or placed charts) of the current worksheet.

1-2-3 does not care what is in the print range. By default, labels, numbers, charts, and drawn objects are all treated the same.

To see how basic printing works, select File Open CONCOST. The CONCOST file contains two worksheets, with the tab names Estimator and Form Letter. Click on the Estimator tab if it is not current. Then click on the Print icon or select File Print. You will see the Print dialog box, as shown in Figure 6.1.

FIGURE 6.1

The Print Dialog Box

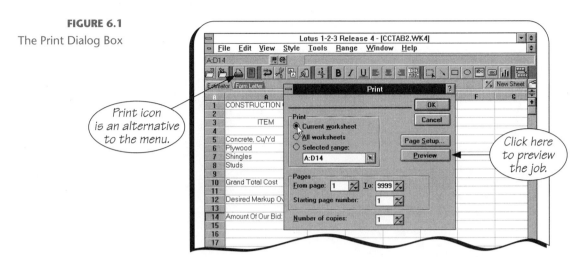

FIGURE 6.1

The Print Dialog Box

The currently selected option button is Current worksheet. The current worksheet is our Estimator. If you click on OK, 1-2-3 prints the entire **active area** of your Estimator. The active area goes from A1 to the intersection of the lowest row and rightmost cell containing data or graphics.

The active area of the Estimator goes from A1 to D14 because row 14 is the lowest row in use and column D is the rightmost column in use. By default, this is the area that 1-2-3 will print. If you aren't sure how big the active area is, press END HOME. The cellpointer then moves to the lower right corner of the worksheet's active area.

PREVIEWING THE PRINT JOB

Note that the File Print dialog box contains a Preview button. If you click on it, 1-2-3 shows you an onscreen mock-up of what the printed page will look like, including margins and the placement of the data on the page. It is a good idea to preview the print job before sending it to the printer so you can fine-tune the job without wasting time and paper.

You also can preview from Ready mode by clicking on the Preview icon or by selecting File Print Preview. Figure 6.2 shows the Print Preview dialog box.

FIGURE 6.2

The Print Preview Dialog Box

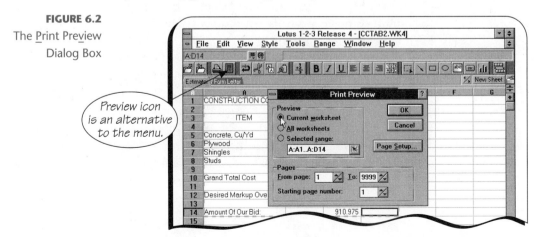

By default, the preview is of the current worksheet. Figure 6.3 shows the Print Preview screen for the Estimator sheet in CONCOST. The Print Preview screen has its own small set of icons; we have labeled them 1 through 7 in Figure 6.3.

FIGURE 6.3
What a Print
Preview Looks Like

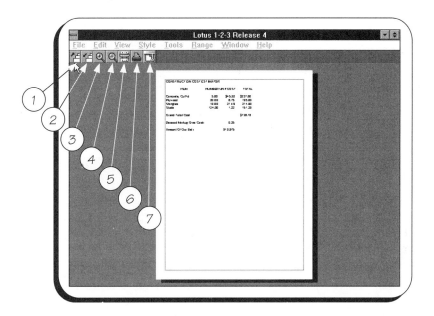

Table 6.1 shows the correspondence between icons and keys you can use to manipulate the preview.

TABLE 6.1   Print Preview Icons and Keyboard Equivalents

Icon Labeled	Keyboard Equivalent	Effect
1	ENTER or PageDown	Display next page.
2	PageUp	Display previous page.
3	Gray Plus	Zoom in to make larger.
4	Gray Minus	Zoom out to make smaller.
5	File Page Setup	Change page setup (display Page Setup dialog box).
6		Print.
7	ESC	Close Print Preview window.

SENDING THE JOB TO THE PRINTER

Once the preview looks the way you want, simply click on the Print icon or press ESC and select File Print. Then click on OK or hit ENTER to send the job to the printer.

Be sure the printer is turned on and online. If you are using a dot matrix printer, check to be sure the print head is near the top of a page perforation.

Printing Files Containing Multiple Worksheets

If we wanted to print only the Form Letter sheet of CONCOST, we could click on the Form Letter tab and repeat the process we used to preview and print the Estimator tab. If we wanted to print both worksheets at the same time, we could click on the All Worksheets option button in the Print dialog box.

Print Text and Charts Together

As we noted earlier, 1-2-3 prints anything in the selected print range—text, charts, or drawn objects. To get some experience at mixed printing, select File Close; then open the SMEDLEY file.

In the SMEDLEY file, select the range A1..G20. Then click on the Print icon or select File Print. Your screen should look like Figure 6.4.

FIGURE 6.4
Preparing to Print
a Selected Range

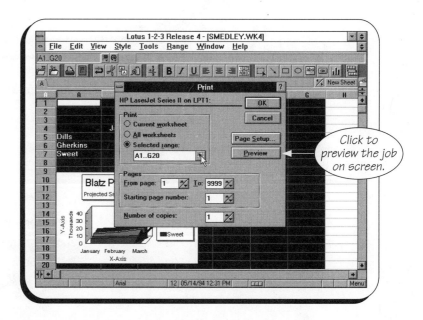

Now select Preview from the Print dialog box. Your screen now should look like Figure 6.5.

FIGURE 6.5
Print Preview
Including Charts
and Graphics

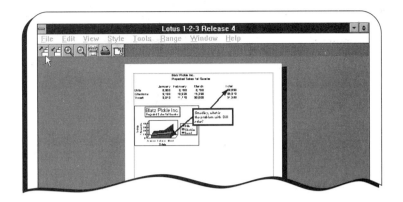

Go ahead and print the selected range in SMEDLEY. Your printout will look exactly like the print preview, complete with text, the area chart, and the arrows.

SELECTING AND PRINTING ONLY A CHART

You can print a chart by itself, without printing the other worksheet elements. For example, select only the area chart (by clicking inside it). Select Preview. Your screen should look like Figure 6.6.

FIGURE 6.6
Previewing the
Selected Chart

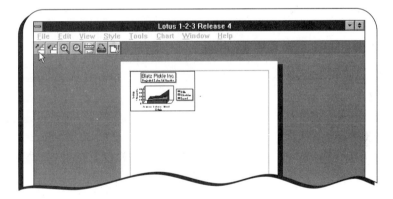

Changing the Print Size of a Chart

If you want to print a full-page version of the selected chart, select File Page Setup Size. The Fill page option resizes the chart to fill the entire page. Chart proportions probably will be altered. The Fill page but keep proportions option keeps the chart's current proportions while coming as close as possible to filling the page.

PRINTING LONG AND WIDE REPORTS

If all your print jobs would fit on a single sheet of paper, this chapter could end right here. Of course, they won't. Some jobs will be wider than a standard page; some will be longer than a page; and some will be both wide and long.

Your SMART disk contains a file called BIGPRINT. BIGPRINT is not a gradable SMART problem; it is just a long, wide worksheet. We will use BIGPRINT as the guinea pig as we explore printing multipage reports. Close SMEDLEY.

Select File Open or click on the File Open SmartIcon. Open the BIGPRINT file and select File Print Preview. Cycle through the pages; note that four pages are required to show the entire file. Figure 6.7 shows the four preview pages.

FIGURE 6.7
Previewing the Pages of a Larger Print Job

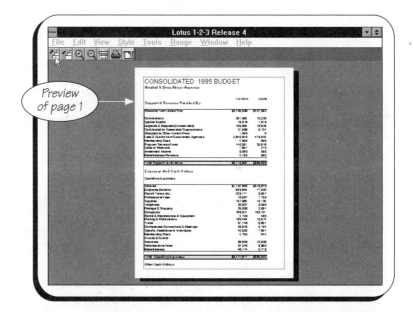

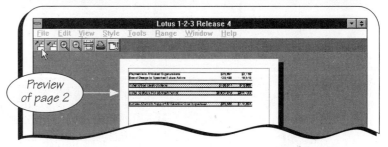

FIGURE 6.7
Continued

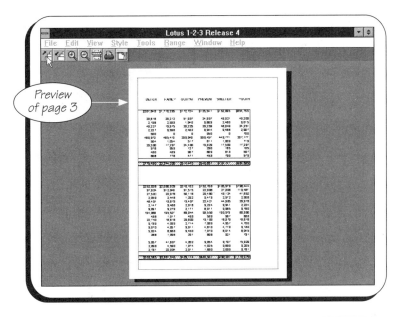

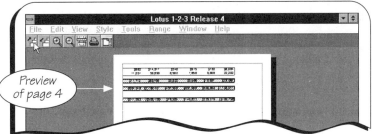

If you printed the file as it shows in the preview, you would need scissors and transparent tape to reassemble the parts into a readable report. Fortunately 1-2-3 offers several tools for rearranging the "lay" of large print jobs.

Shrinking the Job Size

One avenue for dealing with BIGPRINT is to shrink its size to the point that it all fits on a single page. To shrink BIGPRINT, select File Page Setup. You should see the File Page Setup dialog box, as shown in Figure 6.8.

FIGURE 6.8

The Page Setup
Dialog Box with
Size Selected

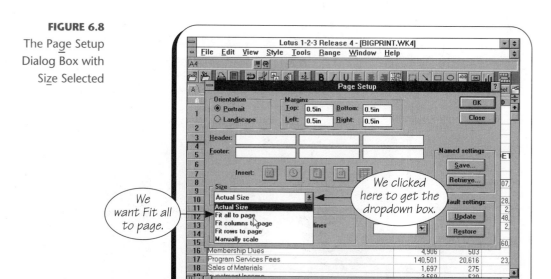

In Figure 6.8, we clicked on the Size arrow. Note the dropdown box. We are going to select Fit all to page, but there are other choices. These are the options under Size and their meanings:

Option	Meaning
Actual size	Is the default.
Fit all to page	Shrinks both columns and rows so that the entire report fits on a single page.
Fit columns to page	Shrinks only the columns so that all the columns fit on a single page. Rows are not shrunk. If you select this option, BIGPRINT requires two pages (up and down) to print, rather than four.
Fit rows to page	Shrinks only the rows so that all the rows fit on a single page. Columns are not shrunk. If you select this option, BIGPRINT still requires two pages (side by side) to print, rather than four.
Manually scale	Lets you enter a percentage from 15 to 1000 in the text box. Fifteen is tiny; 1000 is huge.

With Fit all to page selected, let's preview the job. Click on OK to close the dialog box. Then select File Print Preview. You should see a print preview like Figure 6.9.

If your screen does not look like Figure 6.9, use the Print Preview dialog box to set the selected Range to A1..I59.

FIGURE 6.9
Print Preview with
Fit All to Page
Selected

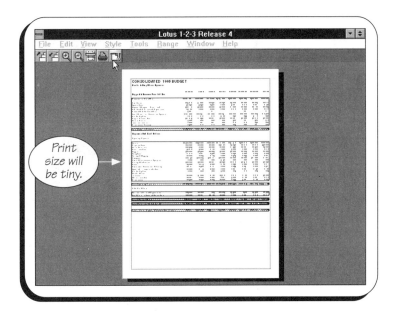

Hmmm. We *did* get the entire report on a single page, but we would have to issue magnifying glasses to the readers. Let's try another avenue for dealing with the report.

Changing Page Orientation

The default orientation is portrait, meaning that the page is upright, like the page you are reading right now. Under File Page Setup you can select Orientation to flip the report for landscape orientation (sideways printing). By using landscape orientation to print sideways, you can get more columns across a page. The price you pay is fewer rows per page.

Let's try that. Select File Page Setup and click on Landscape. Fit all to page is still selected. Your print preview should look like Figure 6.10.

FIGURE 6.10
Preview with
Landscape Option
in Effect

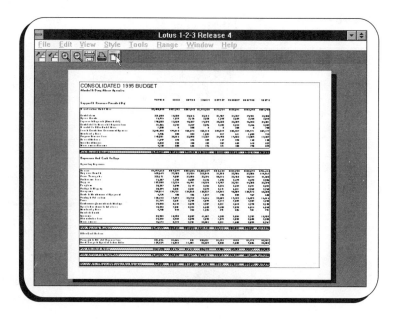

FIGURE 6.10
Preview with
Landscape Option
in Effect

That looks much better. With landscape orientation, all the columns fit across a single sideways page. If you don't mind squinting, the print size is readable. We can make the print size a bit larger by using the following technique.

Select Page Setup Fit columns to page. This choice fits all the columns onto a single page without shrinking the rows. The preview result is shown in Figure 6.11.

FIGURE 6.11
Landscape Option,
Fit Columns to Page

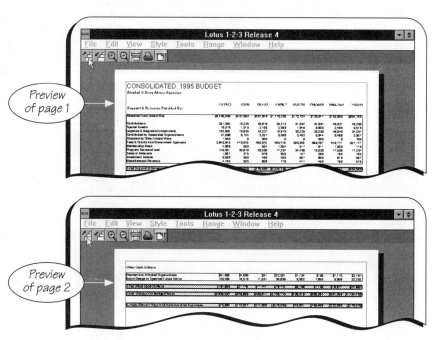

Adding Page Breaks

Page breaks are markers that cause 1-2-3 to spit out a page and begin a new page. Vertical page breaks occur in print jobs that have more lines than will fit on a page. Horizontal page breaks occur in print jobs that require more columns than will fit on one page.

1-2-3 automatically places page breaks if a job requires more than one page. However, the automatic page breaks may not produce eye-pleasing output. For example, in a long job they may put column headings at the bottom of one page and data on the following page.

If you do not like 1-2-3's placement of page breaks, you easily can change them. Our report might look better if we broke it at a different place. Let's insert page breaks that force the Revenue report onto one page and the rest of the report on a second page.

Put the cellpointer on cell A23. To add a page break, select Style Page Break from the menu (this command is not on the Print dialog box). Your screen should look like Figure 6.12.

FIGURE 6.12

Selecting a Page Break

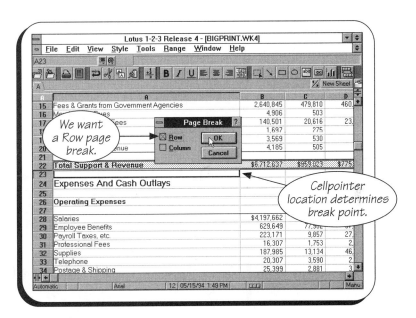

Note that dashed lines appear at the page break point. Select File Print Preview to see how the new page break would affect the printout. The preview consists of two pages; for economy of space they are shown side by side in Figure 6.13.

FIGURE 6.13
Print Preview
with Page Break
at Row 23

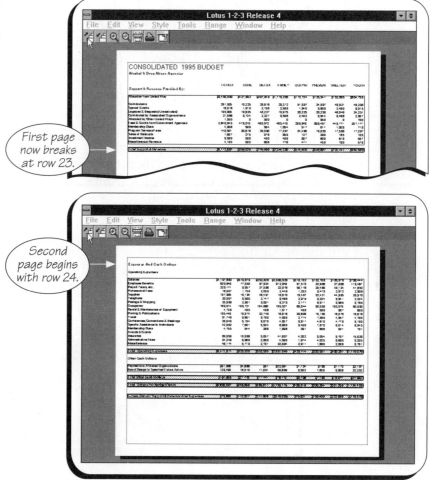

Removing Page Breaks

To remove page breaks, select a cell below and to the right of the page break. Choose Style Page Break and unselect the check box (by clicking on it to remove the mark). Then click on OK.

ADDING HEADERS AND FOOTERS

A **header** is information that prints at the top of each page of a print job; a **footer** prints at the bottom. Let's add a header to our job. Select File Page Setup. In the Header boxes, enter the information shown in Figure 6.14.

FIGURE 6.14

Using File
Page Setup to
Add a Header

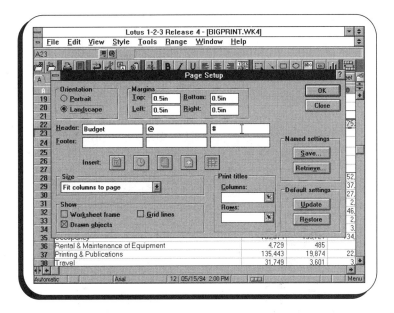

The entry "Budget" in the first header box appears at the top left corner of each printed page. The at sign (@) in the middle box places the system date at the top center of each printed page. The pound sign (#) places sequential page number at the upper right corner of each page. You can select the boxes and then click one of the Insert icons instead of typing the symbols.

Figure 6.15 shows your print preview with the header information in place.

FIGURE 6.15

Print Preview
of Page 1 with
Header Information

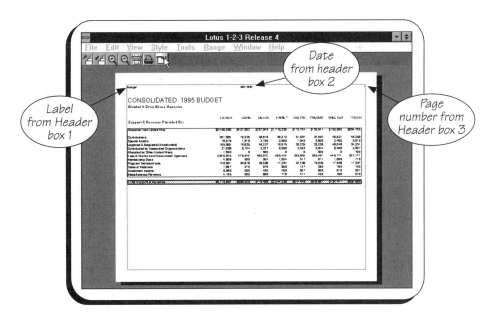

SAVING AND REUSING PAGE SETUP SETTINGS

After using File Page Setup, you can save your settings for future use on other files. This makes sense if you need to print different files but with the same margins, orientation, and so forth.

To save your current settings, select File Page Setup to bring up the dialog box. In the dialog box, select Named Settings Save. In the File name text box, enter a name of up to 15 characters. Select OK. Your settings are saved in a special, non-worksheet file with the extension AL3.

To apply named settings to some other worksheet, open the worksheet. Then select File Page Setup Retrieve. Select the named setting you want and click on OK. To see what your printed worksheet will look like with the newly applied setting, select Print Preview.

CHANGING MARGINS

To change top, left, bottom, or right margins for the print job, click on the respective Margins box in the Page Setup dialog box. After changing margins, it is a good idea to preview the print job before committing it to paper.

1. Open the file JOEBOB3 (you prepared the worksheet at the end of Chapter 2). Select File Print and print it.

2. Print only the range A1..F18 of JOEBOB3.

3. On your SMART disk there is a file named 11CU30. Open that file. Shade the range B54..B200 with light shading. Specify a header line that says:

```
Fraben Assembly Date        date page#
```

where date is today's date and page# is provided by the automatic page numbering feature. Then print the range A54..C200.

3. Open the LONESTAR file (on you SMART disk). Print the range A24..E57; then print the range A70..E102.

None for this chapter. The SMART checker isn't quite smart enough to evaluate a printed page!

PART ONE
BASIC LOTUS 1-2-3

The six chapters in this section cover
skills that all 1-2-3 users need to know.
After mastering this section, you will be
able to create, format, and print basic
1-2-3 worksheets and charts.

A Deeper Look at Functions and Formulas

OBJECTIVES   After studying this chapter, you should know how to:

- Create relational expressions.
- Create @IF functions.
- Use complex operators in @IF functions.
- Use date functions and date arithmetic.
- Use the @PMT function.
- Seal a worksheet.

Chapter 3 discussed the basics of functions and formulas. This chapter provides a deeper look at the capabilities of functions and formulas.

RELATIONAL EXPRESSIONS   A **relational expression** is a special kind of formula that uses relational operators to make a comparison. The formulas we have used up to this point are **computational**; that is, they create a value by using arithmetic operators to add, subtract, multiply, divide, or exponentiate.

There are times when you need to compare the relationship between cells, rather than make arithmetic computations. For example, you may need to know whether or not one cell is equal to another, or greater than another, or less than another. To make a comparison, you have to build a relational expression using relational operators. Table 7.1 presents these operators.

TABLE 7.1 Relational Operators

Operator	Meaning
=	Equal to
>	Greater than
<	Less than
<>	Not equal to
<=	Less than or =
>=	Greater than or =

All of these operators are used sandwich-fashion in relational expressions.

You build relational expressions by placing relational operators sandwich-fashion between two cell references, constants, or formulas. It makes no sense to start or end an expression with a relational operator. For example, >A5 has no meaning. *What* is greater than A5? There must be something to which to compare A5.

The worksheet in Figure 7.1 offers some examples of relational expressions. They all reference cell A1. If the expression is true, the cell containing the expression has a value of 1. If the expression is false, the cell where the expression is has a value of 0. That is, 1-2-3 uses a 1 to send you a signal: The expression is true. A 0 sends the opposite signal: the expression is false.

FIGURE 7.1
How Relational
Operators Work

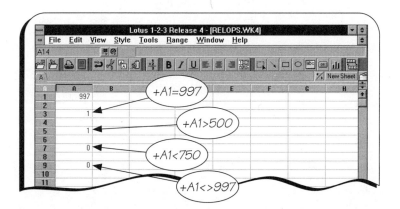

The preceding examples are standalone relational expressions. Later you will use them in database work, but their immediate application is to make a test to see whether a condition is true or false, and then *use* the test result directly.

THE @IF FUNCTION Except for database work, the main use for relational expressions is in @IF functions. Up to now we have used formulas to give cells a single value rule that always remains the same. However, sometimes you need to switch a cell's value rule, based on the outcome of some relational comparison. This is what an @IF function does.

@IF functions are expressed in mathematical form, but the logical structure can be thought of like this:

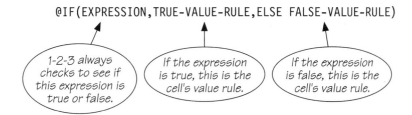

```
@IF(EXPRESSION,TRUE-VALUE-RULE,ELSE FALSE-VALUE-RULE)
```

1-2-3 always checks to see if this expression is true or false.

If the expression is true, this is the cell's value rule.

If the expression is false, this is the cell's value rule.

The expression is always a relationship that 1-2-3 tests to see if it is true or not. If it is true, 1-2-3 bases the cell's value on the true-value-rule. If the expression is false, 1-2-3 bases the cell's value on the false-value-rule.

To @IF or Not to @IF: An Example

Assume that we need a worksheet to compute state income tax for our small business. The state's rules are: If you have taxable income greater than zero for the year, you pay a tax of 8% of taxable income; if you have negative taxable income, you pay no tax. However, if you have a loss year, it is your tough luck—the state does *not* give any rebate of prior taxes paid.

Set up the worksheet shown in Figure 7.2. As it stands, the worksheet uses only a simple, arithmetic formula to compute the tax.

FIGURE 7.2

Naive Formula for Computing Tax

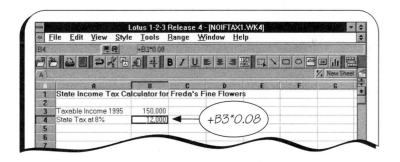

The formula in B4 (Figure 7.2) works very well so long as taxable income is positive. But what if the firm suffers losses and has negative taxable income? Change cell B3 by entering -10000. Remember that you type a negative sign—a minus—to get negative numbers, but cells B3 and B4 are in Comma,0 format, so they show ( ) instead of a minus sign for negative numbers. Figure 7.3 shows the outcome of entering -10000 in cell B3.

FIGURE 7.3

Naive Formula Gives
Incorrect Results

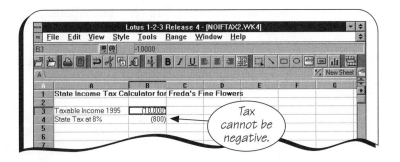

In Figure 7.3, cell B4 now indicates a negative income tax—the state owes us money! This goes against the state's tax rules; the bureaucrats probably will not be amused if we send them a bill for $800.

What we need is a switch-hitter formula; a formula in B4 that computes tax due if taxable income (cell B3) is positive, but computes a tax of 0 if cell B3 is zero or negative. That is, we need to test the value of cell B3 and base the value rule in B4 on the outcome of the test. Relational operators give you the vehicle for making the comparison, and @IF functions can use the outcome of the comparison to set the value rule for a cell. Cell B4 needs a value rule that says: If cell B3 is greater than zero, use the value rule B3*.08; otherwise, use the value rule 0.

Now let's return to our tax calculator. We can fix the problem with an @IF function. In place of the naive formula we used earlier, put this @IF function in cell B4: @IF(B3>0,B3*.08,0). Figure 7.4 shows the result of placing the @IF function in cell B4.

FIGURE 7.4

Using an
@IF Function
to Compute Tax

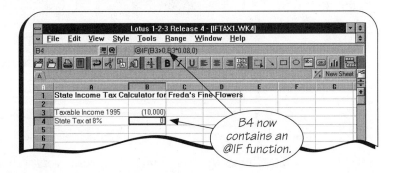

In Figure 7.4, the tax cell, B4, computes a value of zero because the test expression, B3>0, is false. B3 is a negative amount and thus *not* greater than zero. Since the test is false, 1-2-3 ignores the true-value-rule and bases the cell's value on the false-value-rule. Try putting a positive figure in the taxable income cell, B3, and see what happens. You will find that a positive tax value is calculated because the test expression is now true. Thus B4's value rule becomes the true-value-rule, B3*.08.

Think of the @IF function in the preceding example (taxable income less than 0) like this:

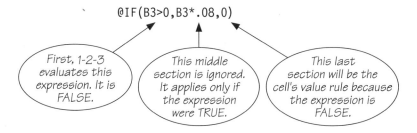

```
@IF(B3>0,B3*.08,0)
```

First, 1-2-3 evaluates this expression. It is FALSE.

This middle section is ignored. It applies only if the expression were TRUE.

This last section will be the cell's value rule because the expression is FALSE.

This power to make cell value rules flip-flop based on some test is extremely important. You cannot construct sophisticated worksheets without @IF.

Using Labels in @IF Functions

Either the true- or false-value-rule, or both, can be labels rather than formulas. For example, if we wanted to show the label "NO TAX" if taxable income were <= 0, we would modify our @IF function as shown in Figure 7.5. Note that the label must be enclosed in double quotes inside the @IF function.

FIGURE 7.5

Using Labels Inside an @IF Function

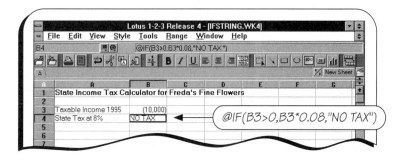

Nested @IF Statements

A single @IF function can only handle an either-or situation. If you need to evaluate more than two possibilities, you can put one @IF function inside another. This process is called **nesting** @IF functions.

To understand nested @IFs, remember the overall logic of any @IF function:

```
@IF(EXPRESSION,TRUE-VALUE-RULE,ELSE FALSE-VALUE-RULE)
```

The true-value-rule itself can be an @IF function; so can the false-value-rule. For that matter, both can be @IF functions, and the nested @IF functions can contain @IF functions. You can nest @IF functions many layers deep, but the logic quickly becomes very hard to follow. We are only going to examine a one-level nest, which can handle three-way decisions.

Here is an example of a nested @IF. For simplicity we have used literal numbers instead of cell references.

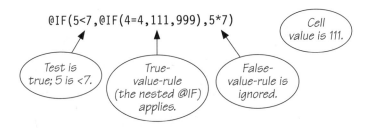

In the preceding example, the test in the outside @IF is true, so the cell value will be based on the true-value-rule, which itself is an @IF. 1-2-3 evaluates the nested @IF to see if its test is true. It is—4 does equal 4—so the cell value will be based on the true-value-rule of the nested @IF, that is, 111.

Here is a rework of the nested @IF. Now the test in the outside @IF is false:

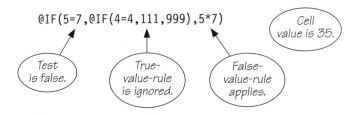

The nested @IF gives its cell a value of 35, based on the false-value-rule, 5*7. The true-value-rule (the nested @IF) is ignored.

We also could have an @IF for the false-value-rule instead of having 5*7. Or, we could have another level of nesting inside the nested @IF. As you can see, nesting can get complicated in a hurry. But you are in luck. You can accomplish the same result of multiple tests by using Boolean operators in plain, unnested @IF functions.

LOGICAL OPERATORS

There are three logical operators: AND, OR, and NOT. The logical operators AND and OR give you a way to make more than one test before deciding what value a cell should have. The NOT operator is largely surplus baggage in 1-2-3, so we will not discuss it much.

All three logical operators share a common characteristic with the relational operators: Their main use is as part of the test expression in an @IF function.

The #AND# Operator

When #AND# is used, it is *always sandwiched* between two relational expressions. Except for the math, #AND# works just like the "and" you use in conversation. For example, I could say "If my son AND my daughter both say yes, we will go hiking." The implication being that *both* my son and my daughter have to say yes or there will be no hike. If one says yes but the other says no, we do something else. If both say no, we do something else.

Let's look at 1-2-3 example of using #AND#. Say you want to set up a real, working corporate tax calculator. The corporate tax structure works in stair-step fashion; the corporation has to pay different rates on each of the first four $25,000 chunks of taxable income. We will assume the applicable rates are (they change at the whim of Congress):

Amount of Taxable Income	Rate
First $25,000	15%
Second $25,000	18%
Third $25,000	30%
Fourth $25,000	40%
All > $100,000	46%

For example, if a corporation has a taxable income of $20,000 it pays a tax of (20,000*.15). If the firm has taxable income of $40,000 it pays (25,000*.15 + 15,000*.18). If it has taxable income of $300,000, it pays:

.15*25,000

+ .18*25,000

+ .30*25,000

+ .40*25,000

+ .46*200,000   (everything above the first 100,000)

To set this step-fashion calculation up in 1-2-3, you can use five @IF functions, and then sum the values provided by the @IFs. However, you have to use #AND# to check for two true relationships. Set up the worksheet shown in Figure 7.6. Put the @IF functions in cells B5..B10. They are shown in Text format in the figure.

FIGURE 7.6

AND Operators in @IF Functions

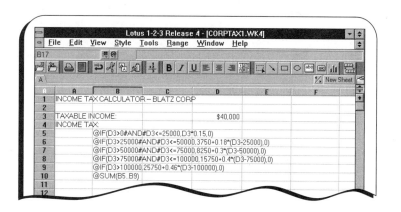

With $40,000 as taxable income, your #AND#-ed @IF functions produce the results shown in Figure 7.7.

FIGURE 7.7

Tax Computation
at $40,000

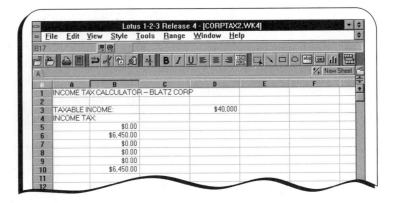

Try changing the taxable income (cell D3) to $100,000. After the change, you should see the display shown in Figure 7.8.

FIGURE 7.8

Tax Computation
at $100,000

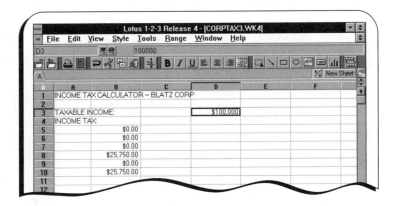

Finally, try changing taxable income to $3,300,405. You should see the effect shown in Figure 7.9.

FIGURE 7.9

Tax Computation
at $3,300,405

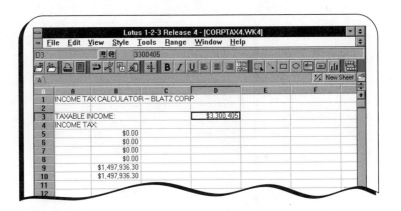

Save your worksheet. Call it TAXCALC. Later we may want to use it to set up a pro forma financial planning model.

The #OR# Operator

When #OR# is used, it is always sandwiched between two expressions, just as #AND# is. The #OR# operator is much looser than #AND#. With #AND#, both of the adjacent expressions have to be true in order for the relationship test to be true. With #OR#, the relationship test is true if *either* adjacent expression is true. #OR# works like the usual English "or"; for example, "If either my son OR my daughter say yes, we will go hiking."

As an example of using #OR#, let's set up a simple credit rating worksheet for businesses. Assume you are a banker who is willing to loan money to any business that has either a current ratio of >2 or a debt ratio of <.5. By the way, these criteria are not presented as good lending standards—they are just a convenient way to illustrate the use of #OR#.

Clear your worksheet and set up a model like the one shown in Figure 7.10. The @IF function in cell C7 shows a value of "GOOD", based on the true-value-rule. The test is whether C3 is greater than 2 or C4 is less than .5. In this case, C3 is in fact greater than 2; this makes the #OR# evaluates to true, even though the debt ratio is greater than .5.

FIGURE 7.10

Applying the #OR# Operator

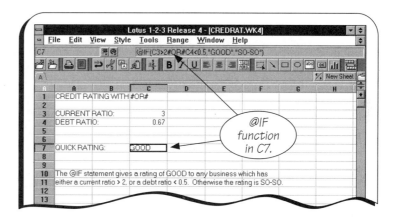

The #NOT# Operator

This complex operator is not much used in 1-2-3. It is a one-sided operator; #NOT# is never used sandwich-fashion, for example,

```
@IF(#NOT#(A5=7),999,111)
```

This @IF function could be handled more easily and less confusingly by saying:

```
@IF(A5<>7,999,111)
```

In fact, any #NOT# expression you can think of can be duplicated with the relational operators. Maybe that is why #NOT# is not much used in 1-2-3.

DATE FUNCTIONS AND DATE ARITHMETIC

1-2-3 has a built-in scheme for keeping track of the passage of time: the date functions. These functions can be used for very simple applications such as dating worksheets, or for more complex applications such as building calendars and determining how much time has elapsed between two dates.

1-2-3 keeps track of time by using December 31, 1899, as day zero. January 1, 1900, is day 1; January 1, 1901, is day 366, and so forth. The program can handle any date out to December 31, 2099, by giving the date an integer representing how many days have elapsed between day zero and the specified date.

The most generally useful date functions are:

Function	Meaning
@DATE(YEAR,MONTH,DAY)	Computes the specified date.
@NOW	Returns current date and time of day.
@TODAY	Returns current date without time.

The @DATE Function

First let's examine how the @DATE function works. Close your current worksheet. Put your cellpointer on cell B2. We are going to assume that the current date is November 22, 1995. In cell B2, enter this:

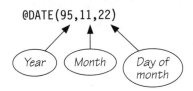

Your worksheet should now look like Figure 7.11.

FIGURE 7.11

A Date Number

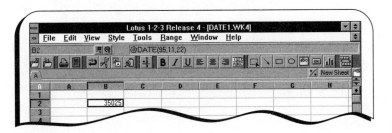

The number 35025 is the number of days that have elapsed between December 31, 1899, and November 22, 1995. If you want to convert the integer into human-readable form—which you do—be sure cell B2 is selected and then select

Style Number Format. Your screen should look like Figure 7.12. Note that several formats make numbers look like dates. We are going to select the 31-Dec-93 format, which you see highlighted in the figure.

FIGURE 7.12
Available
Date Formats

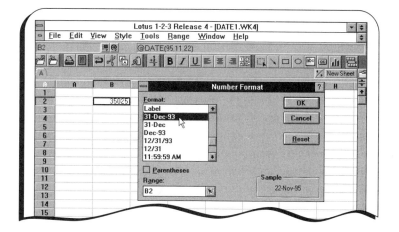

If you take the second choice, only the day and month 22-Nov show in the cell. The third menu choice shows Nov-95 in cell B2. For most purposes, the DD-MMM-YY format is used. Take that choice by selecting OK.

If you see asterisks in cell B2, it means column B is too narrow to show your selected format. To fix the problem, widen column B. Your screen now should look like Figure 7.13.

FIGURE 7.13
Formatted
Date Number

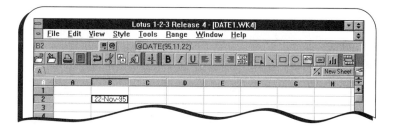

This may seem like a great deal of trouble compared to the alternative of typing the text entry '22-Nov-95. In fact, if all you want is a date stamp on the worksheet, it is simpler to type the date as a text entry. But there is an important distinction between the text entry '22-Nov-95 and the display created by formatting the @DATE function. A text entry is just a label; you cannot use it in arithmetic operations. The @DATE function is numeric and yields a number value—35025, in this case.

Remember the distinctions between value rules, values, formatting masks, and screen displays. You merely squeezed the 35025 through a special formatting mask to get the text-like screen display. The numeric value created by @DATE is still in the cell.

In 1-2-3 Release 4, you can enter a valid date number, such as 11/22/95, without using the @DATE function. However, do not begin the entry with a label prefix.

By using the @DATE function, you can do date arithmetic with cell values. The worksheet in Figure 7.14 illustrates such a real-world application of the @DATE function: An apartment management worksheet, in which we are using @DATE functions to automatically compute tenants' duration of occupancy.

The RENTED and VACATED fields contain the @DATE for those events, formatted with Style Number Format as DD-MMM-YY. The DURATION formula is an @IF function.

In Figure 7.14, set columns A through D to a width of 14. Use Style Column Width to change the default settings. Also right align the labels in B1..D1, so they appear directly above the data under them (select B1..D1 and click on the Right-align icon).

FIGURE 7.14

Date Functions in Action

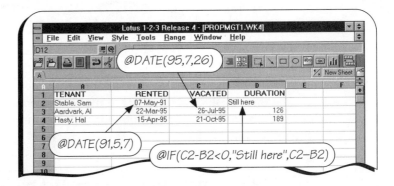

All of the underlying formulas for this worksheet are shown in Figure 7.15.

FIGURE 7.15

Date Functions and @IF Functions

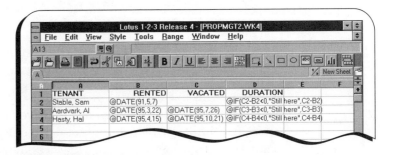

The object of the @IF functions in column D is to compute how many days a particular tenant remained before moving. However, we do not want to show a number under DURATION for tenants who have not moved out, such as Stable Sam. We want to flag current tenants with the label "Still here."

The DURATION column yields a value for the two tenants who have vacated, but not for Stable Sam. The @IF function is controlling whether a value shows under DURATION. The first term of the @IF function in cell D2 (C2–B2<0) is true only IF the number in C2 is smaller than the one in B2. For Stable Sam, cell C2 is blank, meaning he is a current tenant. A blank cell has a value of zero, so for Stable Sam it is TRUE that C2–B2<0.

The true term of the @IF function is the "Still here" label. So the @IF function uses the label as the value rule IF C2–B2 is less than zero. This avoids sending current renters into a time warp! If no entry has been made for VACATED, a simple subtraction of column B from column C would show negative duration— zero minus the RENTED value.

Select File Close. If you want to save the worksheet, do so now. A logical filename would be TENANTS.

The @TODAY Function

The @TODAY function is a handy way to display the current date within a worksheet. When you place @TODAY in a cell, 1-2-3 looks on the computer's internal clock and computes the number of days that have elapsed since the turn of the century. For example, if you placed @TODAY in a worksheet cell and the current date was August 29, 1995, you would see the number 34940 in the cell because 34,940 days have elapsed between December 31, 1899, and August 29, 1995. You can use Style Number Format with a date selection to make the date number understandable to humans.

The @TODAY function (and also the @NOW function) are "alive"—they check the computer's internal clock every time the worksheet recalculates. This means that if you File Save a worksheet containing the function and then File Open the same file tomorrow, the cell containing @TODAY will show a different number.

The @NOW Function

The @NOW function is used to get the current date *and time* from the computer's internal clock. To see how it works, set up the worksheet shown in Figure 7.16. Widen column A to 22, and widen column B and C to 16. Type the label shown in cell A2. Then in cells B2 and C2, enter the @NOW function. The number you see in cells B2 and C2 depends on the date when you do the exercise because the @NOW function picks up the current date as noted earlier. The example in Figure 7.16 assumes that today's date is May 16, 1994.

FIGURE 7.16
Date Numbers
Generated
by @NOW

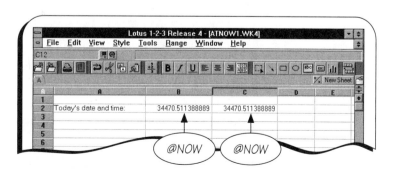

In Figure 7.16, the number in B2 has a whole number part and a fractional part. The whole number is the number of days since the turn of the century; the fractional part shows what fraction of today has elapsed. For example, the fractional part of 34470.511388889 means it is 12:16 PM.

You can use the Style Number Format to make the numbers sensible to humans. In Figure 7.17, cells B2 and C2 have been formatted as indicated.

FIGURE 7.17
@NOW Values
Formatted as
Date and Time

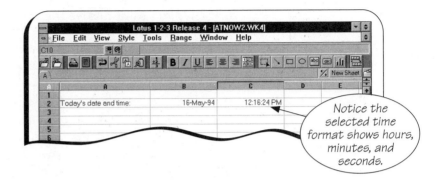

Freezing the Date and Time

You may be wondering why you need these functions since you can look at the bottom of your screen and see the current date and time. Their most common application is for date-stamping and time-stamping some event. If we destroy the functions but leave their computed values, the cells will always show the same date and time.

To try this out, select the range B2..C2. Then select Edit Copy, followed by Edit Paste Special Formulas as values. The functions are destroyed, but their *computed values* remain. We will have a permanent, chronological record of whatever event you were working with.

The Speedo Trucking Corporation worksheet in Figure 7.18 shows an example of this technique. When truck TX123R arrived, the dockmaster recorded its license, entered the @NOW function in cell B6, and killed the function in B6. When TX123R left, the dockmaster entered @NOW in C6 and killed the function. The formula in D6 is +C6–B6, which computes the elapsed days between arrival and departure. Watch out, truckers. Big Brother is watching.

FIGURE 7.18
Monitoring
Elapsed Time

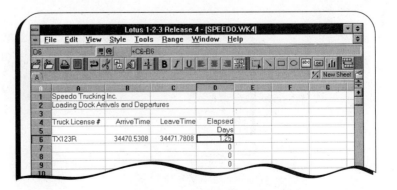

THE @PMT FUNCTION

The @PMT function has a very restricted use: All it does is calculate the periodic payment on an equal-payment amortized loan such as a mortgage or car payment. It works like this:

@PMT(principal,interest-rate-per-period,number-of-periods)

Here are two examples:

- @PMT(100000,.145/12,360)—for a home mortgage of $100,000 at an annual rate of 14.5% for 360 months. Note that the formula, .145/12, converts the annual rate to a monthly rate.
- @PMT(12500000,.16/4,20)—for a $12,500,000 business loan at an annual rate of 16%, paid quarterly with 20 quarterly payments (5 years).

You can also use cell references rather than literal numbers. Close your worksheet and set up a car payment calculator like Figure 7.19.

FIGURE 7.19

A Worksheet for Car Payment Computations

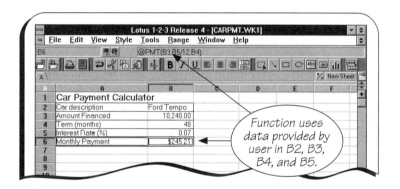

That is all there is to the @PMT function. Very handy if you need it. Save this file; call it CARPMT.

SELECTIVELY SEALING A WORKSHEET

With only the default settings, worksheet modifications are very easy to make; sometimes they are *too* easy to make. A simple case in point is our CARPMT worksheet.

Our intention was that anyone using the worksheet would enter data only in the B2..B5 range. However, there is nothing to stop the user from accidentally overwriting the labels in column A, or cell B6, which contains the function @PMT(B3,B5/12,B4).

Style Protection and File Protect Seal

You can use the Style Protection and File Protect Seal commands to protect worksheets against accidental (or intentional) changes. The two commands are independent, but usually both are needed.

File Protect Seal locks the entire worksheet, except for ranges you specifically unprotect. If no ranges are unprotected (with Style Protection), File Protect Seal prevents users from making any entries at all. For most applications, users need to make entries in some cells.

The CARPMT worksheet needs user input only in the B2..B5 range. Let's modify the worksheet to allow input only to that range. Select the B2..B5 range; next select Style Protection. You will see the Protection dialog box shown in Figure 7.20.

FIGURE 7.20
Unprotecting
Input Cells

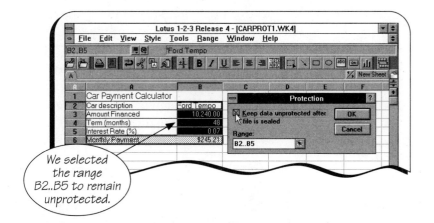

Click the Keep data unprotected option box. Then click on OK. Next, select File Protect to get the Protect dialog box shown in Figure 7.21.

FIGURE 7.21
Sealing the
Worksheet

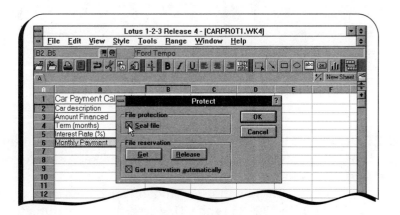

Click the Seal file option box; then click on OK.

The File Reservation box is not needed unless you are sharing a worksheet on a network. The Get choice keeps other network users from changing the file while you have it open. The Release choice lets others change the file even though you still are using it.

1-2-3 displays the Set Password dialog box as shown in Figure 7.22. If you supply a password, users must know the password to open the file. If the worksheet contained confidential data, a password would be appropriate, but we do not need one for the car payment worksheet, so click on OK without providing a password.

If you attach a password, be sure to remember both the password and its upper- and lowercase character combination. If you do not type the password exactly as you input it, you cannot open the file.

FIGURE 7.22

The Set Password Dialog Box

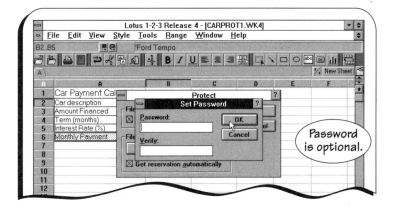

The file is now protected. Users can make entries only in the B2..B5 range. Figure 7.23 shows the result if a user tries to enter data outside the allowable range.

FIGURE 7.23

No Input Allowed Outside Unprotected Range

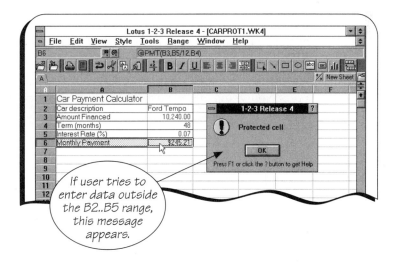

When to Seal Files

If you are preparing worksheets for use by others in your organization, unprotect the data areas and seal the file before distributing copies. Otherwise, some user, somewhere, will corrupt the worksheet.

A Note on Deleting Files

Each file you create and save requires disk space. Get in the habit of deleting unneeded files. There is no command in the 1-2-3 Release 4 menu for deleting files. However, you can use the older, classic menu to do the job. To delete a file using the classic menu, press the slash (/) key. Select File from the first menu; select Erase from the second. If you want to erase a worksheet file, select Worksheet from the third. A list of files appears. Use the arrow keys to select the file you want to delete; then press ↵.

Olive Oil

Assume you just got a job with BankCorp 1, a large East Coast bank. BankCorp 1 is considering a loan of $17,500,000 to a new customer, Spartacus Imports, Incorporated (SPI hereafter). SPI says it specializes in importing and wholesaling Italian olive oil. SPI has offered to pledge 57 huge tanks of olive oil as security for the loan. Assuming the tanks actually are full of olive oil, they will be good security for the loan. The immediate question, of course, is: Is there really olive oil in the tanks? If so, how much?

BankCorp 1 knows you are a 1-2-3 master. They are relying on you to develop a worksheet for logging sample data on each tank. Of course, BankCorp 1 also expects you to take the samples. The bank plans to give you a very long tape measure, a long jointed measuring rod (a dipstick), a portable computer, a highway map (of New Jersey, where the tanks are), and keys to a rental car. Good luck.

Set up your template in the following format. When you finish, unprotect the input cells and seal the file.

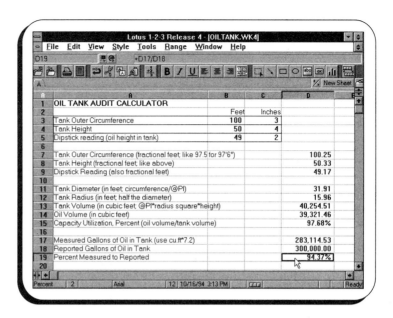

The image shows a Lotus 1-2-3 spreadsheet window titled "Lotus 1-2-3 Release 4 - [OILTANK.WK4]". Cell reference D19 with formula +D17/D18.

	A	B	C	D	E
1	OIL TANK AUDIT CALCULATOR				
2		Feet	Inches		
3	Tank Outer Circumference	100	3		
4	Tank Height	50	4		
5	Dipstick reading (oil height in tank)	49	2		
6					
7	Tank Outer Circumference (fractional feet; like 97.5 for 97'6")			100.25	
8	Tank Height (fractional feet; like above)			50.33	
9	Dipstick Reading (also fractional feet)			49.17	
10					
11	Tank Diameter (in feet; circumference/@PI)			31.91	
12	Tank Radius (in feet; half the diameter)			15.96	
13	Tank Volume (in cubic feet; @PI*radius square*height)			40,254.51	
14	Oil Volume (in cubic feet)			39,321.46	
15	Capacity Utilization, Percent (oil volume/tank volume)			97.68%	
16					
17	Measured Gallons of Oil in Tank (use cu.ft*7.2)			283,114.53	
18	Reported Gallons of Oil in Tank			300,000.00	
19	Percent Measured to Reported			94.37%	
20					

CASE

Joe Bob LeBouef V

Joe Bob LeBouef, Head Football Coach at Sasquatch University, has been extremely pleased with your earlier templates. He says you almost have an A in the bag in his Phys Ed course. Notice he says "Almost."

Now Joe Bob wants you to create another, more sophisticated, worksheet, like the following one. In the Weather Parameters section, the estimated temperature, rain, and enrollment cells are for user input (Joe Bob wants to be able to change them). Temperature deviation from 72 degrees is a formula: @ABS(72–G5).

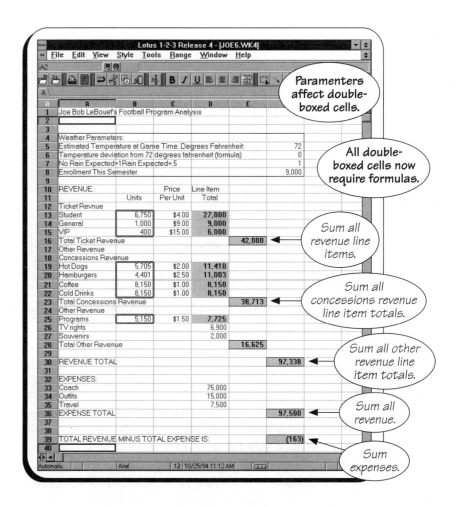

Joe Bob's statistician has developed some mathematical predictors for the items in double boxes:

- Student Ticket Revenue is best predicted by:

  ```
  (Enrollment*0.75)-(Enrollment*(temperature deviation/200)))*the
  rain value
  ```

- General Ticket Revenue is best predicted by:

  ```
  (1000-(1000*(Temperature deviation/200)))*the rain value
  ```

- VIP Ticket Revenue is best predicted by:

  ```
  (400-(400*(Temperature deviation/200)))*the rain value
  ```

- Unit Hot Dog Sales are best predicted by:

  ```
  @SUM(total units of tickets sold)*0.7
  ```

- Unit Hamburger Sales are best predicted by:

  ```
  @SUM(total units of tickets sold)*0.54
  ```

- Unit Coffee Sales are best predicted by:

  ```
  @SUM(total units of tickets sold)-@SUM(total units of tickets
  sold)*(0.01*temperature deviation)
  ```

- Unit Cold Drink Sales are best predicted by:

  ```
  @SUM(total units of tickets sold)+@SUM(total units of tickets
  sold)*(0.02*temperature deviation)
  ```

- Program Sales are best predicted by:

  ```
  Unit VIP ticket sales+Unit General ticket sales*.7+Unit Student
  ticket sales*.6
  ```

Enter the formulas. Then play "what-if." For example, change the predicted temperature to 100 while leaving other factors constant. Your new bottom line figure should be (13,709).

1. Using 1-2-3 as an expensive desk calculator: Put your cellpointer on A5. Multiply your age by your weight.

2. Edit A5 from Exercise 1. Expand the formula by appending *IQ, where IQ is a number representing your intelligence quotient. The resulting formula should be your age*weight*IQ. If the result is too big to fit in the cell display, widen column A.

3. In cell A10, add your age to your IQ and then divide the result by your weight.

4. Set up a worksheet to calculate the weight of a metal sphere (e.g., a buckshot, a cannonball, Darth Vader's Death Star, or whatever). Assume the metal in question weighs 650 pounds per cubic foot. Supply your own figure for the radius. The formula for volume of a sphere is 4/3*@pi*radius^3. Your worksheet should look like this:

   Radius of sphere: some number
   Volume of sphere: use a formula
   Weight of sphere: use a formula

5. Assume a basketball, dropped from a height of x feet (say, 10 feet) rebounds to a height of .8*x (e.g., to 8 feet on first rebound). Each successive rebound is .8*the previous one. Set up a table showing the rebound number and the ball's rebound height for 30 rebounds. Provide a setup cell where the user can enter the height from which the ball is assumed to drop.

6. Set up a worksheet that gives a tabular analysis of Norwegian lemming population for the next 20 years, based on the facts that the current lemming population is 5321, and the population will increase at a rate of x% per year (you supply the rate). Your worksheet should be set up like this:

```
        Beginning population:  5,321  <—comma zero format
        Growth rate:........:   .445
End of
Year            Population
    1              use a formula
    2              that references
    3              the beginning population
   20
```

7. Set up a worksheet to compute the compound growth of a starting sum, year by year, given some starting amount of money and some annual growth rate. The general formula for compound growth is:

```
Amount at end of Period n = Beginning Amount*(1 + growth rate)ⁿ
```

The user of your worksheet should be able to change the beginning amount and/or the annual growth rate in decimal form and get an instant recomputation of the year-by-year future amounts. Set your worksheet up like this:

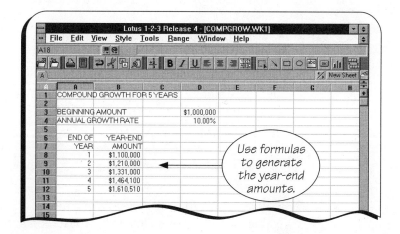

8. Do a File Close to get a clean worksheet. With your cellpointer in cell H20, enter an @SUM function that adds up all the values in the range A1..F19. Since all the cells in the range are blank, presumably cell H20 now will show a zero value. Move your cellpointer into the range A1..F19; enter some numbers. Note that the function in H20 automatically picks up each new number you insert into the range.

9. Use File Close to clean your worksheet. In cell A1, enter 5. In cell B1, enter 6. In cell D5, set up an @IF function that gives the cell the value 999 if the value of cell A1 is 5; otherwise, the cell should have the value 111.

10. In cell D7, set up an @IF so that D7 has the value 99999, if cell A1 = 5 and cell B1 = 5; otherwise, D7 should have the value 11111.

11. In cell C12, set up an @IF so that C12 has the value 99999 if either A1 or B1 have the value of 5; if neither A1 or B1 has the value of 5, cell C12 should have the value 11111.

1. **07AU15** is a workout in @SUM and relative versus absolute formula copying. As practice at changing column widths, several columns have been narrowed to ridiculously small widths. Use Style Column Width to make them legible. Some columns need to be wider than others.

2. **07AU20** is a general review problem. Refer to the problems at the end of Chapter 6 for details since not all the necessary tips and hints are provided in the worksheet itself.

3. **07AU22** is a mildly complex budget for the City of Drakensburg. It requires various sorts of formulas to compute revenue and expenditure changes. The problem is commented sufficiently that even non-business students can complete it successfully.

4. **07BU10** is a payroll worksheet that requires @IF functions to correctly figure employee base pay and overtime pay.

5. **07BU20** emphasizes @IF functions. There are, of course, various ways to set up the @IF functions. One method uses nested @IF functions to determine the middle bracket (column M).

6. **07CU23** is a rather complex application of @IF functions. The purpose is to build an automatic calculator for Federal corporate income tax. Since the FIT is a stair-step calculation, the necessary @IF functions are somewhat involved. The author does not recommend this exercise for non-business students.

Sorting, Importing, and Parsing Data

OBJECTIVES   After studying this chapter, you should know how to:

- Sort data on single or multiple keys.
- Convert 1-2-3 worksheets to ASCII files.
- Use the 1-2-3 Translate program.
- Import ASCII data.
- Parse ASCII data into usable form.

This chapter explains how to sort worksheet data. It also explains how to import data from other programs, and how to parse "foreign" data into standard 1-2-3 format.

SORTING DATA   Sorting means ordering the data in a range in hierarchical order on some key column from highest to lowest, or lowest to highest. Humans have no trouble sorting short lists, but most people go glassy-eyed at the thought of manually sorting hundreds or thousands of records. How would you like, for example, to sort a stack of 2500 mailing-list file cards in ascending zipcode order?

If the mailing list were in a 1-2-3 worksheet, your computer could do the job in about the time it would take you to pour a cup of coffee. A smaller list, say, 300 records, would sort before you could reach for the coffee pot. What's more, unlike a manual sort, the 1-2-3 sort would be free of clerical errors.

Always save your worksheet before you sort. Sorting rearranges data, and it is easy to specify a sort range incorrectly. Reconstructing your data after a bad sort is like trying to put Humpty-Dumpty back together again. Play it safe and save your file before you sort. That way, if you mess up, you can close the file without saving it, and open the good copy.

Sorting a Mailing List

For your first sorting experiment, close your file and set up the small mailing list shown in Figure 8.1. The numbers in Column A indicate the order you entered the data; that is, you entered the data for Smith first, the data for Lopez second, and so forth. There is no requirement that you number your records as you type them in, but it is a good idea in case you want to get them back in original order after a sort.

FIGURE 8.1

An Unsorted Mailing List

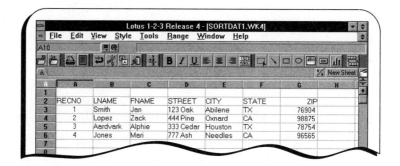

Understanding the Sort Process

If you have a simple, one-column list that you want to sort, there is hardly any way to mess up. However, you normally have several associated columns of data, like our example. When you sort, you want 1-2-3 to rearrange *all the columns* of data, not just the key column.

The rearrangement is always based on a key column, but you must select all the rows and all the columns that make up your table. If you do this, 1-2-3 drags the non-key data along with the key data when you sort. If you do not select the entire range, 1-2-3 rearranges *only the selected part* of your data, and you will be left with a totally scrambled, useless table. Of course, you can recover from the disaster if you remembered to save your work before sorting. If not, you are up the creek with nary a paddle in sight.

One-Key-Column Sorting

The simplest sort uses a single key column. Let's sort the mailing list using the LNAME column as the key. Select the range A3..G6. Do *not* select row 2; if you do, the field names will be sorted, as well as the data!

Using the Range Sort Dialog Box

After selecting A3..G6, select Range Sort. For Sort by, select B3 (or any other cell in column B). All 1-2-3 wants to know is which *column* within the sort range has the key data. The row is immaterial. Your Sort dialog box should look like Figure 8.2.

FIGURE 8.2

The Sort Dialog Box

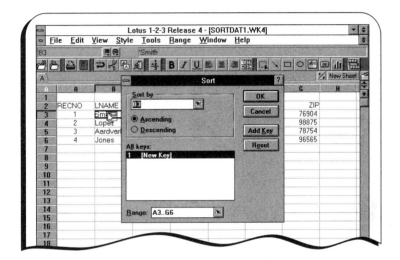

Note the default option is for Ascending sort. If you accept that choice, your table is sorted with Aardvark at the top and Smith at the bottom—alphabetical order. That is what we want.

Completing the Sort

Now click on the OK button in the Sort dialog box. The records sort in a flash. Even if you had several hundred records instead of four, they would sort in a few seconds. Our sorted records should look like Figure 8.3.

FIGURE 8.3

Ascending Sort on LNAME Field

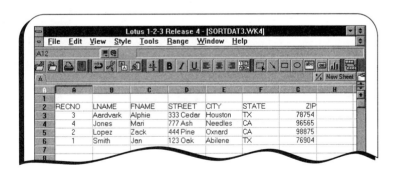

Note that the "Aardvark" record is in first place, Jones is in second, and so forth—entire records have been shifted around to put them in alphabetical name order. Entire records are shifted, rather than just the LNAME fields, because we specified the entire record area A3..G6 as the data range. This forced 1-2-3 to pull the entire records around as it arranged the LNAME fields in ascending alphabetical order.

Resorting in Descending Order

Select Reset to make 1-2-3 forget your earlier sorting instructions. Now sort the table in descending order using the STATE column as the key field. Your screen should look like Figure 8.4 after the sort is complete.

FIGURE 8.4

Descending Sort on the STATE Field

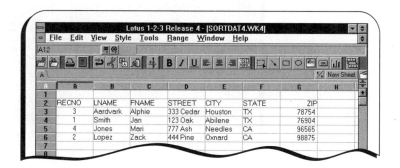

Both records with TX in the STATE field come before the records with CA in the STATE field. Once again, 1-2-3 rearranged entire records, not just the STATE information. This happened because you selected the entire data area (range A3..G6) to be sorted.

A common mistake in sorting is to specify only the key column as the data range. This leads to a totally trashed-out table. For example, if we now decided to sort our table in descending order on LNAME, but specified only B3..B6 as the data range, we would get a screen like the one shown in Figure 8.5. Do *not* actually do what you see in Figure 8.5.

FIGURE 8.5

A Disastrous Sort

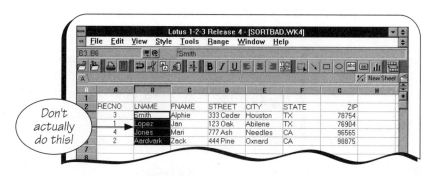

The records in Figure 8.5 are hopelessly scrambled. The sort affected only the LNAME column; the associated data in the other columns remained in place. If you actually did this, the only way to recover would be to close the file and open the copy that we hope you remembered to save before doing the sort!

Sorting on Two Keys: A "Yellow Pages" Sort

It is possible to sort on multiple keys. We now are going to use both a primary key, and a secondary key. This works like the yellow pages in the telephone directory. Businesses are first sorted alphabetically by type; then they are sorted alphabetically within their type. For example, all the Accountants get put ahead of the Bakeries. Then, within the Accountants, Aardvark comes first, Arthur comes second, Boseman comes third, and so forth.

To see how this works, be sure the range A3..G6 is selected. Then select Range Sort. In the dialog box, select Reset to clear your earlier selections. Select F3 (STATE) as the first key, and select the Ascending option. Select Add Key; then select G3 (ZIP) and Ascending. Your Sort dialog box now should look like Figure 8.6. Then select OK. Your mailing list now should look like Figure 8.7.

FIGURE 8.6

Specifying a Two-Key Sort

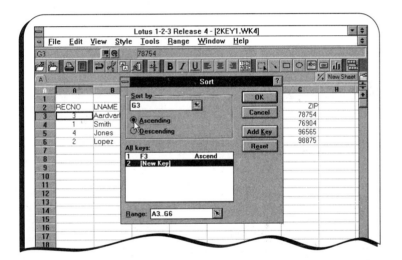

FIGURE 8.7

Two-Key Sort on STATE and ZIP Fields

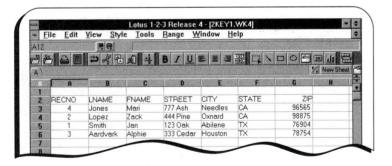

Note that the two records with CA in STATE are above the two with TX in STATE. This happened because you selected the STATE field as the first key, with ascending order. Also note that both the CA records and the TX records are in ascending ZIP order.

1-2-3 first sorted the records by the STATE field; then it resorted to get the CA records in ZIP order, and the TX records in ZIP order. If necessary, you could have specified a third key and a fourth key.

Specifying more than one key field makes no sense unless you have two or more records that have the same thing in the primary key field. It won't hurt anything, but there is simply nothing to sort on the secondary key. It is like a Yellow Pages where there is only one Accountant, only one Bakery, only one Car Repair, and so forth. Once the primary sort is done, there is nothing left for a secondary sort to do.

DEALING WITH THE "WORLD"

As you know, there are many programs besides 1-2-3. In a real-world situation, you cannot depend on finding all the data you need in 1-2-3 format. This section explains how to move "foreign" data into and out of 1-2-3.

1-2-3 Worksheet File Format

A 1-2-3 worksheet file contains not only data, functions, and formulas, but proprietary "file structure" information which 1-2-3 uses to organize the worksheet data in RAM. 1-2-3 can directly read a few "foreign" worksheet files such as Excel Release 4, but generally speaking, 1-2-3 cannot use files generated by other programs. By the same token, other programs have their own proprietary file formats; they cannot necessarily read 1-2-3 files.

The Translate Utility

1-2-3 comes with a Translate utility which converts files to and from these formats:

- 1-2-3 WKS, WK1, and WK3
- dBASE II, III, III+
- DIF
- Enable Version 2.0
- Multiplan 4.2
- Supercalc 4
- Symphony

1-2-3 Release 4 can directly read and write the earlier 1-2-3 formats. However, you need Translate to make a WK4 file usable by an earlier release. The Translate utility is not inside the 1-2-3 program. To use it, click on the Translate icon in the Lotus Applications group in Program Manager. The utility is menu driven and easy to use.

As you can see, the utility works only with a handful of programs. To move data between 1-2-3 and the other 9999 programs in the world, you have to use other techniques.

The ASCII Data Interchange Standard

1-2-3 and nearly all other programs can read and write a standard file structure called **ASCII** (American Standard Code for Information Interchange). ASCII files are the lingua franca of the computer world.

Transferring 1-2-3 Files to ASCII

You can save either a selected range or an entire file in ASCII format. To create an ASCII file from a worksheet file, select File Save As, and select Text as the File type. If you do not supply a different filename, the ASCII file will have the same filename as the worksheet, with a .TXT filename extension. When you click on OK, the ASCII file is saved to disk.

The ASCII version of your worksheet does not contain formulas or any graphic elements such as charts. However, it does preserve some simple formatting elements such as Comma format. Spacing in the ASCII file is the same as in the worksheet.

Transferring ASCII Files to 1-2-3

The "information superhighway" is crowded with useful data. Unfortunately most of it is in ASCII format rather than in 1-2-3 format. This section explains how to bring ASCII data into 1-2-3 worksheets.

Most electronic information sources such as Internet and Compuserve supply data in ASCII format. 1-2-3 can read ASCII files into a worksheet file, so you have access to all sorts of public database information.

Let's assume you have downloaded Bureau of the Census ASCII data on population growth rates by county in New York state. POPDATA.TXT, on your student disk, contains the data.

Select File Close and close your worksheet. We want to start fresh. Our example will be easier to understand if we replace the default font with a monospace font. Select the range A1..H20. Then click on the font selector in the status bar (it probably says "Arial" now). Select Courier. Courier is a monospace font, and it will make the ASCII data appear to line up in columns.

Now select File Open. In the Open File dialog box, select Text from the File type list box. Assuming your student disk is in the A: drive and A: is the default, you should see a screen like Figure 8.8.

FIGURE 8.8

Preparing to
Open an ASCII File

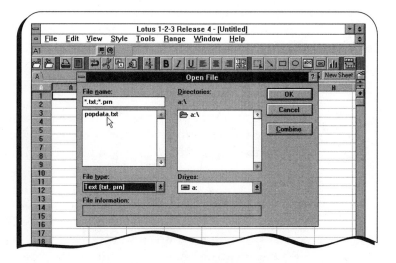

Select POPDATA.TXT in the list box. Then select Combine. You should see
the Combine Text dialog box, as shown in Figure 8.9.

FIGURE 8.9

The Combine Text
Dialog Box

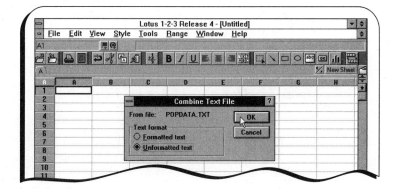

Select the Unformatted Text option button. Then click on OK. 1-2-3 combines
the ASCII data into your worksheet. Your worksheet should look like Figure 8.10.

FIGURE 8.10

ASCII Data
Imported as
Long Labels

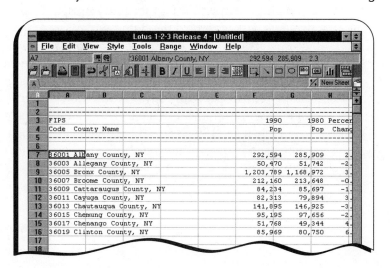

In Figure 8.10, we have selected cell A7. Note the contents box. The entire row of data actually is a long label in A7; the cells to the right contain nothing. The same applies to the other rows. 1-2-3 imported all the data as long labels in column A.

Now we need to break the long labels into 1-2-3 columnar format. This process is called **parsing**. To parse the long labels, be sure you cellpointer is on the first actual data line (A7). Select Range Parse to get the Parse dialog box.

In the Input column box, we need to specify the entire range of labels, A7..A16. You can type the range, or click on the arrow and then select the range by mouse. In the Output range box, we need to specify a place where 1-2-3 can write the parsed results. 1-2-3 overwrites anything that gets in the way, so let's specify the blank area below the long labels. Select A19.

Click on Create to create a format line in the text box. 1-2-3 examines the first line of data and makes a judgment about how to break the label into columns. Your Parse dialog box now should look like Figure 8.11.

FIGURE 8.11
Setup for
Parsing the Text

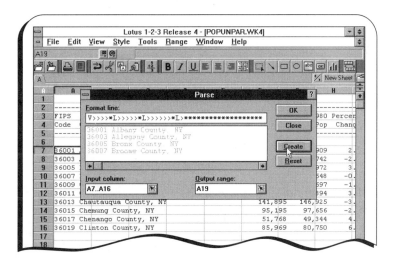

The codes in the Format line box indicate how 1-2-3 plans to break the long labels into columns. You can edit the format line, but let's just accept the default. Click on OK in the Parse dialog box. 1-2-3 executes the parsing operation. Your screen now should look like Figure 8.12.

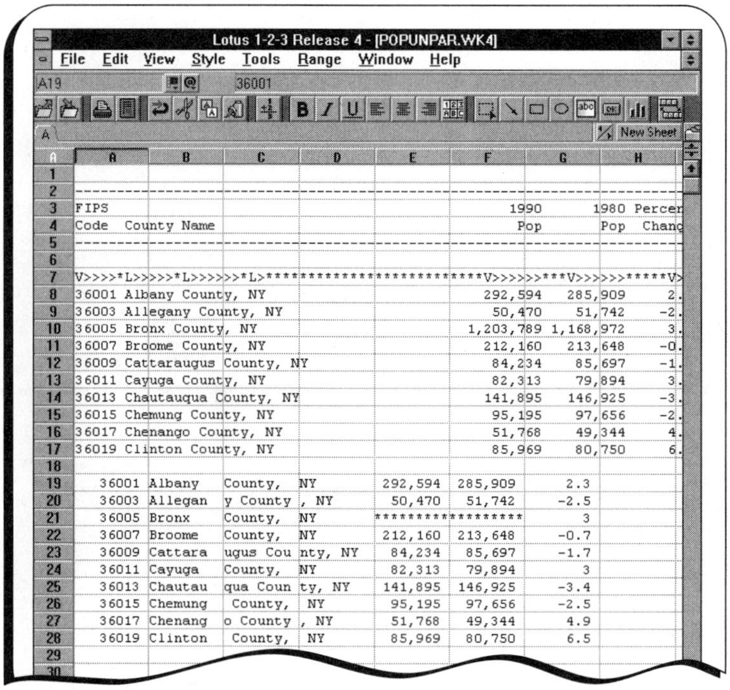

FIGURE 8.12
Parse Operation
Completed

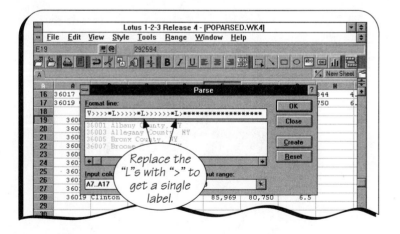

The parsed data in Figure 8.12 looks somewhat ragged because 1-2-3's guess at how to break the labels was not quite right. We could fix the problem by selecting Range Parse and editing the format line, as shown in Figure 8.13.

FIGURE 8.13
Editing the
Format Line

If we now reparse the data, 1-2-3 uses our edited format line. The county and state identifiers would all be rolled together and placed in a single column.

The significant result of the parsing process is that the numeric data now is aligned in columns. In Figure 8.14, we have moved the cellpointer to E19; note the contents box.

FIGURE 8.14

The Payoff
from Parsing

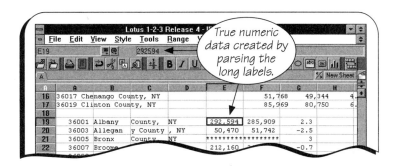

You can operate on the parsed data just as if you had manually entered it into the worksheet. To 1-2-3, there is no difference between data input by parsing and data input by typing.

Importing and Sorting ASCII Population Data

There is an ASCII file on your SMART disk called POPTEX.TXT. Import the file into 1-2-3 and parse it. Then sort it by 1990 population, ascending. Print the sorted data, with this header:

```
County Population, Ascending Order    (date)        (page number)
```

The following exercise requires extensive data input. Similar exercises, with the data preentered, can be found on the SMART disk.

1. Congratulations. You just got a job as a Lotus 1-2-3 guru with Merrill Lunch, Parse, Finner and Spith, a large investment firm. Your boss has given you the following data on quarterly commissions generated by the firm's brokers. Your job is to

   a. Identify the top two brokers (highest two commissions generated) for the first quarter, the second quarter, and for the entire six month period (1st+2nd). The two highest brokers for each quarter get a $500 bonus. The two highest brokers for the entire period (compute an average) get extra-special treatment. These super-brokers each receive tickets (them and spouse) to Honolulu for a 1-week vacation.

   b. Identify the lowest two brokers. These infra-brokers each receive tickets (them only) to Yellowknife, Yukon Territory, next January.

   c. Print the results of each sort.

	COMMISSIONS GENERATED	COMMISSIONS GENERATED
BROKER	QUARTER 1	QUARTER 2
Smith	$99,997	$92,978
Jones	$99,387	$97,450
Harlow	$98,988	$55,396
Welch	$98,719	$54,946
Gomez	$98,530	$70,421
Doe	$98,368	$92,431
Baker	$98,339	$60,102
Donley	$98,030	$87,808
Watson	$97,120	$97,674

2. You just took a job with Waldobooks, Inc., a large bookstore chain, as their resident Lotus 1-2-3 guru. Waldobooks wants you to sort their inventory records in ascending order by the number of copies in stock, so management can see whether there are any excessive numbers of copies on hand. Print a copy of the sorted list. Then, management wants you to sort in ascending order using book-title as the primary key. Print a copy.

TITLE	AUTHOR	CODE	COST	RETAIL	NUM
THE MERRY TINKER	BRANZ, JOE	AA	7.53	12.95	1
LEARN TO LOVE DBASE	GREEN, ADAM	AD	8.63	69.84	8
WOODWORKING	HANDY, HANK	AG	7.27	9.95	5
LAWN CARE	GREEN, G.G.	AH	12.74	18.95	5
LAWN CARE	GREEN, ADA	AI	8.63	11.95	9
SAILBOAT THEORY	RUDDER, JOE	AJ	16.32	23.95	7
SEVEN STITCHES	SIMPLE, SIMON	AK	8.77	12.49	8
AXMANSHIP EXPLAINED	STUBB, JOCK	AL	10.95	14.95	11
ON THE BEACH	GRANE, SANDY	AN	0.00	0.00	0
WOODCARVING	NOFINGERS, M.	AQ	8.11	12.95	0
LAWN CARE	GREENE, K.K.	BB	7.66	9.98	5
WHALE BOATS	SPRAY, NEMO	AR	7.11	11.25	0
CRANIAL STRUCTURE	HEDD, JOHN	BA	11.79	21.95	3
FOX HUNTING THEORY	YOICKS, JOSEPH	BB	13.60	22.95	5
LAWN CARE	SPRINKLER, A.	BC	11.21	18.95	3
CAT CARE	JONES, KITTY	AG	4.67	7.95	7
RIDING TO HOUNDS	DOGBREATH, DAN	BH	8.16	11.95	5
THE MARCH UPCOUNTRY	XENOPHON, JOE	CR	8.15	9.98	13
ASTROPHYSICS	LENSMAN, RALPH	CT	19.81	32.25	2
SOARING AS A SPORT	DAEDELUS, F.W.	CY	6.86	9.95	5
DEER HUNTING	SNIPER, CLYDE	CX	9.17	12.49	7
LAWN CARE	TURFF, JOE	BB	5.55	9.95	6

3. Now re-sort the data, using title as the primary key (Ascending) and author as the secondary key (Ascending).

4. Re-sort the data again, using NUM (number of copies on hand) as the primary key (Descending) and COST as the secondary key (Descending).

1. **08AU08** is actually several independent exercises rolled into one SMART worksheet. It requires several sorts, from simple single-column to more complex multicolumn and multikey sorts.

2. **08AU10** has 150 records, showing commissions for stockbrokers. The problem asks you to provide some formulas as well as do some sorts. Some of the questions could more easily be answered with database query techniques, but the problem shows that sorting can be used to provide fairly sophisticated information.

3. **08AU16** requires use of both primary and secondary sort keys. The data is a 100-record bookstore inventory with several fields.

4. **08BU18** is another sorting problem that uses a sizable table of records. Most of the questions involve determining how many records meet a particular condition. Such questions can also be answered using database techniques, of course.

5. **08BU22** requires you to sort an inventory database by assorted criteria.

Consolidations: Multiple Sheets and Files

OBJECTIVES   After studying this chapter, you should know how to:

- Create multiple-sheet files.
- Copy data across worksheets.
- Use Group mode.
- Build multiple-sheet formulas.
- View multiple sheets in perspective mode.
- Combine files.
- Link files on disk to the current worksheet.
- Extract selected ranges of a file to disk.
- Tile and cascade files.

This chapter expands on the usage of multiple sheets in a file. It also looks at how to combine and link files. Finally, the chapter examines techniques for extracting pieces of files from the current worksheet.

MULTIPLE WORKSHEETS REVISITED   In Chapter 3 we created two worksheets in the CONCOST file. Now we need to expand on the concept of multiple worksheets. Assume that you work for a company with three divisions: Argus, Caltex, and Draken. We need a worksheet to keep track of estimated sales for all three divisions.

Create a worksheet like Figure 9.1. Draw a box around cells B3..B9 (by selecting B3..B9 and then selecting Style Lines & Color Outline). The function in B11 is @SUM(B3..B9). After you set up the worksheet, double-click on its tab and name the tab MASTER.

FIGURE 9.1

A Master Budget
Worksheet

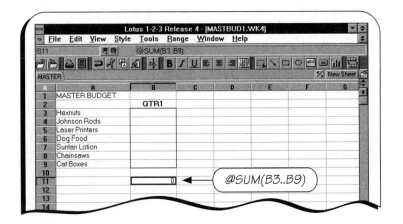

FIGURE 9.1

A Master Budget
Worksheet

Now create three more tabs (by clicking on New Sheet). Double-click on each tab and enter the respective tab names ARGUS, CALTEX, and DRAKEN. After you finish, the tab area of your worksheet should look like Figure 9.2. Note that the MASTER tab is current.

FIGURE 9.2

Four Sheets
with Named Tabs

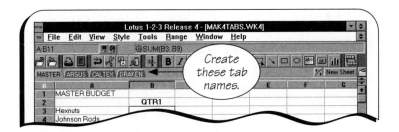

COPYING ACROSS WORKSHEETS

Currently, ARGUS, CALTEX, and DRAKEN contain nothing. We need to copy the area A2..B11 from the MASTER tab to the other three tabs. There are several ways to do the copying job, but we will use this: Select A2..B11 in MASTER. Then select Edit Copy, click on the ARGUS tab and, with the cellpointer on A2 in ARGUS, select Edit Paste.

Repeat the operation for CALTEX and DRAKEN. When you finish, each of the four worksheets will have the same data in their A2..B11 ranges.

GROUP MODE

1-2-3 has a Group mode which ties together all the worksheets in a file. In Group mode, when you select a cell or range in any given worksheet, the same cell or range is selected in all the other worksheets in the group. Data you enter in a selected cell is not copied to the other grouped worksheets, but formats and settings such as column width are applied to all the others. Group mode is the perfect tool for producing multiple sheets with a standardized appearance.

If you insert or delete columns or rows while Group mode is active, all work-sheets in the group are affected—not just the current sheet.

We want all four of our worksheets to share the same format, so select Style Worksheet Defaults and select the Group mode option in the dialog box. Now any formatting changes you make to one worksheet affect all the others. In MASTER, format the range B3..B11 as Comma with zero decimal places. The other three sheets automatically use the same format.

BUILDING TRANS-SHEET FORMULAS

Formulas in one sheet can refer to cells in other sheets. In cell B3 of MASTER, enter the formula

@SUM(ARGUS:B3..DRAKEN:B3)

Then copy the function into the range B4..B9. Figure 9.3 shows how to do it with the right mouse button, in case you've forgotten.

FIGURE 9.3
Copying Down
by Mouse

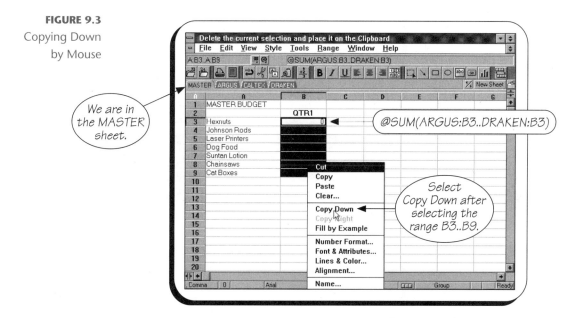

Our MASTER will automatically sum any figures in respective cells of ARGUS, CALTEX, and DRAKEN. Now we need to enter the data into ARGUS, CALTEX, and DRAKEN. Select each tab in turn and enter the data as shown in Figure 9.4.

FIGURE 9.4

Data for the
Subsidiary
Worksheets

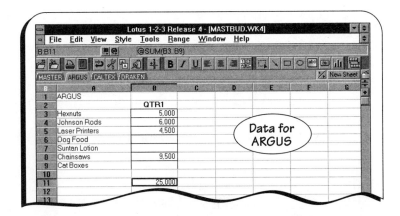

If you now click on the MASTER tab, you should see a screen like Figure
9.5.

FIGURE 9.5
MASTER Sums
Data from
Subsidiary Sheets

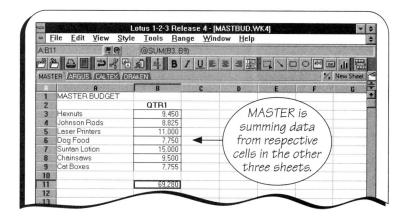

VIEWING SHEETS IN PERSPECTIVE MODE

In a multiple-worksheet file such as MASTBUD, you can view up to three sheets at the same time by selecting View Split. Figure 9.6 shows the Split dialog box. Note that we have selected Perspective option button.

FIGURE 9.6
The View Split
Dialog Box

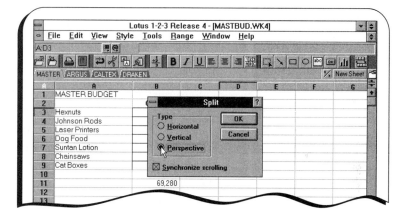

With View Split Perspective set, your screen should look like Figure 9.7.

FIGURE 9.7

Worksheets
in Perspective View

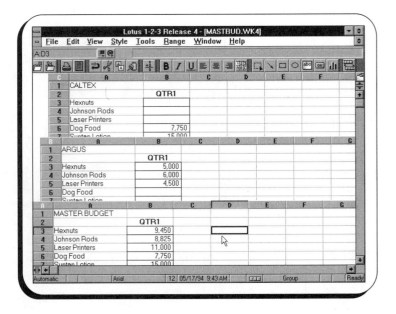

By default, the worksheets are synchronized; that is, they scroll together. When you move the cellpointer inside one sheet, the other sheet displays move in lockstep. If you want to scroll independently, deselect the Synchronize scrolling option box in the Split dialog box.

To move from one sheet to another, press F6 (PANE), or CTRL+PageUp or CTRL+PageDown. To remove the perspective view, select View Clear Split.

1-2-3 cannot provide a perspective view of more than three sheets. If you wanted to drop MASTER and see ARGUS, CALTEX, and DRAKEN in perspective, you could click on the ARGUS tab and then select View Split Perspective.

Close your file, saving it as MASTBUD.

COMBINING FILES

The ability to combine files allows you to bring files, or parts of files, from disk into the current worksheet. The incoming files can replace, add to, or subtract from existing values in the current worksheet.

The incoming file keys on the cellpointer location in the current file. That is, the upper left corner of the incoming file falls at the cellpointer location in the current file.

Replacing Data in the Current File

The File Open Combine Replace Values command replaces existing cell data with data from the incoming file. It is very handy for inserting boilerplate information into the current file. For example, if you need a standard closing statement for reports you prepare, you might set up a worksheet like Figure 9.8 (filename PREPBY).

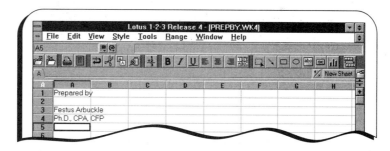

Close the file; name it PREPBY. From a clear worksheet, prepare the wonderfully short budget report shown in Figure 9.9.

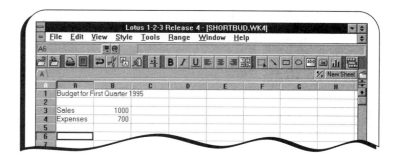

Let's assume that you want to lay the PREPBY boilerplate information into the budget at cell A6. Move your cellpointer to the target location (A6), select File Open, and select File name PREPBY. Then click on the Combine button. You should see the Combine dialog box, shown in Figure 9.10.

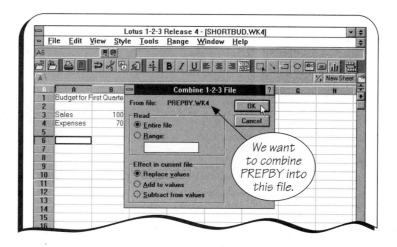

Notice that the Entire file and Replace values options buttons are selected. Click on OK. Your worksheet should look like Figure 9.11 because the PREPBY file is now a part of the worksheet.

FIGURE 9.11

Boilerplate File
Combined into
the Budget

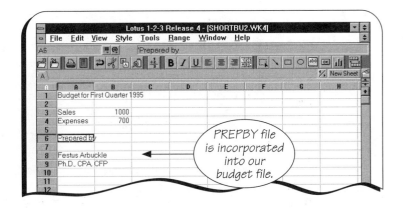

Adding Disk Files to the Current File

The File Open Combine Add command brings in only numeric cells from the disk file, rather than bringing in both text and numbers like Combine Replace. It is used primarily for consolidating divisional financial statements (when they exist as separate worksheets). To get into the proper frame of mind to explore Combine Add, do a little fantasizing.

Assume that you are the vice president for Finance of AMRA Corporation; your headquarters are in Chicago. AMRA has two operating divisions. One, called EASTMISS, operates east of the Mississippi River; divisional headquarters for EASTMISS are in Atlanta. The other, WESTMISS, operates west of the Mississippi; its divisional headquarters are in Denver.

Every month the two divisions use their computers to send financial reports to you in Chicago. In the past, you have had to print out the reports and manually reenter the numbers in your 1-2-3 worksheet in order to consolidate them. You have decided to eliminate the time and hassle of manual consolidation by designing standard report forms and using File Open Combine Add.

First, close your worksheet with File Close and set up the master worksheet for your use at headquarters. Your master worksheet should look like Figure 9.12.

FIGURE 9.12

Master File for
AMRA Corporation

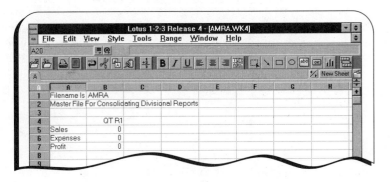

Close the file; save it as AMRA. Switch roles now. Instead of being the vice president at corporate headquarters, you are the divisional manager of Eastern operations in Atlanta. You are preparing to send in your monthly report to headquarters. From your clear worksheet, set up the Eastern divisional worksheet as shown in Figure 9.13.

FIGURE 9.13
EASTMISS
Divisional
Worksheet

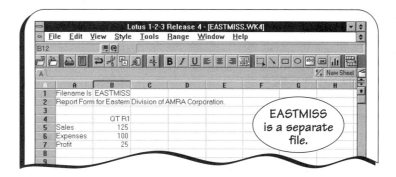

The numeric cells of the divisional report forms *must* be in exactly the same places as those of the AMRA worksheet (the master form). That is, the SALES figure must go in cell B5, the EXPENSES figure must go in B6, and the PROFIT figure must go in B7. The text entries on the divisional report forms are immaterial.

Note that we are calling this file EASTMISS. It is a quarterly income statement for our Eastern divisions. After you have it set up as shown, select File Close and save it to disk under the filename EASTMISS. We assume you have sent the file to corporate headquarters in Chicago. Now at corporate headquarters we have on disk a blank AMRA file and an EASTMISS file containing data for our Eastern operations.

Now switch roles once more. Assume you are the divisional manager in Denver. Set up a report for Western operations as shown in Figure 9.14. To save typing, simply make the changes shown and File Save As WESTMISS.

FIGURE 9.14
WESTMISS
Divisional File

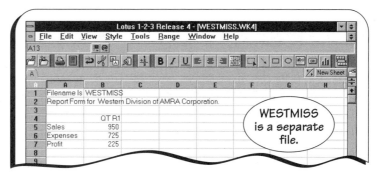

Very good. To simulate telecommunicating the WESTMISS file to corporate headquarters, close the WESTMISS file (and save it). You now have an empty worksheet.

Now mentally transport yourself back to company headquarters. Pretend the two divisions have just sent copies of their files (EASTMISS and WESTMISS) to your disk at headquarters by modem (telecommunications). Your job is to consolidate the divisional files.

Open the AMRA file. Now we are ready to combine (add) the numeric parts of EASTMISS and WESTMISS into AMRA.

After you open the AMRA file, be sure to put your cellpointer on cell A1. The Combine Add command keys on cellpointer location, just like Combine Replace does. If your cellpointer is not in A1 when you combine, the files coming in from disk will not overlay correctly on the master file.

With your cellpointer on A1, select File Open and select the EASTMISS file (Don't hit ↵ or click on OK; if you do, the Combine option will not be activated). Then click on Combine and click on the Add to values option button. Your Combine dialog box should look like Figure 9.15.

FIGURE 9.15

The File Combine Dialog Box

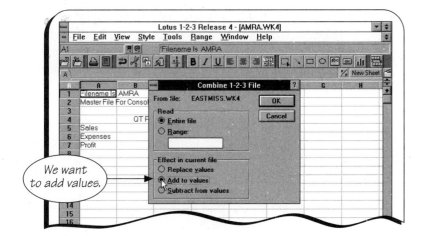

Select OK from the dialog box. The numeric values from EASTMISS are added to the numeric values in the AMRA file; text from EASTMISS is not brought in. You should see the screen shown in Figure 9.16.

FIGURE 9.16

EASTMISS Numeric Data Added to AMRA

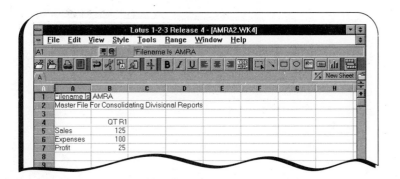

Now, follow the same procedure to add in the values from the WESTMISS file. The finished product should look like Figure 9.17.

FIGURE 9.17
WESTMISS
Numeric Data
Added to AMRA

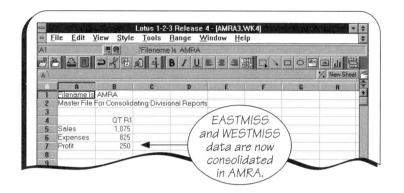

If you had other divisions, you also could consolidate them by the same process. When you finished, you could save the combined file under its own name—say, CONSOL. For that matter, you could save it under the filename AMRA, but then you would no longer have a blank master worksheet. Really the only place you can go wrong is in cellpointer positioning. If you had moved your cellpointer to, say, A12 before you brought in the WESTMISS file, the upper left corner of WESTMISS would start at A12. The WESTMISS numbers would be added to the blank cells B17, B18, and B19 rather than B5..B7 where they belong.

Modify your consolidated file, changing the identifying label to FILENAME IS CONSOL, as shown in Figure 9.18. Then Save As CONSOL.

FIGURE 9.18
AMRA Saved
as CONSOL

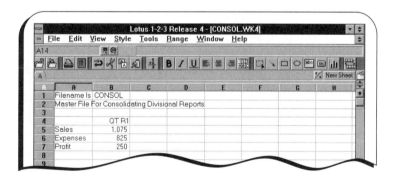

You can use File Open Combine to bring in only a range from a file on disk. The same principle holds; the specified range (or range named area) from the disk file is brought into the current worksheet with the upper left corner of the range falling on the cellpointer location.

LINKING OTHER FILES TO THE CURRENT WORKSHEET

For some applications, you need a "live" hookup between the current worksheet and worksheets in other files. The Combine commands provide only a "dead" connection; after the Combine command, any changes in the combined files are not reflected in the current worksheet unless you repeat the Combine operation.

Linking provides a "live" connection between the master file and the linked files. Each time you change a value in the linked files, the master file updates itself from the linked worksheets.

The formula syntax for creating links to other files is:

```
+<<filename-to-link>>address-to-link
```

Where `filename-to-link` is the name of the file and sheet in the file that contains the cells you want to link into the current worksheet, and `address-to-link` is the cell address to be linked into the current worksheet. If the file is on another drive, include the drive designator.

To examine how linking works, close your file and create the new worksheet shown in Figure 9.19. Note that cells B4 and B5 contain a special type of formula. The formula +<<EASTMISS>>A:B7..A:B7 means "look in the file named EASTMISS and get the contents of cell B7 from EASTMISS." In Figure 9.19, EASTMISS and WESTMISS refer to the worksheets that you created in the previous discussion of File Open Combine.

FIGURE 9.19

Consolidation by File-Linking Formulas

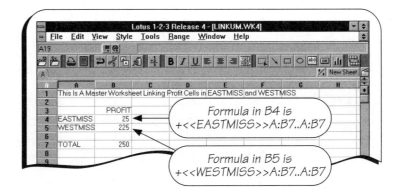

After you set up the worksheet shown in Figure 9.19, save it to disk. Use the filename LINKUM. The linking formulas will be updated every time you open the worksheet. For example, if you File Save LINKUM, then File Open EASTMISS and change the contents of B7 in EASTMISS, your LINKUM cell B4 will reflect the change the next time you File Open LINKUM.

SAVING SELECTED RANGES OF THE ACTIVE FILE

The File Save As command has a Selected range only option box that lets you save a range from the worksheet in memory to a separate disk file, rather than saving the whole worksheet.

Using File Save As Selected range, you can save as a separate disk file anything from a single cell to the whole worksheet. In Figure 9.20 we have selected the range A3..B4 and the filename EASTCUT. Notice that we have clicked on Selected range only.

FIGURE 9.20

Extracting
a Selected Range
to Disk

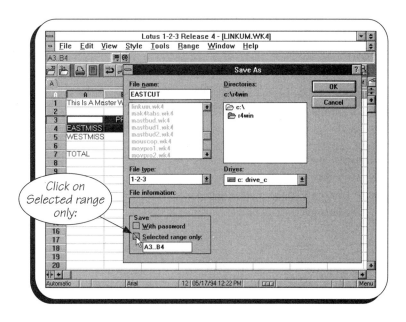

File Save As Selected range leads to another dialog box with two option buttons. You can select either the Formulas and values option (really all four layers of all cells in the range you specify for saving) or the Values only option (the top three layers, discarding the value-rule layer). Label entries and literal numbers are always saved, regardless of which option you take; the choice only applies to formula-based cells.

In Figure 9.21, we have selected the Formulas and values option. If we had selected Values only, the new file would contain only labels and numbers; formulas would have been converted to their values.

FIGURE 9.21

The Save Range
As Dialog Box

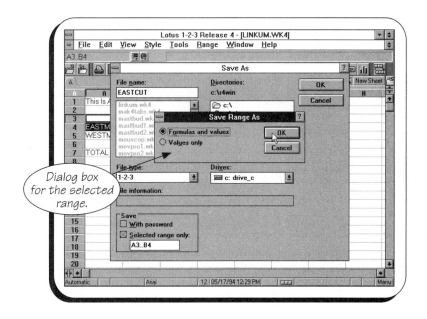

If we select OK in the small dialog box, the EASTCUT file is saved to disk. If we then open the EASTCUT file, it should look like Figure 9.22.

FIGURE 9.22

The New File

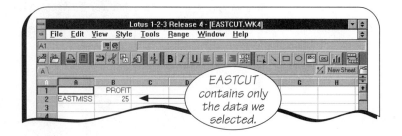

The display in Figure 9.22 is the total worksheet—you saved only the A3..B4 range as a separate file. If you are skeptical, move your cellpointer around and look for the rest of LINKUM. It isn't there. Press the END key and then the HOME key to send the cellpointer to the lower right boundary of the worksheet. The cellpointer goes to cell B2. The formula was saved along with the labels because we selected Formulas and values in the option box.

Saving Values Only

If we opened LINKUM and repeated the process, selecting Values only, we would get the same screen display as the preceding one when we retrieved the new file, except this time, there would be no formulas in the worksheet. The Values only option ignores formulas during the extraction process; it saves only the values, rather than the value rules.

Saving values only is very useful if you want to let someone else look at the results of your work, but not at the formulas behind the results. You can specify the entire worksheet as the range to extract and give others the new file. The recipients will have a perfect copy of your results, but they will not have any of the formulas you used to generate the results.

TILING AND CASCADING FILES

To see more than one file on the screen at one time, open the desired files. Then select Window. You will have two available options, Tile and Cascade. In Figure 9.23, we opened LINKUM, EASTMISS, and WESTMISS, and we selected Window Tile. The currently selected file, WESTMISS, has a darker title bar than the others. WESTMISS is currently selected because it was the most recently opened file.

FIGURE 9.23
Files Tiled with
Window Tile

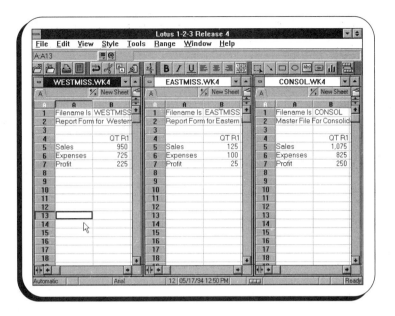

You can switch among the three files by clicking inside them. If you prefer a cascaded look, select Window Cascade. Your screen then should look like Figure 9.24.

FIGURE 9.24
Cascaded Files

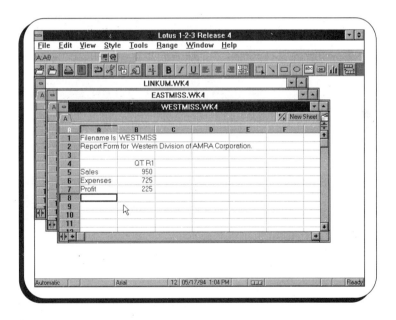

To bring a file to the front of the cascaded stack, click on its name in its title bar. You also can drag elements of the stack (by clicking on the title bar, holding down the left mouse button, and moving the mouse).

To fill the screen with any file, click on its Maximize button. To restore it to a smaller size, click on its Restore button. To size a file, move the mouse to a corner, click, and drag.

To minimize a sheet, click on its Minimize button. Figure 9.25 shows EAST-MISS and LINKUM minimized and the WESTMISS file resized. Note that EASTMISS and LINKUM appear only as icons. To restore them, you would double-click on their icons.

FIGURE 9.25
Resizing and
Minimizing Files

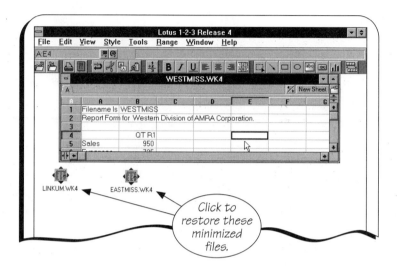

USING EDIT PASTE SPECIAL TO WIPE OUT FORMULAS

To eliminate the formula in a cell (or all the formulas in a range of cells), select the range. Then select Edit Copy, followed by Edit Paste Special Formulas as values. If the paste range is the same as the copy range, the original formulas are replaced with their computed values only. Or, you can specify a different paste range if you want a formula-less copy in a different part of the worksheet.

To destroy the formula in a single cell, you can use another technique. Edit the cell (by pressing F2). Then press Calc (F9), and the formula is destroyed.

Boot up 1-2-3.

1. Open the LINKUM file. Use File Open Combine Entire file Subtract from values to subtract WESTMISS. Close the file without saving.

2. Open your CONCOST file. Put your cellpointer in A1, and combine file EASTMISS into CONCOST, adding values. What happens?

3. Retrieve the CONSOL file. Put your cellpointer in A1. Do a File Open Combine Add to values, specifying CONSOL as the file to use. You just added CONSOL to itself. Now move the cellpointer to B2, and repeat the operation. Notice that everything is jumbled up. What is going on?

1. **09AU06** requires the student to provide linking formulas to bring in selected data from worksheets on disk.

2. **09AU10** requires students to use File Open Combine Add to values to develop a consolidated budget. The problem requires no special skills in finance or ac-counting; any student can do it.

Database Operations

OBJECTIVES   After studying this chapter, you should know how to:

- Create a database.
- Query a database.
- Append records to a database.
- Find and edit records in a database.

A **database table**, or database for short, is a range consisting of field names across the top and records beneath the field names. A **field name** is a column label that categorizes the cells (the **fields**) in the column beneath it. A record is a row of data beneath the field names; the information in each field (each cell) of the record corresponds to the respective field name above it. A database can have up to 256 fields and 8191 records.

WHAT TO DO WITH A DATABASE   1-2-3 users set up mailing lists, customer lists, and other tables of information in database form—with field headings—to take advantage of 1-2-3's query capabilities. You can query the database to extract all the records that meet some criterion.

How to Create a Database

We are going to create a database to hold employee information for Blatz Pickle, Incorporated. The first step is to decide how many categories of information (how many fields) we need.

For each employee, we want to keep track of the employee's last name, the department in which the employee works, the employee's annual salary, and the date the employee was hired. Each of these information categories will be a field in the database. For field names, we will use descriptive labels.

Start with a clear worksheet and set up the field names like Figure 10.1. There is nothing sacred about the choice of field names; we could have used LASTNAME, DEPARTMENT, BUCKS, and FIRSTEMPLOYED instead of the ones shown in the figure. For that matter, we could have used XYZ57K instead of LNAME. 1-2-3 only requires that you have a unique field name label up to 15 characters for each field.

FIGURE 10.1

Field Names
for the Database

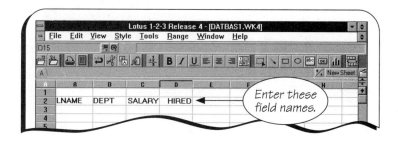

 Use only letters and digits for field names, and don't use field names that look like cell addresses. Field names like DATE-HIRED or BB21 may cause your database to work erratically or not at all.

Now let's enter a record in the database. Reproduce the information you see in row three of Figure 10.2. To enter the date, simply type 11/22/91. Lotus 1-2-3 understands that you are entering a date rather than a division formula.

FIGURE 10.2

Entering a Record

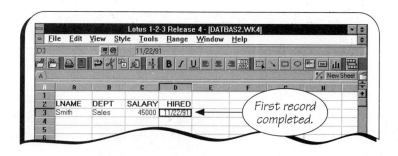

Our record holds information about one unique "thing"—the person Smith. We have Smith's department, salary, and date hired. In a real-world database, we would have to add another field, such as social security number, to make each record unique; a large organization might have fifty Smiths who worked in the sales department.

As you can see, a 1-2-3 database is just another name for a table of information. The only distinguishing feature is the top row—the field names. 1-2-3 uses the field names in all database operations, so they must be there. The field names are a generic classification for all the specific data items that appear below them. For example, cell B2 has the field name DEPT; underneath DEPT we will put the particular department for each record in the database.

We are going to keep the database short and simple, but the same principles work for a database with more fields and more records. Add the records shown in Figure 10.3.

FIGURE 10.3

A Small Database

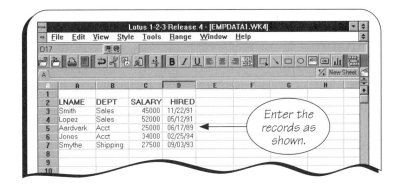

Naming the Database Table

1-2-3 does not require that you name your databases, but an unnamed database is unnecessarily hard to work with. Get in the habit of range naming your databases as soon as you set them up.

After you have entered the additional records, select the range A2..D7. Then select Range Name; enter the Name WORKERS, as shown in Figure 10.4, and click on OK. The range includes the field names in row 2. If you don't include the field names, your database won't work.

FIGURE 10.4

Range Naming the Database

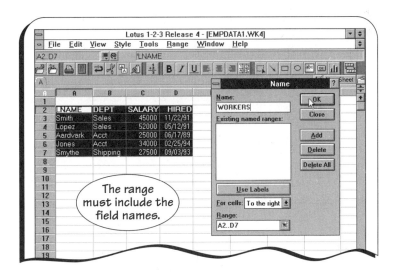

Now select Style Column Width and narrow column E to 2. This is not necessary for the database to work, but it makes your screen look like the examples that follow.

QUERYING A DATABASE

Querying a database means getting information from it. The first time you query a database, you follow setup procedures.

Creating a Query Table

A **query table** is a workspace for holding data that you extract from the database. It looks like a copy of the database, and in effect that is what it is. However, the query table usually is smaller than the database because it contains only the database records you specify. You can work with the query table without affecting any records in the actual database.

At this point in our example, no query table exists. To create a query table, select Tools Database New Query. You should see the New Query dialog box shown in Figure 10.5. In text box 1, enter WORKERS, which is the range name of the database. In text box 3, enter F2..I7, which is the area where we want the query table to appear.

FIGURE 10.5

Using the New Query Dialog Box

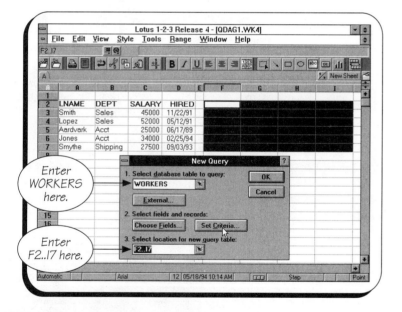

Sizing and Placing Query Tables

If you specify only the upper left corner of the query table (like F2), 1-2-3 automatically uses as much room as is needed for the query table. However, anything that gets in the way of the query table is erased automatically. It is advisable to specifically set the query table range to the same size as the database. On the other hand, if you make the query table range smaller than the database, 1-2-3 may not be able to show all the records you extract.

In real-world applications, you may want to place your query tables in a second sheet. To do so, simply create another tab, and specify the query table location like B:F2. For our examples, we are placing the query table next to the

database, on the same sheet, because it is easier to grasp the concepts when
the database and the query table appear next to each other.

Selecting Fields for the Query Table

You do not need to select the Choose Fields button in the dialog box unless you
want the query table to show fewer fields, or a different order of fields, than the
database. We want the query table to have the same structure as the database,
so we will not select Choose Fields.

Selecting Criteria

Criteria are filters that determine which records get extracted to the query
table. You select one or more criteria (filters) by selecting the Set Criteria button
in the dialog box.

   If you do not select the Set Criteria button, 1-2-3 extracts *all* the records in
your database to the query table. You may find occasions when you want to
do this, but usually you want to extract only those records that meet some
specific set of criteria.

   Let's set the criterion to extract all the records that contain the label Sales
in the DEPT field. Select Set Criteria. Click on the Field arrow to get a list of fields;
select DEPT. Select equals (=) in the Operator box. Select Sales in the Value box.
Your screen should look like Figure 10.6.

FIGURE 10.6
Setting Criteria
for the Query

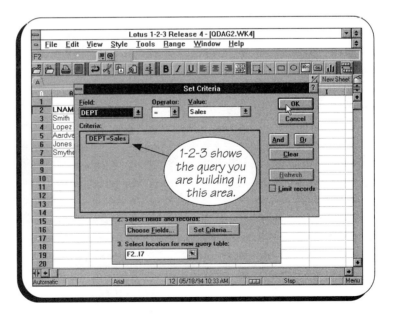

Click on OK in the Set Criteria dialog box and the New Query dialog box.
The dialog boxes go away, and 1-2-3 copies all records that match the criterion
to the query table. Your screen now should look like Figure 10.7.

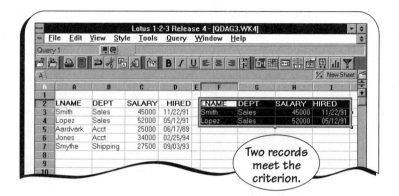

Two records meet the criterion.

The two records in the query table have a common characteristic. Both have the label Sales in the DEPT field because that was your selection criterion. In effect, 1-2-3 put all the database records in an electronic sieve. The ones that failed the criterion fell through, and only the "keepers" were copied into the query table.

Additional Queries

You only need to use Tools Database New Query once for any given query table. 1-2-3 remembers the settings you specified in the New Query dialog box.

You do not have to do all your queries at one time. You can deselect the query table by moving the cellpointer outside it. Then you can do anything you want, and return to the query process later.

In Figure 10.8 we have moved the cellpointer to A1; the query table is deselected. To reselect it, move the mouse pointer to the query table boundary (the pointer changes shape, as shown in Figure 10.8). Click to reselect the table.

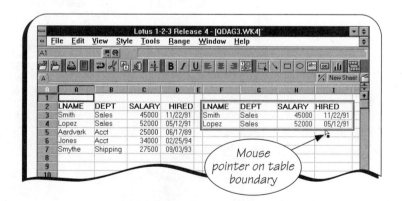

Mouse pointer on table boundary

Now let's do another query. When you select a query table, the menu choice changes to Query and new SmartIcons appear. Select Query Set Criteria to get the Set Criteria dialog box. Change your criterion, as shown in Figure 10.9. The figure shows both the dialog box and the results. You no longer see the dialog box after you click on OK.

FIGURE 10.9
Query Table
for SALARY > 50000

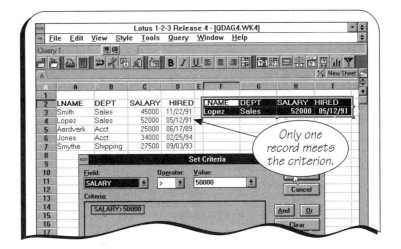

Now select HIRED > 1/1/92 as your criterion and click on OK. Your screen should look like Figure 10.10.

FIGURE 10.10
Query Table
for HIRED > 1/1/92

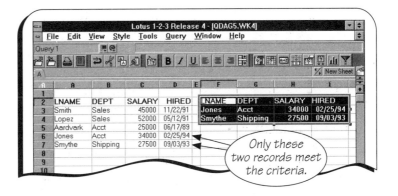

Wildcard Queries for Labels

For label fields, you can specify either of two wildcard characters as part of the search criterion. The wildcards are asterisk (*), meaning "accept any characters after this," and question mark (?), meaning "accept any single character in this position."

Figure 10.11 shows the result of querying for LNAME=S*. Two records were extracted and both begin with the letter S.

FIGURE 10.11

Wildcard Query
for LNAME = S*

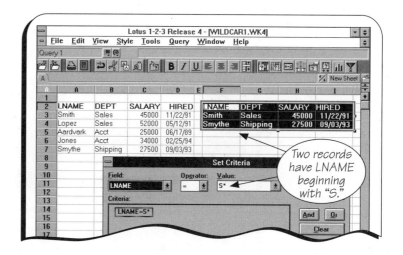

Figure 10.12 shows the result of querying for LNAME=?O*. The meaning is "extract all records whose LNAME field begins with any character, whose second character is O (or o—1-2-3 searches are not case sensitive), and accept any characters after the O."

FIGURE 10.12

Wildcard Query
for LNAME = ?O*

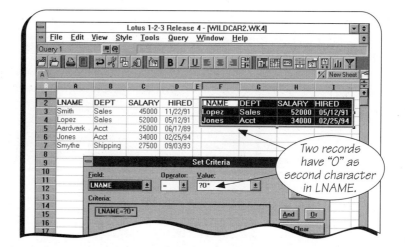

Multiple Criteria

You are not restricted to querying for a single criterion. You can query for all records meeting one criterion *and* other criteria. You also can query for records meeting one criterion *or* other criteria.

Using the And Button

Let's assume you are the boss, and you are feeling mellow and generous. Maybe you should give raises to everyone hired before January 1, 1994, who makes less than $30,000. To get a list of the lucky employees, you need to specify two criteria with the And button.

Select Query Set Criteria. Select SALARY < 30000. Then click on the And button. Select HIRED < 1/1/94. Then select OK. Figure 10.13 shows all records meeting both those criteria.

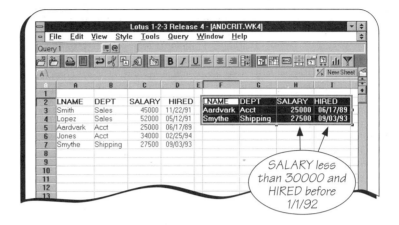

If you wanted a list of all employees making between 30000 and 40000, you could use the And button to specify an upper and lower bound for the SALARY field. Figure 10.14 shows how to set up this operation.

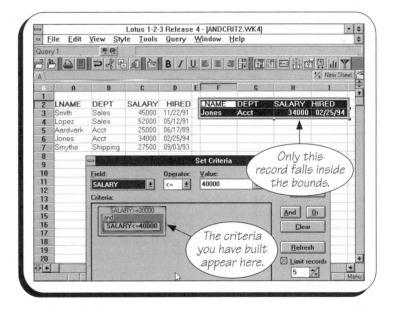

Using the Or Button

Let's assume that, in a fit of generosity, you decide to give raises to all employees who *either* work in the shipping department *or* who were hired before January 1, 1990. To extract the records, select Query Set Criteria; specify DEPT = Shipping; then click on the Or button. For the "or" condition, specify HIRED<01/01/90. Click on OK in the dialog box. Your query table should look like Figure 10.15.

FIGURE 10.15

Query Table for
DEPT = SHIPPING or
HIRED < 1/1/90

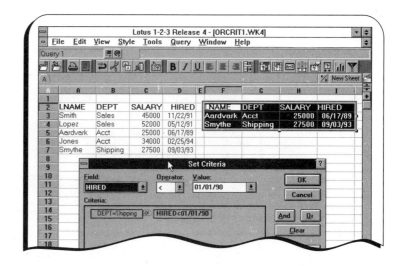

Sorting the Query Table

To sort records in a query table, the table must be selected. If it is not selected, click on its border.

Before sorting the query table, let's extract everyone making more than 25,000. Select Query Set Criteria. Click on the Clear button until all existing criteria are deleted. Then specify the criterion SALARY>25000, and click on OK. All records except Aardvark's appear in the query table.

Select Query Sort. In the Sort dialog box, select Sort by LNAME and click on OK. Figure 10.16 shows both the Query Sort dialog box settings and the resultant sort.

FIGURE 10.16

Sorting the Query
Table by LNAME

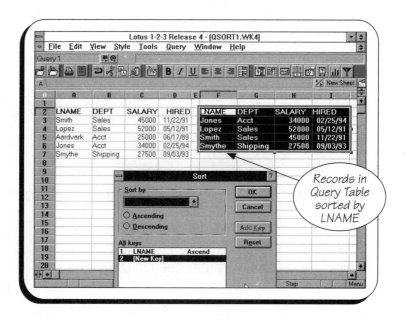

APPENDING
RECORDS

The naive way to append records to a database is simply to move the cellpointer to the row immediately below the last record and type the new data. However, then you must use Range Name to expand the database range; otherwise, 1-2-3 will not know that the new records exist.

The better way to append records is to select Tools Database Append Records. This command automatically expands the database to include the appended records. Let's add a record to our database using this technique. First move the query table to M1 (by the standard click-and-drag technique) so your screen looks like the example.

Follow these steps to prepare an area for new record entry:

1. Copy the field names (A2..D2) to another location. We are going to copy to F1..I1. Do not retype the field names; any slight difference invalidates the Append operation.

2. Name the range where you plan to input new records. For our example, the range F1..I10. Any name will do, but we are using the name NEWRECS. Note that we include the copied field names in the range. As a reminder of the size of the range, draw a box around it (choose Style Lines & Color Outline).

Now enter the records shown in Figure 10.17.

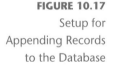

FIGURE 10.17
Setup for
Appending Records
to the Database

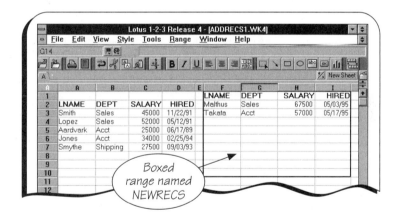

Now select Tools Database Append Records. You should see a dialog box like the one in Figure 10.18. Enter NEWRECS in the Append records from box, and enter WORKERS in the To database table box.

FIGURE 10.18

The Tools Database Append Records Dialog Box

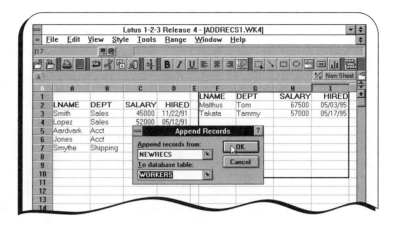

Select OK from the dialog box and your screen should look like Figure 10.19. Note that the records for Malthus and Takata have been appended to the bottom of the database.

FIGURE 10.19

Records Appended to the Database

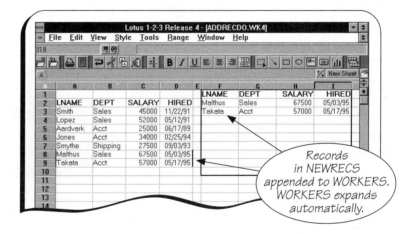

1-2-3 automatically expands the WORKERS range (the database) to include the appended records. If we now did another query, 1-2-3 would look at the new Malthus and Takata records, as well as the old ones.

DELETING RECORDS FROM A DATABASE

Let's assume that Aardvark, our underpaid accounting, just told you to "take this job and ...". We need to delete Aardvark from the WORKERS database.

It is an extremely good idea to save your file before deleting any records. Then if you mess up, you can close the bad file, open the good one, and try again.

Select Tools Database Delete Records; specify WORKERS as the database table; and select the criterion as LNAME=Aardvark. Your dialog box should look like Figure 10.20.

FIGURE 10.20
The Tools Database
Delete Records
Dialog Box

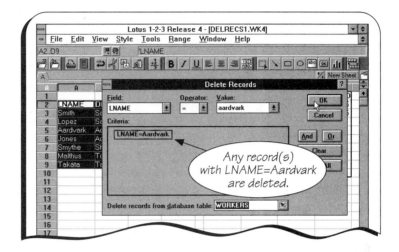

Select OK. The Aardvark record disappears from your database, and your worksheet should look like Figure 10.21.

FIGURE 10.21
Aardvark Deleted
from the Database

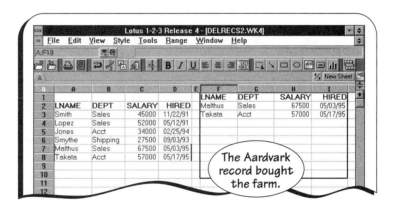

FINDING AND EDITING RECORDS

To find and highlight records inside a database, select Tools Database Find Records. After you provide criteria, 1-2-3 highlights all matching records. You can browse among them and make any changes you wish.

In our database, let's find all the records where DEPT=Acct. After our experience with Aardvark, maybe we should give them a raise. Select Tools Database Find Records; select WORKERS as the database table; and select DEPT=Acct as the criterion. Your Find Records dialog box should look like Figure 10.22.

FIGURE 10.22

The Tools Database
Find Records
Dialog Box

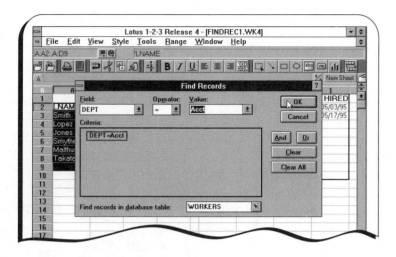

When you click on OK in the dialog box, your screen should look like Figure 10.23. The two records that meet your criterion are selected (highlighted). *Do not* click your mouse, move the cellpointer with the arrow keys, or press ESC. If you do, the "found" records will be deselected.

FIGURE 10.23

1-2-3 Highlights
Matching Records

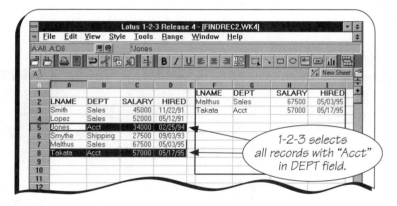

In a large database, the Find command is handy for selecting a class of records that need to be edited. Table 10.1 shows the keys you can use to move around the highlighted records and edit them.

TABLE 10.1   Editing "Found" Records

Action	Key
Edit current field.	F2; ⏎ when finished
Move to next field.	⏎
Move to previous field.	SHIFT+⏎
Move to next record.	CTRL+⏎
Move to previous record.	CTRL+SHIFT+⏎
Deselect the found records.	ESC, arrows, or click

In our worksheet (Figure 10.23), cell A5 is selected. To give Jones a raise, press ENTER twice to select Jones' SALARY field. Hit F2 to edit the field. Hmmm. Give Jones a $500 raise. Do the same for Takata. Now close your file.

SETUP PROCEDURES FOR DATABASES

1-2-3's database capabilities are powerful and useful. However, certain setup errors can cause frustration. When you set up your own databases, follow these rules:

1. Use labels for all field names; numbers or formulas do not work reliably as field names.
2. Use only letters and digits in field names; special characters may cause erratic results.
3. Don't use field names that 1-2-3 might mistake for cell addresses (such as EX3).
4. Never use the exact same field name twice in one database.
5. Put field names in adjacent columns; don't leave blank columns inside the database.
6. Don't put a separator row between the field names and the records.
7. Don't leave blank rows in the database.
8. Use the same data type for all entries in the same field.
9. Give the database a range name; include the field names in the range.

Open your DATABASE file.

1. Perform a query which pulls all records where LASTNAME begins with the character S.
2. Query for SALARY between 20,000 and 40,000 inclusive.
3. Query for SALARY between 20,000 and 40,000 inclusive and HIRED greater than January 1, 1992.
4. Delete all records where HIRED is less than January 1, 1992.
5. Add a record for Charles Dickens, a new employee. His salary is 31,500. He was hired on October 14, 1995.

1. **10AU08** involves both database techniques and application of functions such as @AVG. It also requires that columns be widened if you want to see the data. The data set is fairly large.

2. **10AU14** could be done by sorting, but it is much easier with database techniques. Some formulas and formatting are thrown in to keep you fresh on those topics.

3. **10AU18** requires application of database techniques to analyze data from a consumer preference survey.

Advanced Analytical Techniques

OBJECTIVES   After studying this chapter, you should know how to:

- Create frequency distributions.
- Use the database statistical functions.
- Create What-if tables.
- Generate regression analyses.

Chapter 3 discussed several simple statistical functions. This chapter applies them in a more complex setting and covers some of 1-2-3's more specialized tools for data analysis.

SOME DATA TO CRUNCH: THE METRO TRANSIT CASE   Several years ago an Eastern metro transit authority paid big bucks to a consulting firm for a statistical analysis of people's seating space requirements. The transit authority was planning to have a number of new vehicles built, and there was a question about how narrow the seats could be without inconveniencing the riders.

The transit authority hired a consulting firm, which collected a random sample of 1000 posterior dimensions. The consultants pocketed a very nice fee for gathering and analyzing the measurements. Unhappily the author does not have the raw data. We are going to simulate gathering a sample of 1000 posterior widths, and then do our own statistical analysis.

Begin with a clear worksheet. In cell A1, enter the label SAMPLEWIDTHS. In cell A3, enter this formula:

```
+11+(@RAND+@RAND+@RAND)*6
```

The formula gives us an excellent simulation of posterior width measurements. The basic idea is that the @RAND function gives us a random number between 0 and 1; we add three of them together, multiply by six, and add 11 (remember the rules for evaluating arithmetic expressions?). This gives us fanny widths scattered in a bell curve around an average of about 20 inches.

Copy your formula in cell A3 into A4..A1002 to get 1000 normally distributed fanny width simulations. Probably no two widths will be exactly the same—just like in real life. To make the numbers line up, format the range A3..A1002 as Fixed with two decimal places.

Now, only one problem remains. The @RAND function makes the values unstable. If the worksheet recalculates, the numbers change. When we begin analyzing the figures, we will have a moving target. We need to kill the value rules—the formulas—behind the fanny widths and leave only the values themselves.

To kill the formulas, select the range A3..A1002. Select Edit Copy. Then select Edit Paste Special Formulas as values. Note that the value rules are gone—nothing is there but pure numbers.

As our first effort at making sense of the data, we have entered the @PURE-COUNT, @PUREAVG, @PUREMAX, @PUREMIN, and @PURESTD functions in the range C3.. C7. We discussed all these functions except @PURESTD in Chapter 3. The @PURESTD function computes the standard deviation of a range of values; it is a measure of scatter around the average value. Figure 11.1 shows the current worksheet setup.

FIGURE 11.1

Simulated
Metro Transit Data

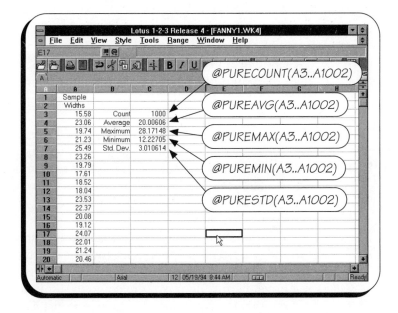

Your values will not be exactly the same as mine, of course (except for the 1000 produced by @PURECOUNT). Although your values will not be identical, notice that they are very close to mine. In particular your average will be very close to 20, and your standard deviation will be very close to 3. This is so because we used the same formula to generate the 1000 simulated fanny widths. Even though the exact values are different, we both were sampling from the same simulated "universe." The same thing would happen in real life if we both went to the same city and took random samples of 1000 fanny widths. With such a large sample size, there would be little difference in our statistics.

FREQUENCY DISTRIBUTIONS

At this point we have summary statistical figures for our observations, but we can't see how, or even if, the data is grouped. We need a frequency distribution. A 1-2-3 **frequency distribution** is an electronic tally sheet that counts values by their size class. Frequency distributions are a useful tool for summarizing the data characteristics of a large mass of observations such as ours.

Creating a Set of Class Intervals

The first step in doing a 1-2-3 frequency distribution is to decide what class interval you want. To set your bin (class interval) range, look at the MIN and MAX values. Your bin range should take in both values. The easy way to generate the bin range is to enter 12 in E2; select the range E2..E19; then click your right mouse button and select Fill by Example. Your screen now should look like Figure 11.2. The labels BIN and DISTRIBUTION (E1 and F1) are not required, but they help you remember what is where.

FIGURE 11.2

Class Intervals Covering Minimum to Maximum Values

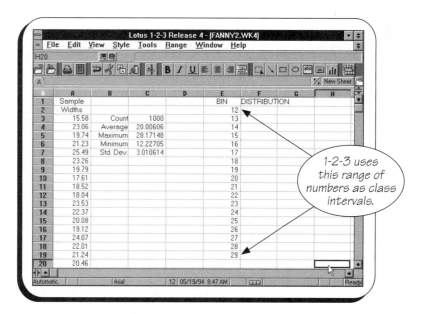

Generating the Distribution

To generate the frequency distribution, select Range Analyze Distribution. Select A3..A1002 as the Range of values. Select E2..E19 as the Bin range. Figure 11.3 shows what your dialog box should look like.

FIGURE 11.3

The Range Analyze
Distribution
Dialog Box

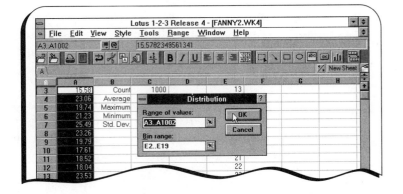

Click on OK in the dialog box. Your screen should look approximately like Figure 11.4. The first number under DISTRIBUTION is zero; it tells you that no values in the range A3..A1002 are less than 12, the first BIN number. The second number under DISTRIBUTION is 3, meaning there are three values greater than 12 but less than or equal to 13, the second BIN number. The final zero at the bottom of the DISTRIBUTION column tells you that no values are greater than 29, the last number in the BIN range. Your distribution may be slightly different because of the effect of @RAND in the original formulas in column A.

FIGURE 11.4

The Resulting
Frequency
Distribution

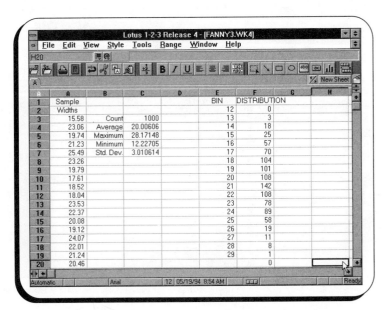

Charting the Frequency Distribution

To keep your graphics skills sharp, let's chart the frequency distribution. Select the range F2..F19. Click on the Chart icon. Create a 3-D bar chart like the one shown in Figure 11.5.

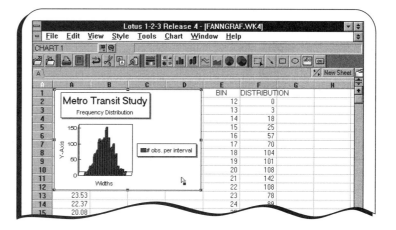

Notice the almost perfect "bell curve" shape of the histogram. The fanny widths bunch around the average value of 20; the number of items in each class interval falls as the intervals move away from the average on either side. Even though the data are simulated, this is the pattern you would find in an actual frequency distribution of a physical characteristic.

THE DATABASE STATISTICAL FUNCTIONS

1-2-3 has a set of functions for automatic statistical analysis of databases. These are stand alone functions; they do not require you to use the Tools Database command. These functions have this general form:

```
@FUNCTION-NAME(Input Range,"Field", Criterion Range)
```

The Input Range includes the database field names and all the records. The "Field" is the name of the field on which you want to operate; it must be in quotes inside the function. The Criterion Range is a copy of the database field names and the row beneath. To make the functions work, you place any desired criteria in the criterion range; the analysis happens automatically. The database statistical functions are shown in Table 11.1.

TABLE 11.1 Database Statistical Functions

Function	Description
@DCOUNT(argument)	Counts the nonblank cells in the specified field of the selected records.
@DAVG(argument)	Averages the specified field of the selected records.
@DSUM(argument)	Sums the specified field of the selected records.
@DMIN(argument)	Finds the smallest value in the specified field of the selected records.
@DMAX(argument)	Finds the largest value in the specified field of the selected records.
@DSTD(argument)	Finds the standard deviation of the values in the specified field of the selected records.
@DVAR(argument)	Finds the variance of the values in the specified field of the selected records.

To experiment with the database functions, set up the worksheet shown in Figure 11.6. It shows an example of using the @DAVG function.

FIGURE 11.6

Analyzing a Database with @DAVG

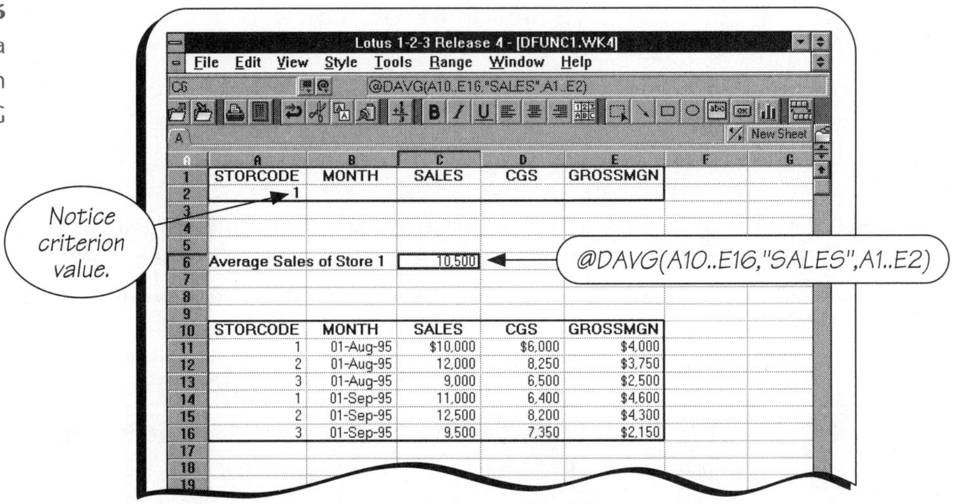

Cell C6 contains the function @DAVG(A10..E16,"SALES",A1..E2). Its meaning is "Search the input range A10..E16 for records that match the criterion in the criterion range A1..E2, and average the SALES field only of those records." 1-2-3 obtains the value of 10,500 by averaging the two records that meet the criterion—a STORCODE field of 1—and computing the average of the SALES field of those two records.

Figure 11.7 shows another example of using the @DAVG function, with a different field.

FIGURE 11.7

Adding a
Second @DAVG

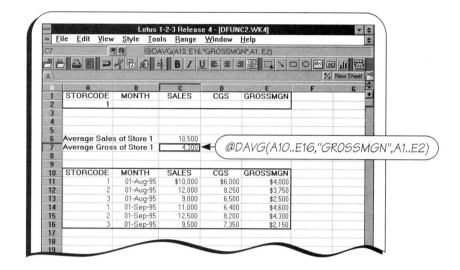

In the preceding case, 1-2-3 selects records whose STORCODE is 1 and computes the average of the GROSSMGN field for those records.

As a final example, consider the worksheet shown in Figure 11.8, which adds a second criterion range and a second set of functions to compute values for store 2.

FIGURE 11.8

Analyzing a
Second Store

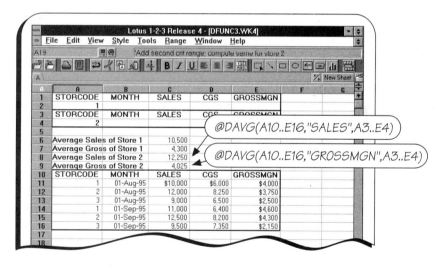

We could extend our worksheet to provide automatic computations for all four stores, not only for average sales and gross margin, but for maximums, minimums, and any other statistics we wanted to compute. By combining these techniques with the database input techniques discussed in Chapter 10, we could create a very powerful, easy-to-use system for tracking the performance of every entity in the database.

WHAT-IF ANALYSIS If you wanted to analyze the effect of different interest rates on the monthly payment on the new car you are planning to buy, you could do the analysis either of two ways: You could repeatedly substitute different interest rates into the @PMT function, or you could build a table of interest rates and make 1-2-3 do the substituting for you.

1-2-3 has built-in tools for creating what-if tables with one, two, or three variables. The command is Range Analyze What-if Table.

A One-Variable What-if Table

The Range Analyze What-if Table 1 command is designed for automatic "what-if" analysis. Let's assume you want to examine the effect on the monthly payment of interest rates of 0.10, 0.11, 0.12, 0.13, 0.14, 0.15, 0.16, 0.17, 0.18, 0.19, and 0.20. The simple, and slow, way to do the analysis would be to set up the worksheet shown in Figure 11.9 and begin changing cell B4, the interest rate.

FIGURE 11.9
Monthly
Payment Data

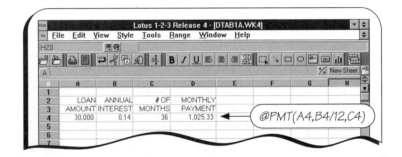

Alternatively you could copy A4..D4 down the worksheet and change column B to generate a table of monthly payments at each of the different interest rates. Neither approach is as flexible or powerful as using the What-if command.

Before you use this technique, you need to have done some preliminary work. First, you need to set up a column of variables. In our case, the variables are the interest rates we want to plug into the payment function. Select the range B8..B18; add a column of interest rates by using Range Fill. In the dialog box, specify a starting value of .1 and an increment of .01. You are not required to use Range Fill, but at this point in your 1-2-3 education, you may as well begin habitually using shortcuts.

Next you need to reproduce the payment function above and to the right of your interest rate column. Your column of interest rates starts in B8, so the function goes in C7. You can do this either by retyping the formula or by using a cell reference. Unless you used absolute cell references in the initial @PMT formula, you cannot copy it because the cell references will change. Your worksheet now should look like Figure 11.10.

FIGURE 11.10

Setup for a
One-Variable
What-if Table

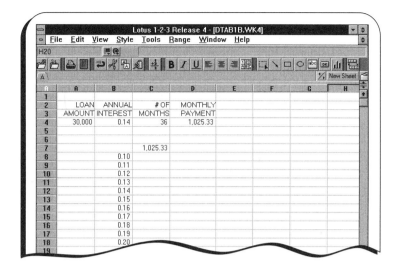

Now you are ready to use the command. Select Range Analyze What-if
Table. In the dialog box, specify Number of variables as 1; specify Table range
of B7..C18. The table range must include the formula cell and the column of
values. Next specify B4 as Input cell 1. The input cell is the cell into which you
want 1-2-3 to sequentially substitute the values in the column you built. In this
example, we want 1-2-3 to substitute the various interest rates into the interest
cell, which is B4. Your What-if Table dialog box now should look like Figure
11.11.

FIGURE 11.11

The What-if
Table Dialog Box

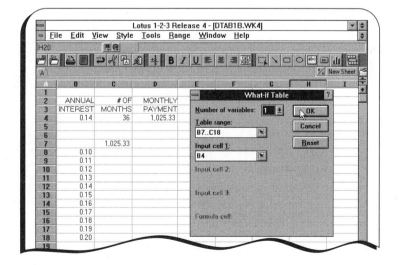

Select OK. Figure 11.12 shows the result of the analysis.

FIGURE 11.12

Output
from the One-Way
What-if Analysis

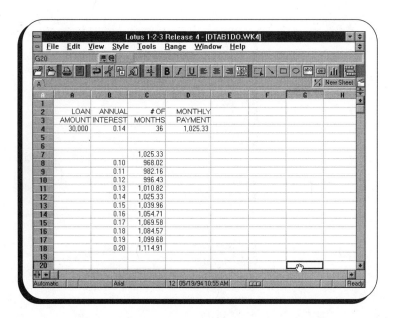

If you position your cellpointer on any of the computed monthly payments in C8..C18, you will see that there are no underlying formulas. In effect, 1-2-3 made the computation and performed an Edit Calc to strip off the formulas and leave only the values.

A Two-Variable What-if Table

Now let's assess the effect of changing *both* the interest rate on your car loan *and* the number of months to maturity. Save your one-variable analysis; call it ONEWAY. Then select File Save As and specify the filename TWOWAY. We are going to use TWOWAY to illustrate a two-variable what-if table.

Format the C8..F18 range as Comma with 2 decimal places. Modify your TWOWAY file as shown in Figure 11.13.

FIGURE 11.13

Setup for a
Two-Variable
What-If Table

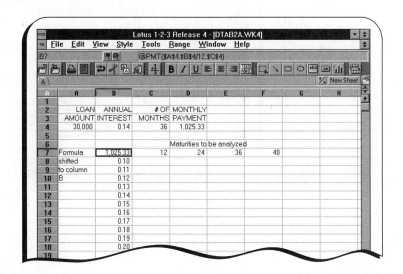

Note that the formula that was in cell C7 for the one-variable operation is now in B7, and we have added a horizontal row of months to maturity in C7..F7. We are preparing to build a table or matrix that shows the monthly payment for each maturity at each interest rate.

Select Range Analyze What-if Table. In the dialog box, input the settings shown in Figure 11.14. The B7..F18 range is your table range; it includes both the interest rate column and the maturity row. Cell B4 is still the Input cell 1, just as it was for the What-if Table 1 operation earlier. Input cell 2 is C4. Cell C4 is the loan maturity cell referenced by the @PMT functions; we want 1-2-3 to substitute different maturity values into it.

FIGURE 11.14
Preparing the
Dialog Box

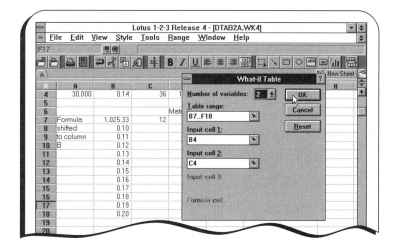

Select OK from the dialog box. 1-2-3 computes a monthly payment for every possible combination of interest rate and maturity in the table. Your screen now should look like Figure 11.15.

FIGURE 11.15
Output
from the Two-Way
What-if Analysis

	A	B	C	D	E	F	G	H
4	30,000	0.14	36	1,025.33				
5								
6				Maturities to be analyzed				
7	Formula	1,025.33	12	24	36	48		
8	shifted	0.10	2,637.48	1,384.35	968.02	760.88		
9	to column	0.11	2,651.45	1,398.24	982.16	775.37		
10	B	0.12	2,665.46	1,412.20	996.43	790.02		
11		0.13	2,679.52	1,426.25	1,010.82	804.82		
12		0.14	2,693.61	1,440.39	1,025.33	819.79		
13		0.15	2,707.75	1,454.60	1,039.96	834.92		
14		0.16	2,721.93	1,468.89	1,054.71	850.21		
15		0.17	2,736.14	1,483.27	1,069.58	865.65		
16		0.18	2,750.40	1,497.72	1,084.57	881.25		
17		0.19	2,764.70	1,512.26	1,099.68	897.00		
18		0.20	2,779.04	1,526.87	1,114.91	912.91		

If you have trouble understanding what is going on in Figure 11.15, try substituting some of the values in column B and row 7 into cells B4 and C4, respectively. The payments that appear as your answers in D4 also exist in the table. For example, as the worksheet stands now, cell D4 is computing the payment for an interest rate of .14 and a maturity of 36 months; note that the same value, 1,025.33 appears in the column E, row 12.

REGRESSION
ANALYSIS

Lotus 1-2-3 has a very easy-to-use multiple regression analysis capability in the Range Analyze Regression menu. **Regression analysis** is a tool for determining the relationship between a dependent variable and one or more independent variables. If you are not statistically minded, think of regression as a way to plot a line of best fit through a scattergram. Come to think of it, we already have a scattergram. In Chapter 5 we created a scattergram chart of rainfall versus corn yield, and we saved it as the file RAIN. Let's use regression analysis on the data in that file.

Close your file and open the RAIN file. Save as RAINREG so we have a separate file for our regression analysis. Click on the chart and move it to M1. Then select Range Analyze Regression. In the dialog box, the first job is to select the X-range (the independent variable) as B5..B20. Common sense indicates that rainfall affects corn yield, rather than the other way around.

Next select C5..C20 for the Y-range (the dependent variable). Finally, select E8 as the Output range. Your dialog box should look like Figure 11.16.

FIGURE 11.16
The Range
Analyze Regression
Dialog Box

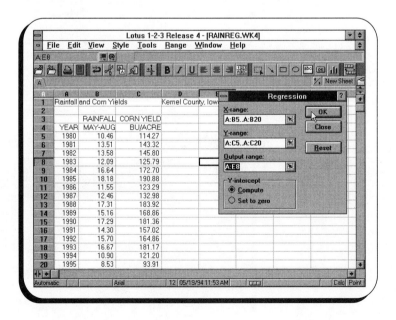

Click on OK and 1-2-3 generates your regression analysis. Your results should look like Figure 11.17.

FIGURE 11.17

Output from the
Regression Analysis

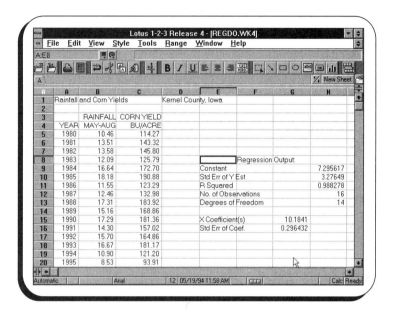

Plotting a Regression Line

Thinking in terms of the equation for a straight line, Y=A+B*X, cell H9 in Figure 11.17 is the A in the equation—the intercept with the Y-axis when X is zero. This is what 1-2-3 calls the "Constant." The number in cell G15 is the B in the equation—the number that you multiply times the X value. So, to predict what the Y value—Corn Yield—will be for any value of X, all you have to do is set up a cell with the formula +H9+G15*(the value of X).

We are going to use this idea to make Lotus plot the line of best fit through the actual data points. To do this, put your cellpointer on cell D5 and enter the equation +$H$9+$G$15*B5.

The formula in cell D5 is the "predicted" value of Y (as opposed to the actual historical value) for the given value of X (in this case, 10.46). Notice that the formula uses dollar signs to freeze H9 and G15. We do this because we need to copy the formula down the worksheet; if we do not freeze those two cells with $ signs, they will adjust during the copy operation and we will have nonsense values for the predicted value of Y.

Copy D5 into the range D6..D20. Now your worksheet should look like Figure 11.18.

	A	B	C	D	E	F	G	H
1	Rainfall and Corn Yields			Kernel County, Iowa				
2								
3		RAINFALL	CORN YIELD					
4	YEAR	MAY-AUG	BU/ACRE					
5	1980	10.46	114.27	113.8213				
6	1981	13.51	143.32	144.8829				
7	1982	13.58	145.80	145.5958				
8	1983	12.09	125.79	130.4214		Regression Output:		
9	1984	16.64	172.70	176.7591	Constant			7.295617
10	1985	18.18	190.88	192.4426	Std Err of Y Est			3.27649
11	1986	11.55	123.29	124.922	R Squared			0.988278
12	1987	12.46	132.98	134.1896	No. of Observations			16
13	1988	17.31	183.92	183.5825	Degrees of Freedom			14
14	1989	15.16	168.86	161.6866				
15	1990	17.29	181.36	183.3788	X Coefficient(s)		10.1841	
16	1991	14.30	157.02	152.9283	Std Err of Coef.		0.296432	
17	1992	15.70	164.86	167.1861				
18	1993	16.67	181.17	177.0646				
19	1994	10.90	121.20	118.3024				
20	1995	8.53	93.91	94.16603				

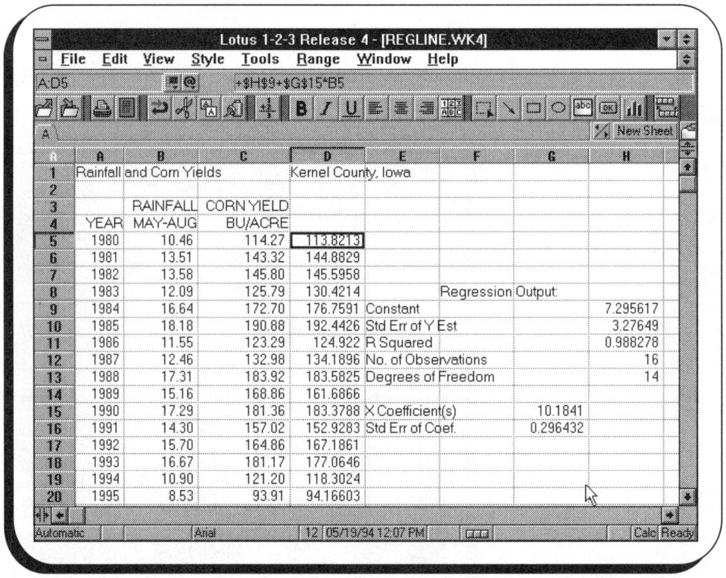

FIGURE 11.18 Data for the Line of Best Fit

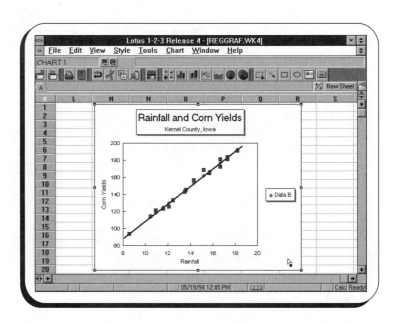

Graphing the Line of Best Fit

If you chart the X, A, and B ranges using an XY scatter plot, everything will be much clearer. Your X range should be B5..B20; your A range should be C5..C20; and your B range should be D5..D20. Your chart now will have data points for the line of best fit superimposed on the scattergram. By selecting Tools Draw Line, you can lay a line of best fit through the point, and your chart should look like Figure 11.19.

FIGURE 11.19 Scatterplot with Line of Best Fit

The regression line—the estimated Y value for each actual X value—is a very handy tool for graphically estimating Y values for projected X values. Regression analysis is widely used in both the business and academic worlds.

1. Open the 10AU14 file. Save the worksheet under a new name: WALDO.

   a. Set up a bin range with these class intervals:

   5
   10
   15
   20

   Create a frequency distribution of retail prices.

   b. Use @DCOUNT to determine how many books have a retail field greater than 15.

   c. Use @DAVG to determine the average retail price of books whose CODE starts with the letter C.

2. This is a big integrative problem; it covers database, statistics, and graphics.

   A marketing research firm has offered you a consulting job. They have conducted a survey for a client; a small sample of the survey results are as follows:

AGE	SEX	INCOME	Q1	Q2	Q3	Q4	Q5
53	F	20707	N	N	1	N	N
63	F	62162	N	Y	2	N	Y
47	M	15102	N	N	0	N	N
38	M	11747	N	N	1	N	N
22	F	13871	Y	N	0	N	N
52	M	50979	N	N	3	Y	Y

   The AGE column shows the age of the survey's respondents; the SEX column shows whether they were male or female; the INCOME column shows their annual income. The answers in the Q columns are from these questions:

   Q1:   WOULD YOU VOTE FOR ALFRED A. NEUMAN FOR PRESIDENT?
   Q2:   DO YOU THINK SOCIAL SECURITY BENEFITS SHOULD BE RAISED?
   Q3:   HOW MANY VEHICLES (CARS, TRUCKS) DO YOU OWN?
   Q4:   DID YOU GRADUATE FROM A 4-YEAR COLLEGE?
   Q5:   DO YOU HAVE AN ACCOUNT WITH A STOCKBROKER?

There is a SMART disk version of this problem; it contains 303 records rather than the handful shown in the preceding table. Use the survey data to answer these questions:

a. How many females were included in the survey?
b. How many males were included in the survey?
c. What was the minimum age of those who want an increase in Social Security benefits?
d. What is the average income of respondents in the age range 20–39 (inclusive)?
e. What is the average income of respondents in the age range 40–59 (inclusive)?
f. What is the average income of college graduates age 22–29 (inclusive)?
g. What is the average income of college graduates age 30–45 (inclusive)?
h. What is the average income of non-college graduates age 22–29 (inclusive)?
i. What is the average income of non-college graduates age 30–45 (inclusive)?
j. What is the average income of those who would vote for Alfred E. Neuman?
k. What is the average income of those who have a brokerage account?
l. What is the standard deviation of incomes for those who have an account with a stockbroker?
m. What is the average age of those with two or more vehicles?
n. What is the average income of females?
o. What is the average income of males?
p. What is the maximum income in the entire list?
q. What is the minimum income in the entire list?
r. What is the range of incomes?
s. What is the range of incomes for college graduates?
t. What is the range of incomes for non-college graduates?
u. How many people responded "N" to Q1 and Q2 and Q4 and Q5? That is, how many said "N" to all four of those questions?
v. How many females between the ages of 20 and 40 owned two or more vehicles and graduated from a 4-year college?
w. Print a sorted list of those respondents who were males and said they would vote for Alfred E. Neuman for president. The sort key should be income, descending order.
x. Print a list of *only* the top five incomes in descending order. The secondary key should be age, in descending order.
y. Provide a chart of the frequency distribution of income by income brackets 10,000–100,000 (10,000 increments). The first title should be FREQUENCY DISTRIBUTION, INCOME.

1. **11AU10** is a straightforward exercise in use of Range Analyze Regression.

2. **11AU11** requires both database statistical techniques and the application of range names. On this problem, SMART checks the contents of range names that you create, instead of checking static cell addresses.

3. **11CU18** is a fairly difficult problem. To do it with the least expenditure of time requires use of the @D database statistics functions. The problem also requires complex criteria such as +A40>=22#AND#A40<=39.

4. **11CU30** is a rather difficult problem involving analysis of differential component assembly times by several production teams. It requires use of database stat functions, and the fact situation is complicated.

Financial Analysis and Planning with 1-2-3

OBJECTIVES After studying this chapter, you should know how to:

- Create loan amortization tables.
- Use present value and future value functions.
- Create financial projections.
- Generate breakeven analyses.
- Create versions and scenarios.

Electronic spreadsheets were originally used for financial analysis and projection. That still is perhaps their most common use. Lotus 1-2-3 has a number of functions that stem from that heritage, including @NPV, @PV, @FV, @IRR, and @PMT. This chapter examines the use of these analytical functions and also looks at the broader field of deterministic financial modeling.

LOAN AMORTIZATION Many business loans, as well as consumer loans and home mortgages, are **amortized**, or paid off in equal installments over a number of periods. An amortization table shows the financial profile of an amortized loan during its life.

The @PMT function, which was introduced in Chapter 3, provides the basis for amortization tables. The function automatically calculates a loan payment large enough to pay the required interest, with enough left over to gradually reduce the loan balance. The balance falls to zero with the final payment.

Although an amortized loan's periodic payments are the same each period, the proportions of the payment going to interest and principal repayment change. Each period the interest component decreases and the principal repayment increases. This happens because each period's interest is based on the previous period's principal balance, not on the beginning principal balance.

To create your own amortization table, set up a worksheet like Figure 12.1. The user enters values in cells B1, B2, and B4. The worksheet is formatted as text so you can see the formulas in the other cells.

FIGURE 12.1

Amortization
Table Setup

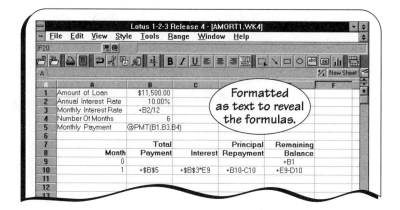

After entering the formulas in the range B10..E10, copy them to B10..B15. Then fill the range A10..A15 with sequential numbers. To keep the first amortization table short, we are doing only a six-month loan.

Figure 12.2 shows the worksheet values, given the loan balance, the annual interest rate, and the number of months the loan runs. The initial principal balance at month zero (the time the loan was made) is $11,500, but at the end of month 1 it has dropped to $9,622.88.

FIGURE 12.2

Completed
Six-Month
Amortization Table

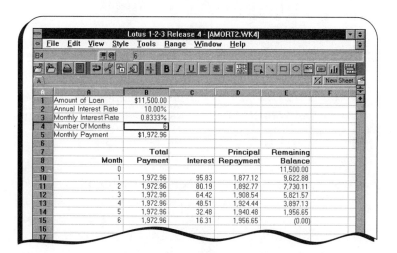

By the end of the sixth period, the loan balance has dropped to zero. However, you might find the monthly payments a bit steep. To see the effect of a longer loan period, enter 24 in cell B4. Figure 12.3 shows first six months of the resulting schedule.

FIGURE 12.3
First Six Months of 24-Month Amortization Table

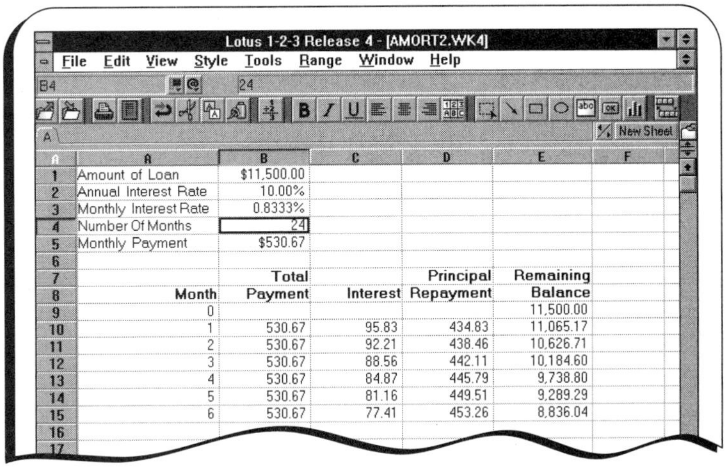

	A	B	C	D	E	F
1	Amount of Loan	$11,500.00				
2	Annual Interest Rate	10.00%				
3	Monthly Interest Rate	0.8333%				
4	Number Of Months	24				
5	Monthly Payment	$530.67				
6						
7		Total		Principal	Remaining	
8	Month	Payment	Interest	Repayment	Balance	
9	0				11,500.00	
10	1	530.67	95.83	434.83	11,065.17	
11	2	530.67	92.21	438.46	10,626.71	
12	3	530.67	88.56	442.11	10,184.60	
13	4	530.67	84.87	445.79	9,738.80	
14	5	530.67	81.16	449.51	9,289.29	
15	6	530.67	77.41	453.26	8,836.04	
16						
17						

The good news from extending the term of the loan from 6 periods to 24 is that the monthly payments get smaller. The bad news is that, at the end of six months, you still owe $8,836.04, and you have another 18 payments to make!

As the table stands, it does not show the other 18 months of the schedule. To complete your 24-month amortization schedule, you would have to copy the formulas in B15..E15 downward through the twenty-fourth month.

THE @NPV FUNCTION

NPV is an acronym for **net present value**. However, the @NPV function does not calculate *net* present value, but merely *present* value. It does the same thing you can do with pencil, paper, and calculator using the formula

$$PV = Cashflow1/(1+i)^1 + Cashflow2/(1+i)^2 + \ldots + Cashflow(n)/(1+i)^n$$

where n is the final period number and i is the discount rate in decimal form. That is, the @NPV function computes the present value of a series of cash flows. The cash flows are assumed to occur at the end of each period.

The general structure of the function is:

```
@NPV(discount rate in decimal form,row or column range)
```

The discount rate can be a literal number such as 0.1, or it can be a cell reference. The range of cells tells 1-2-3 where the cash flows to be evaluated are.

Close any open files and set up the worksheet shown in Figure 12.4; in cell C5 enter the function `@NPV(0.1,C2..F2)`.

FIGURE 12.4

Computing Present
Value with @NPV

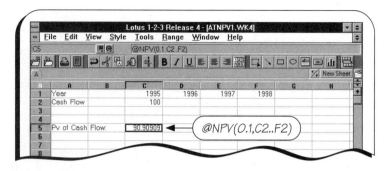

You could cover the same cell range and get the same answer—90.90909—
if you put this formula in cell C5:

$$+C2/(1+.1)^1+D2/(1+.1)^2+E2/(1+.1)^3+F2/(1+.1)^4$$

The @NPV function just saves you the trouble of building present value formulas. Now put another number in your range, as shown in Figure 12.5.

FIGURE 12.5

Function Picks Up
Second Cash Flow

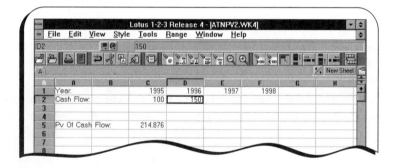

The function automatically picked up the second cash flow (150 in D2) because D2 lies in the function's cell range. If you added flows in E2 and F2, the function would also evaluate them. At this point, the function is telling you that the present value of 100 at the end of one year and of 150 at the end of the second year, discounted at 10%, is 214.87.

The elegant way to use the @NPV function is to use a cell reference, rather than a literal number, for the discount rate. Add a discount-rate cell to your worksheet and modify your function as shown in Figure 12.6.

FIGURE 12.6

Using a Cell
Reference for the
Discount Rate

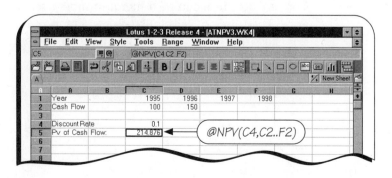

The advantage of using a cell reference, rather than a literal number, for the discount rate is the familiar one: You can play "what-if" without having to modify anything except the value in the cell being referenced. If you now change the discount rate in cell C4 to 0.25, 1-2-3 recalculates the present value of the cash flows at the new discount rate. Give it a try (pv of cash flow changes to 176).

The @NPV function works on either uneven cash flows or annuities. In the preceding example, the cash flows are uneven—100 in the first period and 150 in the second period. For an annuity example, change your cash flows to 100 100 100 100 in cells C2..F2, respectively. If you leave your discount rate at 0.25, the answer will be 236.16.

The least confusing way to use the @NPV function to compute net present value is to supply a figure for the outlay on the project and subtract the function's value from the outlay. For example, if we shell out $100 to buy a cash flow of $50 per year for three years, we could find the net present value of the investment as shown in Figure 12.7.

FIGURE 12.7
Computing
Net Present Value

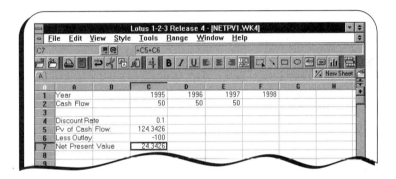

THE @IRR FUNCTION

By playing "what-if" with the discount rate in cell C4 (Figure 12.7), you could eventually find the **internal rate of return** (IRR) of the project. You could fiddle the discount rate until you eventually got the net present value in cell C7 to zero. The discount rate that makes the present value of the cash inflows equal to the cost of the project is the IRR—the true rate of return on the project. However, this would be a time-consuming business. 1-2-3 provides a fast, direct way to calculate the IRR.

The @IRR function is actually a small built-in program that does the "what-if." It fiddles the discount rate until it finds a rate that gives a net present value of zero.

The general form of the function is:

```
@IRR(guess at discount rate, cell range)
```

The guess at the discount rate should be some decimal figure like 0.10. The guess serves no purpose other than to give 1-2-3 a starting point; it has nothing to do with the eventual answer yielded by the function. The author always uses 0.1; that works as well as any other decimal number.

Add the @IRR function to your worksheet, as shown in Figure 12.8.

FIGURE 12.8

Using the

@IRR Function

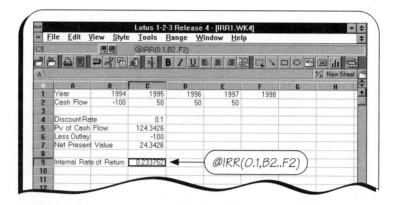

The @IRR function in cell C9 is telling you that 0.233752 is the discount rate that forces the present value of the inflows (50,50,50) to equal the cash outlay in cell B2 (–100).

For fun, change the discount rate in cell C4 to the value of the IRR cell, 0.233752. Notice that the net present value becomes zero because the 0.233752 discount rate brings the present value of the cash flows to 100. This should give you some insight into how @IRR works—it hunts for the discount rate that equates the present value of the inflows with the value of the outlay.

THE @PV FUNCTION— CALCULATING THE PRESENT VALUE OF AN ANNUITY

The @PV function is also a specialized function. It has this general form:

```
@PV(annuity-payment,interest-rate-per-period,term)
```

@PV calculates the present value of an ordinary annuity. As you probably know if you are reading this chapter, an ordinary annuity is a level stream of two or more payments with each payment coming at the end of a time period. This is an example of an ordinary annuity:

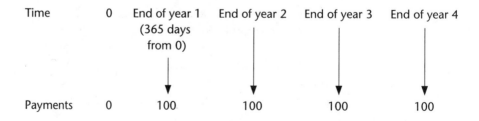

You could calculate the value of this ordinary annuity with the @NPV function. The only drawback is that you would have to set up the payments in a cell range. A quicker way is to use the @PV function. There are four periodic payments of 100; assume the periodic interest rate is 12%. The function @PV(100,0.12,4) would yield a value of 303.73. Remember that @PV does not work for a stream of uneven payments. For example, if the payments in years 1, 2, 3, and 4 were, respectively, 100, 100, 155, and 126, you could not use the function.

THE @FV FUNCTION— COMPUTING THE FUTURE VALUE OF AN ANNUITY

Other than pension planners, not many people are interested in calculating the future value of an annuity. But if you are, here is the function to do it:

```
@FV(annuity-payment,interest-rate-per-period,term)
```

@FV differs from @PV only in the function name; the argument is the same. You might use @FV to figure whether you will be eating beans or steak when you retire. It tells you how much money you will have at future date Z if you put X dollars into a pension fund and earn Y interest-rate.

For example, if your pension fund contribution is $1000 per month, you earn 1% per month interest, and you plan to retire in 360 months, you can express the function as: @FV(1000,.01,360). The result of this function indicates that you will have $3,494,964.13 in your fund at the projected retirement date; it looks like steak for you.

On the other hand, if you contribute $100 per month, earn 1/2% per month interest, and plan to retire in 120 months, the function would be: @FV(100,.005,120). On this basis, you will have only $16,387.93 in your retirement fund when you get the gold watch, and it will be beans, beans, beans.

FINANCIAL STATEMENT ANALYSIS

1-2-3 is custom-made for doing ratio analyses and common-size income statements. The normal practice is to set up a blank form as a master analysis worksheet and to insert specific data into a copy of the blank master form.

A Note About ERR

Usually, many of the formula cells in the blank master contain divide operations. For example, the formula for computing the current ratio is current assets divided by current liabilities. In a blank master, the simple formula gives an ERR result because it is impossible to divide anything by zero. As a rule, it is a good idea to trap possible ERRs. Sometimes an ERR can propagate through the worksheet, and it becomes very difficult to figure out which cell is causing the problem.

To see the effect, set up the worksheet shown in Figure 12.9. The formula is shown in text format.

.

.

.

FIGURE 12.9
Formula with a
Zero Denominator

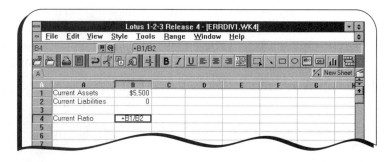

Division by zero is a mathematical impossibility. Figure 12.10 shows the result.

FIGURE 12.10
Result of a
Zero Divide

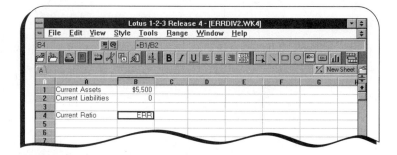

The @ISERR function can detect ERR results such as you see in cell B4 in Figure 12.10. The function has a value of 1 if the argument is true, that is, if the argument creates an ERR condition. If there is no ERR condition in the argument, @ISERR gives a value of 0, meaning false. Replace the formula in B4 with this: @ISERR(B1/B2).

Since B1/B2 results in an ERR condition, the @ISERR function evaluates to a 1, meaning "it is TRUE that the argument B1/B2 gives an ERR condition." With @ISERR(B1/B2) in cell B4, your worksheet would look like Figure 12.11.

FIGURE 12.11
The @ISERR Function

The @ISERR function is almost never used as a standalone function. Instead it is incorporated into @IF statements as a way to trap ERR conditions. For example, if you changed the formula in B4 to @IF(@ISERR(B1/B2),0,B1/B2), the current ratio cell would show a zero if B2 was zero or blank; it would compute the current ratio in all other cases.

A Blank Master for Ratio Analysis

The @ISERR function commonly is used with @IF to trap zero divides in financial analysis worksheets. Figure 12.12 shows a ratio analysis template; all the formulas are set up as @IF statements. The comparison uses the @ISERR function. @ISERR is true if the expression in parentheses is true. For example, the formula for current ratio is:

$$@IF(@ISERR(C22/C29),0,C22/C29)$$

The meaning is "IF dividing C22 by C29 gives an ERR, put a zero in the cell instead of the ERR message; if dividing C22 by C29 does not give an ERR, use the value rule C22/C29."

FIGURE 12.12

Applying @IF and @ISERR in a Ratio Analysis Template

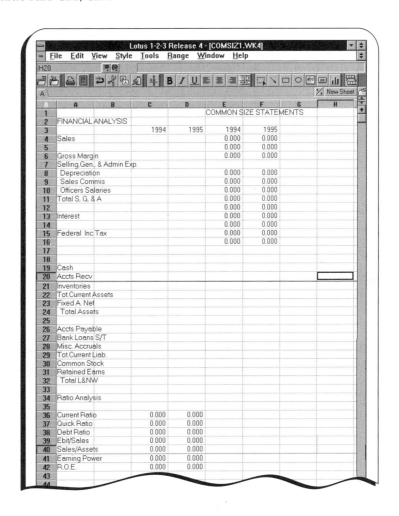

The ratio formulas in the Figure 12.12 worksheet are as follows:

```
C36: CURRENT RATIO: @IF(@ISERR(C22/C29),0,C22/C29)
C37: QUICK RATIO: @IF(@ISERR((C19+C20)/C29),0,(C19+C20)/C29)
C38: DEBT RATIO: @IF(@ISERR(C29/C24),0,C29/C24)
C39: EBIT/SALES: @IF(@ISERR(C12/C4),0,C12/C4)
C40: SALES/ASSETS: @IF(@ISERR(C4/C24),0,C4/C24)
C41: EARNING POWER: @IF(@ISERR(C39*C40),0,C39*C40)
C42: @IF(@ISERR(C16/(C30+C31)),0,C16/(C30+C31))
```

By plugging numbers into columns B and C, you can generate an immediate ratio and common-size analysis. Figure 12.13 shows the output of the analysis.

FIGURE 12.13
Results Generated

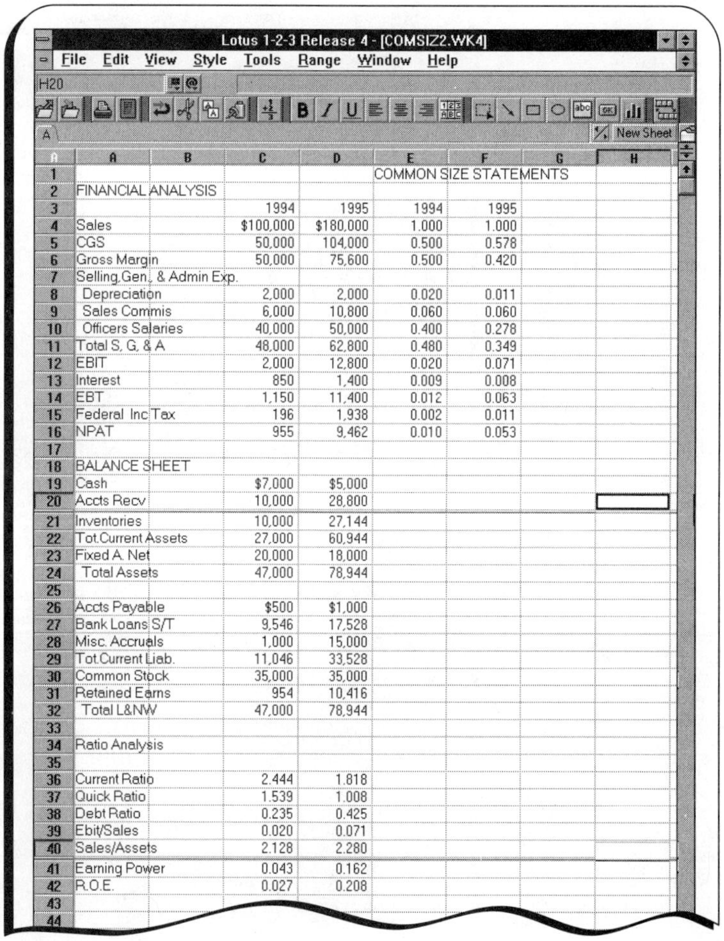

Lotus 1-2-3 Release 4 - [COMSIZ2.WK4]

	A	B	C	D	E	F	G	H
1					COMMON SIZE STATEMENTS			
2	FINANCIAL ANALYSIS							
3			1994	1995	1994	1995		
4	Sales		$100,000	$180,000	1.000	1.000		
5	CGS		50,000	104,000	0.500	0.578		
6	Gross Margin		50,000	75,600	0.500	0.420		
7	Selling,Gen., & Admin Exp.							
8	Depreciation		2,000	2,000	0.020	0.011		
9	Sales Commis		6,000	10,800	0.060	0.060		
10	Officers Salaries		40,000	50,000	0.400	0.278		
11	Total S, G, & A		48,000	62,800	0.480	0.349		
12	EBIT		2,000	12,800	0.020	0.071		
13	Interest		850	1,400	0.009	0.008		
14	EBT		1,150	11,400	0.012	0.063		
15	Federal Inc Tax		196	1,938	0.002	0.011		
16	NPAT		955	9,462	0.010	0.053		
17								
18	BALANCE SHEET							
19	Cash		$7,000	$5,000				
20	Accts Recv		10,000	28,800				
21	Inventories		10,000	27,144				
22	Tot.Current Assets		27,000	60,944				
23	Fixed A. Net		20,000	18,000				
24	Total Assets		47,000	78,944				
25								
26	Accts Payable		$500	$1,000				
27	Bank Loans S/T		9,546	17,528				
28	Misc. Accruals		1,000	15,000				
29	Tot.Current Liab.		11,046	33,528				
30	Common Stock		35,000	35,000				
31	Retained Earns		954	10,416				
32	Total L&NW		47,000	78,944				
33								
34	Ratio Analysis							
35								
36	Current Ratio		2.444	1.818				
37	Quick Ratio		1.539	1.008				
38	Debt Ratio		0.235	0.425				
39	Ebit/Sales		0.020	0.071				
40	Sales/Assets		2.128	2.280				
41	Earning Power		0.043	0.162				
42	R.O.E.		0.027	0.208				
43								
44								

Pro Forma Financial Forecasting

Ratio analysis is very useful for analyzing what *did* happen; the worksheet also can help you examine what *may* happen in the future as a result of a particular set of policies. Forecasting the future financial condition of the firm is called **pro forma forecasting**.

In Chapter 4, as an example of how to copy formulas, we constructed a rudimentary pro forma income statement and saved it under the filename PROFORMA. Open the PROFORMA file. We are going to use it as the basis for a somewhat more sophisticated forecasting worksheet. If you do not have the file on disk, set up the worksheet shown in Figure 12.14.

FIGURE 12.14

Formulas
for the Pro Forma
Income Statement

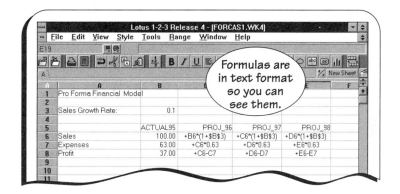

Column B represents actual, historical data for the year 1995. Columns C, D, and E are a three-year projection. Modify the column headings to distinguish between actual and projected data.

Next, modify cells C6..E6. Originally those cells computed sales by multiplying prior year's sales by B3. For the purposes of Chapter 4, this approach was all right. However, growth rates normally are stated in decimal form. Change cell C6 to +B6*(1+$B$3). Then copy C6 into D6..E6. Then change cell B3 to 0.1—a growth rate of 10%. While you are making changes, use Comma,2 format on the range B6..E20. After these changes, your worksheet should look like Figure 12.15.

FIGURE 12.15

Projection at Sales
Growth Rate of 0.1

Let's assume the worksheet in Figure 12.15 is a projection for a business that you own. The figures in columns C, D, and E show the sales, expenses, and profit you expect during the next three years of business.

For planning purposes, you also need a set of pro forma balance sheets. Sales and profit projections depend on the existence of sufficient assets and financing sources. Add the simple balance sheet categories shown in Figure 12.16, and punch in the "actual" balance sheet figures for 1995.

FIGURE 12.16

Historical
Balance Sheet Data
Added to Model

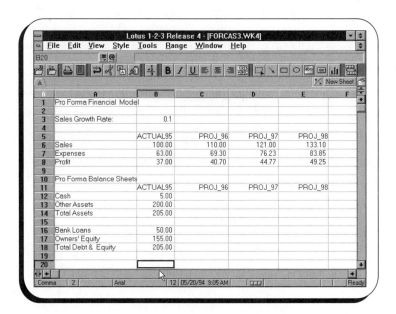

For the projection, we need to describe the relationship between sales and the various balance sheet categories that are affected by sales. In this model, we assume that OTHER ASSETS at year-end are always 200% of sales for the year. The OTHER ASSETS category includes accounts receivable, inventory, plant and equipment, and so on—everything except cash. This is the historical relationship, based on sales of 100 for 1995, and the 200 figure for other assets.

Also, let's assume that you need cash equal to a minimum 2% of annual sales. More cash would be fine, but the business must have cash of at least 2% of sales. This minimum is somewhat less than the historical relationship, which is 5%.

By using @IF statements, it is fairly easy to link the income statements and the related balance sheets together so that the balance sheets take into account any income statement changes, and still balance.

Our model is still too simple for real-world application, but it is just the right size to illustrate the mechanics of linking income statements with balance sheets.

Linking Balance Sheets with Income Statements

As the projected income statement data changes, the projected balance sheet accounts also should change. Enter these formulas in your model:

```
Cell C12: @IF(C13+0.02*C6>C17,C6*0.02,C17-C13)
Cell C13: +C6*2
Cell C14: +C12+C13
Cell C16: @IF(C17>C13+C6*0.02,0,(C13+C6*0.02)-C17)
Cell C17: +B17+C8
Cell C18: +C16+C17
```

At this point your worksheet should look like Figure 12.17.

FIGURE 12.17

Balance Sheet Formulas for Initial Year of Projection

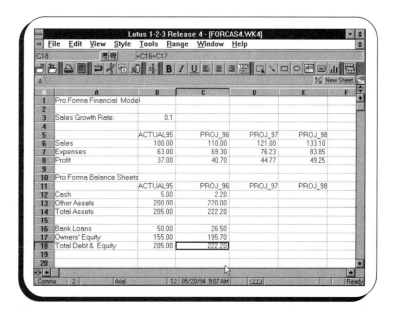

The projected balance sheet for 1996 automatically picks up the profit generated during 1996. The formula in C17 for Owners' Equity is +B17+C8, which tells 1-2-3 to compute the 1995 owners equity as the previous year's balance plus the profit for 1994. OTHER ASSETS for 1996 keeps the relationship of 200% of sales for 1996.

If you are an accounting or finance person, you should be stunned and delighted to see that the projected balance sheet automatically balances. Thanks to the @IF statements in Cash (C12) and Bank Loans (C16), 1-2-3 automatically computes the amount of bank loan needed and the amount of cash on hand.

To understand how the automatic balancing feature works, consider first the @IF statement in C12:

```
Cell C12: @IF(C13+0.02*C6>C17,C6*0.02,C17-C13)
```

The test—C13+0.02*C6>C17,—is whether the sum of other assets plus the minimum acceptable cash balance (2% of sales) is greater than internal financing (in this case, owners equity is the only internal financing source). If the test is true, there will be no surplus cash because we would have to borrow to maintain surplus cash. Consequently, if the minimum assets needed to run the business exceed internal financing, the cash balance will be the true-value-rule—sales*0.02.

If minimum assets required (other assets plus 2% of sales in cash) are equal to internal financing, the same logic applies. On the other hand, if minimum required assets are less than internal financing, we will have surplus cash, and a total cash balance equal to internal financing minus other assets.

The @IF in the bank loan cell, C16, is:

```
@IF(C17>C13+C6*0.02,0,(C13+C6*0.02)-C17)
```

The test here is whether or not internal financing is greater than minimum assets required to run the business. If that is true, there is no need for a bank loan; the true-value-rule is 0. Otherwise, the bank loan is equal to minimum assets required minus internal financing.

Now copy the formulas in C12..C18 into D12..E12. Your model should look like the one shown in Figure 12.18.

FIGURE 12.18

The Pro Forma Model, 10% Sales Growth Rate

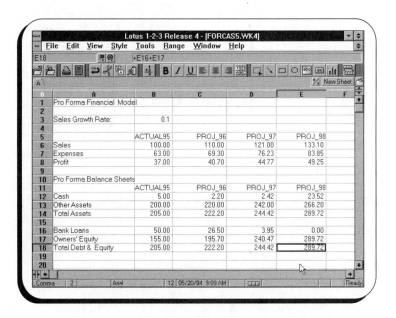

Now proceed to play "what if." Change the projected sales growth rate to 0.8 and watch the changes ripple through the model. With the new (and phenomenally high) growth rate, your model should look like Figure 12.19.

FIGURE 12.19
The
Pro Forma Model,
80% Sales
Growth Rate

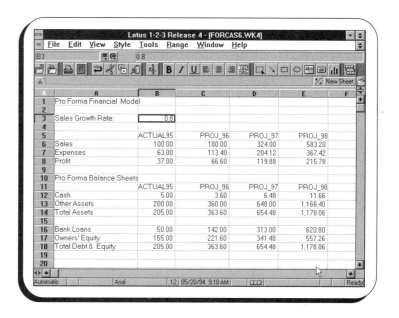

Even after the change in projected sales growth rate, we still have a perfectly articulated, balancing, interlocked set of pro forma financial statements. Models of this sort provide illuminating insights into the financial consequences of different business scenarios. For example, the extremely rapid projected sales growth rate modeled in Figure 12.19 shows an ominous increase in the firm's bank loans relative to equity.

BREAKEVEN ANALYSIS

Breakeven analysis shows how many units of product a firm must sell in a given period to cover operating costs. It is commonly used to evaluate the feasibility of new ventures *before* undertaking them. Computing the breakeven point is the financial equivalent of looking before you leap.

Pretend you are a businessman, say, a book publisher. You are trying to decide whether or not to print a how-to book called *How to Repair Your Own Computer*. Would you just flip a coin to decide, or would you analyze the economics of the deal to see whether or not you could make money by printing the book? If your answer is "flip a coin" and you are a business student, see your faculty advisor immediately about a change of degree plan. If you answered "analyze," go to the head of the class. The publisher would estimate probable sales of the book, analyze production costs, and see if the book promised to at least break even.

Breakeven analysis is a valuable real-world planning tool—the time to figure out that *How to Repair Your Own Computer* is a loser is *before* you set up for production, not afterward! Let's set up a new worksheet for a breakeven point analysis and graph of the book project. Set up a worksheet like Figure 12.20.

FIGURE 12.20

Breakeven Analysis

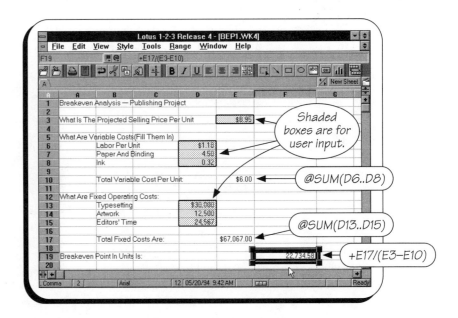

The worksheet in Figure 12.20 is a "what-if" model for calculating how many units of product your firm has to sell to cover all the costs of production, that is, to break even. The costs of production are made up of two elements. The first is fixed costs such as typesetting and artwork (in this example), which stay the same regardless of whether the firm produces a lot of the product or a small amount.

The other cost element is variable costs, which vary with how much product is produced. Our worksheet has the two main variable costs—production labor and materials. If the firm produces only a few units of product, material usage drops and production workers get laid off. If the firm doubles its production, twice as many workers are needed and twice as much material is used.

To figure out how many units the firm has to sell to cover costs (both fixed and variable costs), the fixed costs are divided by the contribution per unit. **Contribution** is the spread between the selling price and the variable costs. The way the worksheet is set up now, the firm sells its products for $8.95 a unit. Variable costs per unit—materials and labor—are only $6.00 per unit. Thus each unit sold contributes 8.95 – 6.00, or 2.95, to covering the fixed costs—or to profit, once fixed costs are covered.

To break even in the current price-cost scenario, the firm has to produce and sell 22,734.58 units. Obviously the firm really can't sell 58/100 of a unit, but that is a minor quibble. If the firm is lucky enough to sell more than 22,735 units, it makes a profit. If it sells fewer, it takes a loss.

Now, play some "what-if." Try changing the selling price and/or the expenses. Watch what happens to your breakeven point.

CREATING VERSIONS AND SCENARIOS

In financial planning, managers commonly create multiple versions of projected budgets. With earlier versions of 1-2-3, each version had to be stored in a different worksheet or a different file. Release 4 offers a much simpler tool for managing different versions of the same worksheet: the Version Manager.

The Version Manager saves different versions (different data sets) of named ranges and, on command, lays the data back into a single worksheet. With Version Manager you do not need to create multiple worksheets to see the effects of data changes.

To explore Version Manager, create a worksheet like Figure 12.21. Select the range B4..C4. Use Range Name with the range name TOTALSALES. Save your worksheet as FLEXBUD.

FIGURE 12.21

The FLEXBUD Worksheet

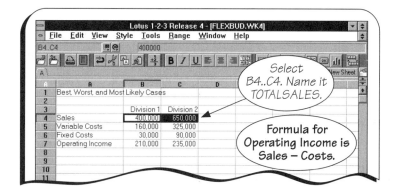

Currently the TOTALSALES range contains our most optimistic sales projection for each of the two corporate divisions. By using Version Manager, we can save the contents of the range as a version name and lay it back into the worksheet whenever we want to.

Be sure the cellpointer is in the TOTALSALES range. Select Range Version. You should see the Version Manager dialog box, as Figure 12.22 shows. Note that we have placed the mouse pointer on the Create box.

FIGURE 12.22

The Version Manager Dialog Box

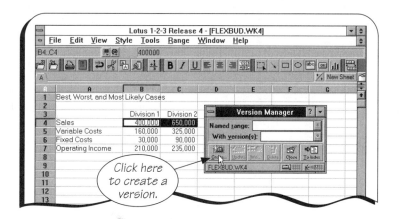

Click to select the Create box. You should see the Create Version dialog box shown in Figure 12.23. TOTALSALES appears automatically in the Range name text box because your cellpointer is in that range. Select the Version name text box; enter HISALES for the Version name. 1-2-3 stores the *current contents* of the TOTALSALES range under a version name called HISALES.

You also can attach a comment to the version. Enter "Most optimistic sales projection for both divisions." in the Comment box.

FIGURE 12.23

The Create Version
Dialog Box

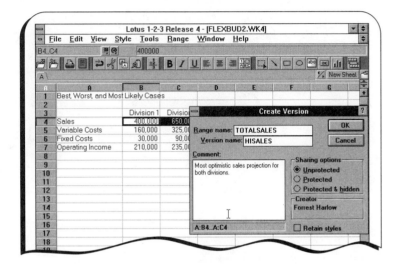

Click on OK in the dialog box. The Version Manager dialog box reappears, as Figure 12.24 shows. The Version Manager is telling you that the TOTAL-SALES range currently contains the HISALES data version. HISALES, of course, is the version you just created.

FIGURE 12.24

HISALES Version
Created and in Effect

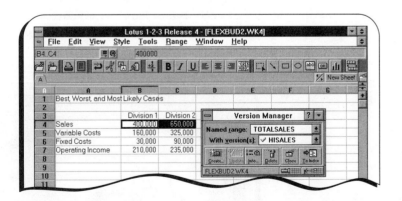

Now let's create a low sales version of the TOTALSALES range. To create the low sales version, enter 200,000 in B4 and 400,000 in C4. Select B4..C4. Then select Create Version from the Version Manager dialog box; specify LOWSALES for the Version name; enter "Most pessimistic sales projection for both divisions." in the Comment box. Click on OK to return to the Version Manager. Your screen should look like Figure 12.25.

FIGURE 12.25

LOWSALES Version
Created and in Effect

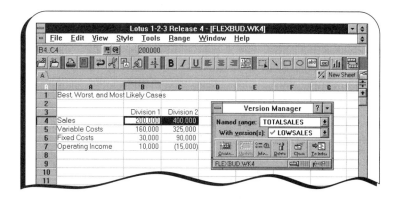

Save your worksheet. The Version Manager settings are saved as a part of the worksheet. Now we can flip back and forth between the two versions at any time.

To close the Version Manager dialog box, click on Close. To use it again, Select Range Version. The dialog box reappears. To see the HISALES version, click on the With versions arrow and select HISALES from the dropdown box. Presto. You now are looking at the HISALES version. Note that the Operating Income line, as well as Sales line, changes as you change versions.

We also could have created a version for most likely sales by the same process. For that matter, we could have named the range B5..C5 and created versions for high and low variable costs.

Using the Version Manager Index

The Index allows you to keep track of versions by version name, creator name, and date of creation or modification. You also can select a version for display, directly from the index.

To bring up the Version Manager Index dialog box, click on To Index in the Version Manager dialog box. Your screen should look like Figure 12.26.

FIGURE 12.26

The Version
Manager Index
Dialog Box

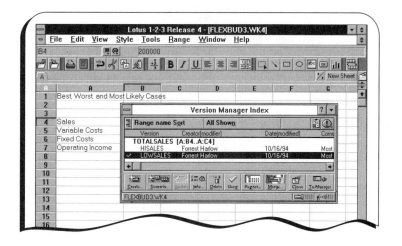

Version Reports

If you click on Report in the Version Manager Index, you get a dialog box like that shown in Figure 12.27. The report allows you to keep track of who has modified any particular version.

FIGURE 12.27
The Version Report
Dialog Box

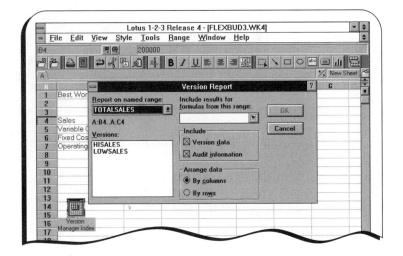

Click on the desired Version to get a report. 1-2-3 automatically creates a new file with a default filename to hold the report. Figure 12.28 shows the result of clicking on HISALES.

FIGURE 12.28
Worksheet Created
by Version Report

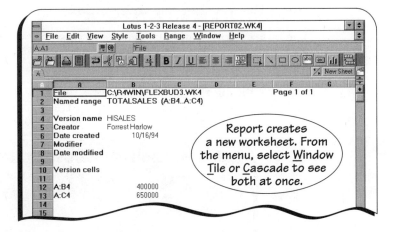

Scenarios

Scenarios are used to group different versions of multiple ranges. For example, if we actually had created a range for variable costs, with versions HIVARCOST and LOVARCOST, we could create a scenario of versions HISALES and LOVARCOST, or one with LOWSALES and HIVARCOST, and so forth.

To create a scenario, choose <u>R</u>ange <u>V</u>ersion. In the Index, hold down CTRL while you click on the versions you want to group into a scenario. After selecting one version for each range, select Scenario.

You cannot include more than one version of the same range in a scenario. It is impossible to show, for example, the HISALES and LOWSALES versions of TOTALCOST in the same scenario.

The Liability Computation Case

Batton, Burton, Barton, and Blatz (BBBB) is a large law firm specializing in personal injury cases. BBBB assesses the monetary damages suffered by a client by determining the present value of the injury-related earnings loss. For example, if a client expected to earn $125,000 a year, but now can expect to earn only $100,000 due to injury, BBBB would sue for the present value of $25,000 (plus a growth adjustment) over the client's remaining working life.

BBBB currently figures the monetary loss by using a pocket calculator. The calculations take a long time, and mistakes tend to creep in. BBBB has heard of your 1-2-3 skills; the firm is offering you a consulting contract for $10,000. Your job is to create a worksheet for computing the present value of lost earning power. The worksheet should generate figures for any number of years between 1 and 20.

The following illustration shows the format BBBB wants. The numeric cells in the boxed Parameters area are for user input. The table should generate appropriate numbers, based on parameters supplied by the user.

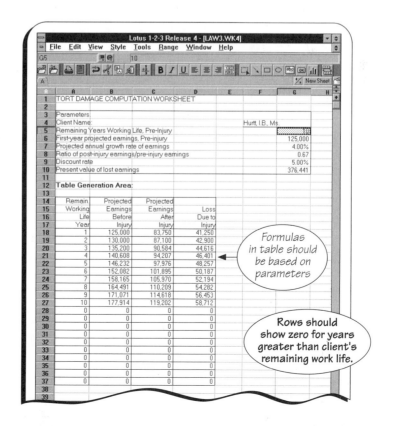

1. Amalgamated Pickle, Inc., bonds pay $80 annual interest, mature in 20 years, and pay $1,000 at maturity. What would the market value of these bonds be if the market interest rate were:

   a. 6%
   b. 9%
   c. 14%

2. Set up a general worksheet that uses the @IRR function to determine the rate of return on a common stock, given the purchase price, annual dividends, holding period, and selling price. Use the Gordon model, that is, present value of all future dividends (+ future dividends implicit in the eventual selling price).

3. Use the @PMT function (and any other tools you need) to build a generalized loan amortization schedule. Use your PAYMENT worksheet as a starting point. *Tip:* Use 12-month loans to test out your model. Then extend the possible period after you have the bugs worked out.

4. Use the pro forma financial planning model to analyze the implications of a sales growth rate of 50% per year. All other setup values should be as shown in the chapter.

1. **12BU14** requires you to set up an amortization table, using @PMT and @IF.

2. **12CU12** requires a fairly sophisticated application of the @VLOOKUP function and @IF statements.

3. **12CU24** is a complex pro forma financial forecasting worksheet. It is not recommended for those with no background in business.

PART THREE
ADVANCED LOTUS 1-2-3

The four chapters in this part cover macro programming. What you have learned about 1-2-3 to this point gives you a great deal of computing power, but the macro facility opens two entirely new vistas of power and control.

1-2-3 macro language changes the way you think about spreadsheets. A program-driven sheet is to a Ready-mode sheet as a Ferrari is to a Model T.

If your ambition is to become a true 1-2-3 guru, you should study all four chapters in this part. However, if you are concerned with ends rather than means, just study Chapters 13 and 16. Chapter 13 grounds you in the bare basics; Chapter 16 presents a unique, time-saving system for creating powerful macros by "snapping together" canned subroutines. The necessary subroutines are in the MACTOOLS worksheet (on your disk).

Macro Basics

After studying this chapter, you should know how to:

- Use the macro recording facility.
- Record simple macro programs.
- Execute macros.
- Debug macros.
- Create macro buttons.

The simplest form of keystroke macros operate on the "monkey see, monkey do" principle. They simply replay the actions you perform from the keyboard. 1-2-3 has a built-in "macro recorder" which you can activate to record your keyboard and mouse actions as macro commands. Using the recorder is the easiest way to build a simple macro. However, you also can write a macro from scratch.

This chapter discusses recording macros and then looks briefly at writing them from scratch.

RECORDING A MACRO: A FIRST EXAMPLE Let's build a macro that enters your name and official title into the worksheet on command. Close your worksheet and move the cellpointer to A1. We are going to walk through the recording process one step at a time.

Show the Transcript Window

This step is not strictly necessary, but it can help you understand how 1-2-3 builds your macro. Select Tools Macro Show Transcript or click on the Show Transcript Window icon. 1-2-3 opens a small window containing the macro code it creates from your actions. Your screen should look like Figure 13.1.

FIGURE 13.1

The Transcript
Window

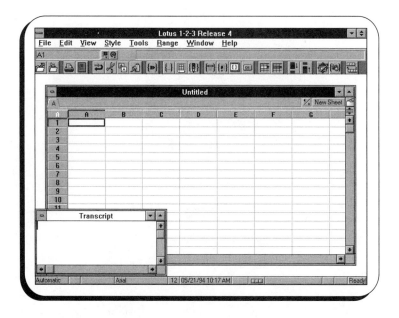

When you select Tools Macro Show Transcript, 1-2-3 automatically resizes your worksheet window and places the Transcript window at the bottom left corner of the screen. Now you are ready to begin recording our macro.

Select Tools Macro Record or click on the Record/Stop Recording icon. The Rec indicator appears in the status bar to show that macro recording is underway. 1-2-3 now converts your keyboard actions into macro code. Recording continues until you turn it off (discussed later).

Type your name in A1 and press the down arrow. Next type your title (pick your own) in cell A2 and press the down arrow. Your screen now should look like Figure 13.2.

FIGURE 13.2

Recording
Keyboard Actions
as Macro Code

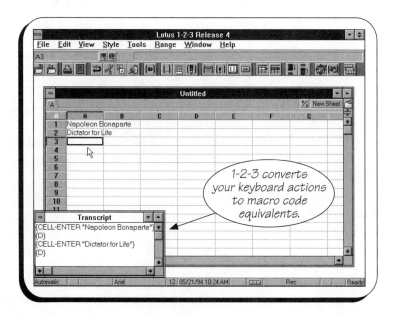

Notice the transcript window. 1-2-3 has recorded your actions, in macro language. {CELL-ENTER "Napoleon Bonaparte"} and {D} is macro-ese for typing the cell contents and pressing the down arrow.

Stop Recording

Now let's quit recording macro code. Select Tools Macro Stop Recording. Now you are back in ordinary 1-2-3; the macro recorder is no longer working. If we decided to record more, we could again select Tools Macro Record.

Place the Code in the Worksheet

To make a working macro, we have to copy the code from the transcript window into the worksheet. Click on the Transcript Window to activate it. Select the four lines of macro code in the window. Then select Edit Copy. Activate your worksheet by clicking in it. Select cell D1 in the worksheet, and select Edit Paste. Your worksheet now should look like Figure 13.3.

FIGURE 13.3

Macro Copied from
Transcript Window
to Worksheet

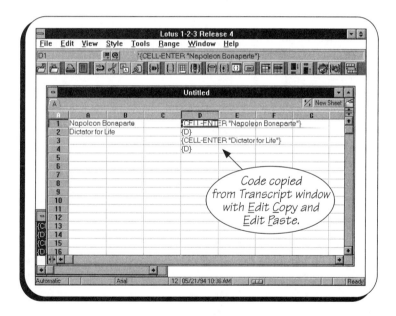

Note that the transcript window cascades behind the worksheet. If we wanted to restore it to the screen, we could click inside it. However, for now we do not need it.

Name the Macro

The final step is to name the top cell of the macro. You could name it with an ordinary range name such as MYTITLE. However, we are going to use a short-hand name consisting of a backslash and a single letter.

Backslash-letter range names always begin with a backslash (\\). An ordinary slash (/) will not work.

Let's use the range name \\N for this macro. We could use \\A, or \\Z, or any letter in between, but \\N offers some help in remembering what this particular macro does—it enters a *name*.

Move the cellpointer to C1. Type a label prefix (') to identify the entry as a label. Then type \\N. If you forget the label prefix, 1-2-3 fills the cell with N's because a backslash from Ready mode is the repeating-label command.

Now with your cellpointer on C1, select Range Name from the menu. In the dialog box, click Use Labels. (Be sure To the right is selected, as Figure 13.4 shows.)

FIGURE 13.4

Naming the Macro
from a Label

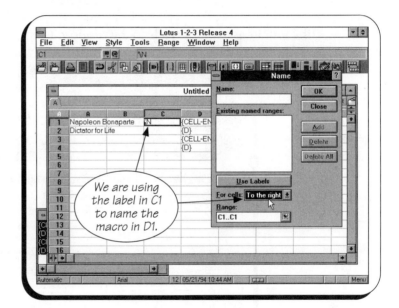

Click on OK to complete the process. 1-2-3 names cell D1 with the label \\N, which it found in C1. We could have placed the cellpointer on D1, selected Range Name, and typed the name into the text box, but naming macros with Range Name Use Labels To the right avoids typo differences between the label and the range name.

Run the Macro

Be sure to move the cellpointer into a blank area before running the macro! When you run the macro, it overwrites anything that gets in its way. For the first run, move the cellpointer to A6.

Macros with a backslash-letter name can be run by pressing CTRL+letter. With your cellpointer in A6, hold down the CTRL key while you press N. Then release both keys. 1-2-3 enters your name in cell A6, moves the cellpointer to

A7, enters your title in A7, and moves the cellpointer to A8. Your worksheet should look like Figure 13.5 after your macro runs.

FIGURE 13.5

Macro Results

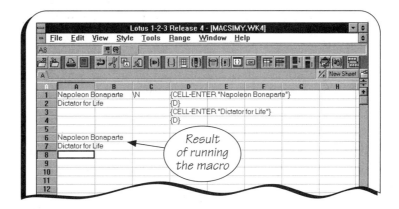

The results of this first macro are rather humdrum, but don't start yawning yet. You can move the cellpointer to any location in the worksheet, press CTRL+N, and reproduce your name and title again and again. You could accomplish the same thing by saving your title as a separate file and using File Open Combine Replace. However, you can do other things with keystroke macros that you cannot do by combining files. We are about to discuss one of them, but first let's recap.

Recap on Creating Macros

1. Select Tools Macro Record or click on the Record/Stop Recording icon. The Rec indicator appears in the status bar to show that macro recording is underway.

2. Perform the action you want recorded, using any necessary keys, menu commands, or icons.

3. When finished, turn macro recording off by selecting Tools Macro Stop Recording or by clicking on the Record/Stop Recording icon.

4. Select Tools Macro Show Transcript or click on the Show Transcript Window icon. 1-2-3 opens a small window containing the macro code it has created from your actions.

5. Click in the transcript window to make the window active.

6. Select the macro commands (all or only some of them) in the window; then select Edit Copy.

7. Click on the worksheet cell where you want to place a copy of the macro code.

8. Select Edit Paste to copy the macro code into the worksheet.

9. Use Range Name to name the top cell of the macro.

Save your macro with the filename MACSIMP. Next we are going to create another macro in the same worksheet. You can have any number of macros in a worksheet.

Clear the Transcript Window

Before beginning our next macro, we need to clear the existing code from the Transcript window. To clear the Transcript Window of all existing commands, follow these steps:

1. Select Tools Macro Show Transcript if the transcript window is hidden.
2. Click in the Transcript window to make it active.
3. Select Edit Clear All.

A SECOND MACRO

Let's create a macro that puts a designer box around the selected range. This is a sequence of actions that cannot be reproduced by combining files because the incoming file loses its formatting instructions.

Select A1..B2. Then select Tools Macro Record. Select Style Lines & Color Designer frame and click on the arrow to get the frame selection. In the frame selection, click on the cornered box at the lower left. Click on OK. Next, select Tools Macro Stop Recording.

Click on the Transcript window to activate it. Select only the second line, which says {STYLE-FRAME "ON";255;12}. Your screen now should look like Figure 13.6.

FIGURE 13.6
Selecting Code
from the
Transcript Window

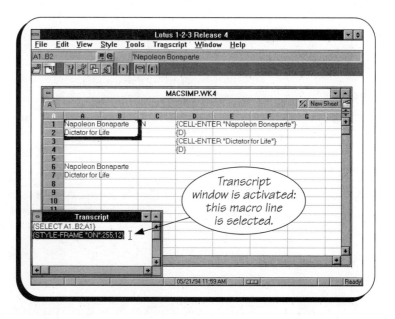

Select Edit Copy; select cell D6 in the worksheet; and select Edit Paste. Place the label FANCY in C6. Select Range Name Use Labels To the Right and click on OK. Your screen now should look like Figure 13.7.

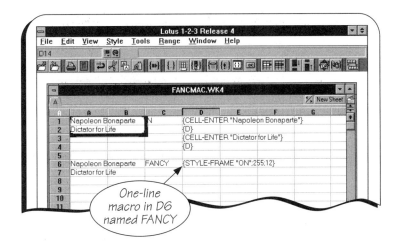

Notice that we are naming this macro FANCY rather than a backslash letter. Macros can be named with ordinary labels (such as SALES). To run a macro named with an ordinary label, you have to select Tools Macro Run and click on the desired macro range name.

Running the Macro with Tools Macro Run

You can run a backslash-letter macro with Tools Macro Run, but the command is more commonly used to run macros with ordinary range names such as FANCY. The FANCY macro places a designer frame around any range we select.

To see FANCY do its thing, select any range. We are going to select D1..G4 and draw a designer box around the first macro. After selecting the range, select Tools Macro Run or click on the Macro Run icon. Select FANCY in the All Named Ranges list box. You should see the Macro Run dialog box, as in Figure 13.8.

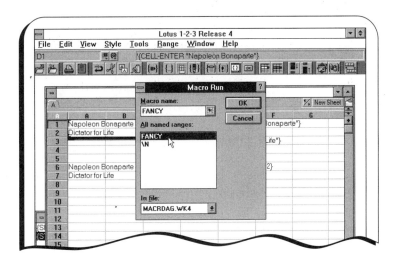

FIGURE 13.8
The Tools Macro
Run Dialog Box

Click on OK in the dialog box. The designer frame is applied to the range D1..G4, as shown in Figure 13.9.

FIGURE 13.9

Output of
the Designer
Frame Macro

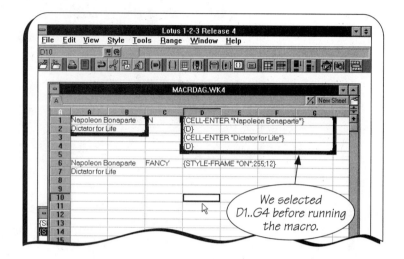

Test-Running Macros from the Transcript Window

Running macros, or parts of macros, from the transcript window is a handy way to check your code before copying it into the worksheet. Before testing a macro by running it from the transcript window, you may need to move the cellpointer to the location the macro is supposed to act on. Then select the transcript window. Select the block of macro code you want to test. You can test a single line, or all the code in the window. After selecting the code, select Transcript Playback.

The transcript window holds only about 200 command lines. Thereafter the earliest commands begin dropping out of the transcript as new commands are added.

Where to Put Your Macros

You can put a macro anywhere on the worksheet, so long as it doesn't get erased or overwritten by your actual worksheet operations. As a rule, a good place for your macros is column Z or AA1. With your macros there, you have plenty of elbow room for your worksheet, without using up an excessive amount of memory. If you have only a small amount of free memory after loading 1-2-3, you may need to economize by setting up your macros just off the portion of the worksheet you actually use in your program.

A PROGRAMMING PRIMER: WRITING MACROS FROM SCRATCH

Sometimes you will need to write a macro partially or entirely from scratch rather than using the recording function. Writing from scratch gives you more flexibility and access to additional commands. For example, the 1-2-3 macro programming commands have no macro recording equivalent.

To write a macro from scratch, you simply pick a location for the macro, from Ready mode, and begin writing. Then you place an identifying label to the left of the macro and Range Name the macro just as you do with a recorded macro. The key representations in Table 13.1 are particularly useful in macro programming.

TABLE 13.1   Macro Keystroke Representations

Symbol	Meaning
~	Press the ENTER key (the ~ is called a tilde).
{UP} or {U}	Press the up arrow.
{UP n}	Press the up arrow n times.
{RIGHT} or {R}	Press the right arrow.
{RIGHT n}	Press the right arrow n times.
{DOWN} or {D}	Press the down arrow.
{DOWN n} or {D n}	Press the down arrow n times.
{LEFT} or {L}	Press the left arrow.
{LEFT n} or {L n}	Press the left arrow n times.
{PGUP}	Press the PageUp key.
{PGDN}	Press the PageDown key.
{HOME}	Press the HOME key.
{END}	Press the END key.
{EDIT}	Press the F2 key (edit current cell).
{BS}	Press the BACKSPACE key.
{DEL}	Press the DEL key.
{NAME}	Press the F3 key—display list of range names.
{ABS}	Press the F4 key—absolute reference.
{GOTO}addr~	Move cellpointer to cell or range name.
{SELECT addr}	Same effect as {GOTO}addr~.
{WINDOW}	Press the F6 key—jump to other pane.
{QUERY}	Press the F7 key—repeat query to database.
{TABLE}	Press the F8 key—repeat data table operation.
{CALC}	Press the F9 key—recalculate the worksheet.
{GRAPH}	Press the F10 key—redraw the current graph.
{?}~	Pause for input from keyboard.
{BEEP} or {BEEP n}	Sounds the computer's buzzer; n from 1 through 4 for successively higher tone.

To understand how to write a macro from scratch, clear your worksheet. Move your cellpointer to D1. Set up the macro shown in Figure 13.10.

FIGURE 13.10

Writing a Macro
from Scratch

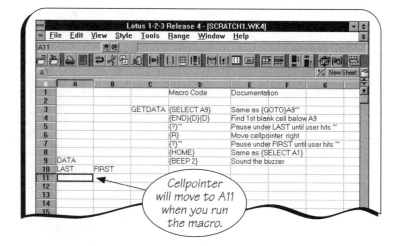

When you run the macro, the cellpointer moves to A9 and then automatically flips to the first blank row below A9. The {?}~ symbol in D5 causes the macro to pause for keyboard input and then resume processing after the user presses ⏎. The {R} in D6 moves the cellpointer right one column. The {?}~ in D7 pauses for user input. Then the {HOME} command sends the cellpointer to A1; the {BEEP 2} command sounds the buzzer at a medium pitch.

Breaking Out of a Macro

If you want to break out of a macro before it finishes running, hold down the CTRL key and press the PAUSE/BREAK key. For example, run the preceding macro again. Press CTRL+BREAK and the dialog box shown in Figure 13.11 appears.

FIGURE 13.11

Halting a Macro
with CTRL+BREAK

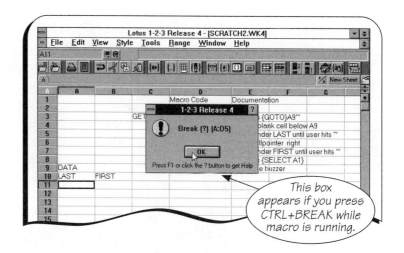

Dealing with Crashes

If there is an error in your code, the macro will crash (quit running unexpectedly). Very few people write perfect scratch macros the first time; you can expect your macros to crash during the development process.

To see the result of a crash, let's deliberately mess up our macro code. Select cell D3, press F2 to edit, and delete the ending curly brace. Then run the macro. Your screen should look like Figure 13.12.

FIGURE 13.12

A Crashed Macro

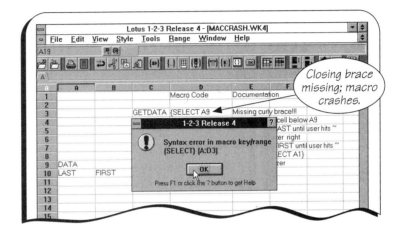

In the error box, 1-2-3 tells you the nature of the problem (a syntax error due to the missing curly brace) and which cell contains the bad code. Click on the OK button, move the cellpointer to D3, and supply the missing brace.

Debugging with Trace and Step

You also can open a Trace window, which shows you each line of the macro as it executes. However, the code flashes through the Trace window very rapidly, so usually you will want to also set Step mode on.

To turn on Trace, select Tools Macro Trace or click on the Trace icon. To turn on Step mode, select Tools Macro Single Step or click on the Step icon.

Fix the error in D3 if you haven't already. Create another error in D8 by changing {HOME} to {HOM}. With Step and Trace on, run the macro. The Trace window will show each line of code; to execute the line, you have to press ENTER (or any other key, but ENTER works best).

Press ENTER to execute each line of code. When you press ENTER with the bad line in the Trace box, your screen should look like Figure 13.13.

FIGURE 13.13

Crash with

Trace Activated

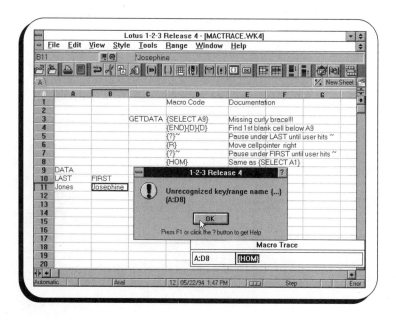

Select OK and fix the mistake that 1-2-3 identified. To get out of Step mode, select Tools Macro Single Step or click on the Step icon. To turn off the Trace window, click on the Trace icon or select Tools Macro Trace.

If Your Macro Won't Run at All

The most common macro error is forgetting to name the top cell of your macro. If you fail to name the macro, 1-2-3 simply beeps at you and does nothing. To see the effect, do a CTRL+Z—presumably you have no macro named \Z. 1-2-3 checks for a macro named \Z; failing to find it yields a beep and no further action. The solution: Name the macro and try again.

Do not be discouraged if your early macros fail to run on the first few tries. Even experienced macro writers spend a good bit of time debugging bad code. Remember to walk through your macro from the keyboard first; then use Step mode as a debugging tool to isolate errors.

CREATING MACRO BUTTONS

A macro button is a clickable object that runs a macro. You can create a macro button anywhere on the screen, and assign a macro range name to it or create the macro directly in the button.

Let's create a macro button to run our macro. Follow these steps:

1. Select Tools Draw Button or click the Button icon.
2. Move the mouse pointer to the spot you have selected for the button (we are starting the button in A2). Click and drag to size the button.

3. 1-2-3 creates the button and opens the Assign to Button dialog box, as shown in Figure 13.14. You can replace the Button text with your own description of what the macro does. We selected the Button text box and typed MY MACRO.

4. Select Range in the Assign macro from dropdown box. Then select the macro range name from the Existing named ranges list box. We selected GETDATA as the range.

At this point your screen should look like Figure 13.14.

FIGURE 13.14

The Assign to Button Dialog Box

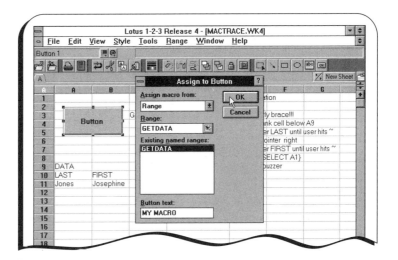

Select OK. Your macro button now should look like Figure 13.15. We moved the mouse pointer onto the button; notice the pointing-hand shape.

FIGURE 13.15

Macro Button with Customized Text

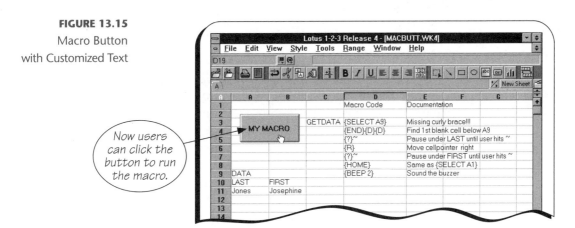

Now users can click the button to run the macro.

To run the macro, simply move the mouse pointer onto the button as shown, and click. If you are building macros for other people to use, it is a good idea to create buttons for them to click. People with no 1-2-3 background are less likely to mess up when they can click on a single button to do a job.

Instead of assigning an existing macro, you can create a (small) macro directly inside the button. Simply select the Enter Macro here text box, and type your macro. Generally it is easier to create and test your macros separately, and then assign them to buttons after they are debugged.

Modifying a Button After Creation

If you want to modify a button, hold down SHIFT and click on the button. Then select Tools Macro Assign to Button.

MACRO SETUP GUIDELINES

Good setup procedures are important in simple macros, as well as in the more complex variety. Bad setup can convert a fairly simple 1-2-3 macro into a mass of hieroglyphics; good style can make even a complex macro easier to read and follow.

Follow these four setup guidelines and your life as a 1-2-3 macro writer will be more serene:

1. Break your macro into easily readable pieces, and arrange the pieces in columnar fashion. 1-2-3 does not care whether you have 3 characters on a macro line, or 30, or 100. 1-2-3 reads whatever is in a macro cell; then it moves down to the next cell in the column, looking for more characters to read. As long as 1-2-3 does not find a blank cell, it keeps reading.

2. Multicell, single-step macros are easy to scan, document, and edit than multiple-step, single-cell macros. As your macros grow in power and complexity, these will be important considerations.

3. Reserve the column to the left of your macros. Use that column as a macro "name" column. In this column, on the same row where each macro starts, enter the macro name as a label. This "name" column has nothing to do with how 1-2-3 reads your macros themselves; it is merely a convenience to humans.

4. Use the column to the right of your actual macro column for comments. Comment religiously. Explain in English what each line of your macro is supposed to do. This may seem silly since you obviously know what you are doing as you create the macro. However, you may want to change something in the macro six months from now. At that time, you may or may not remember how the macro is supposed to work. If you do not remember, and there are no comments to look at, you will have to work back through the logic of the macro, almost as if you were writing it again.

5. Don't let your macros spill over into the adjacent column to the right. Widen the macro column if necessary to prevent spillover. You will need the right column for your comments; if the macro's themselves try to spill over, you will get truncated onscreen lines and nasty, hard-to-read programs.

STANDARD EXERCISES

1. Write a macro that enters a row of month headings, JAN through DEC, across twelve columns beginning at the cellpointer position. Call the macro \M. When you put your cellpointer on a selected cell and press CTRL+M, the macro should enter JAN at the cellpointer location, move the cellpointer right one column, enter FEB, and so forth, until all 12 month headings are entered.

2. Write a macro that uses Edit Calc to kill the value rule in the cell where the cellpointer is located.

3. Retrieve your MASTER file—the worksheet consolidation master file from Chapter 9. Write a macro that automatically combines your EASTMISS and WESTMISS files.

4. Write a macro that drops the cellpointer down ten rows.

5. Write a macro that moves the cellpointer upward five rows and over one column to the right.

6. Write a macro that edits the current cell (wherever the cellpointer is), inserts three blanks to the left to make an indention, and enters the indented material back into the current cell. Don't use this on a numeric cell unless you want to convert it to a label cell.

7. Write a macro that first sends the cellpointer to B3 and then automatically moves the cellpointer down to the first blank cell.

```
        ----A----  ------------B--------------
    1 |
    2 |
    3 |         EMPLOYEES
    4 |         JOE
    5 |         MOE
    6 |         CURLY
    7 |         ALPHIE
    8 |
    9 |
```

SMART DISK EXERCISES

None for the macro chapters.

Macro Programming

After studying this chapter, you should know how to:

- Test for cell attributes.
- Control user input.
- Create macro "do while" loops.
- Execute macro code conditionally.
- Create macro "for" loops.
- Use macro subroutines.

In addition to the keystroke macros discussed in Chapter 13, 1-2-3 provides a set of full-scale programming commands. These commands are what unlock the real power of 1-2-3 macros.

The programming commands are not islands unto themselves; they are used in conjunction with the basic macro techniques discussed in Chapter 13. With the programming commands, macros can be actual computer programs, similar in function to programs you might write in BASIC or C.

The macro recorder cannot create programming commands. You have to enter them manually.

NECESSARY PRELIMINARIES

Before actually writing any macro programs, we need to take a small detour. Many, if not most, macro programs base some of their actions on the current cell's **attribute**. The attribute can be address, or contents, or several other testable features.

Testing the Current Cell's Attributes

The standard tool for this job is 1-2-3's function, @CELLPOINTER("ATTRIBUTE").
There are nine separate ATTRIBUTEs, or characteristics, for which you can test.
Table 14.1 shows the various attributes and what they return.

TABLE 14.1   Testing Cellpointer Attributes

Function with Attribute	Returns
@CELLPOINTER("ADDRESS")	Current cell's absolute address, like $A$6.
@CELLPOINTER("ROW")	Row of current cell, like 57.
@CELLPOINTER("COL")	Column of current cell, where 1=A, 2=B, 255=IV.
@CELLPOINTER("CONTENTS")	Contents of current cell.
@CELLPOINTER("TYPE")	Data type of current cell. Data type can be: B—blank V—number or formula L—label
@CELLPOINTER("PREFIX")	Label prefix of current cell. Can be ', ", or ^.
@CELLPOINTER("PROTECT")	Protection status of current cell. 1—protected 2—unprotected
@CELLPOINTER("WIDTH")	Width of current column.
@CELLPOINTER("FORMAT")	Numeric format of current cell.

The @CELLPOINTER function is not in itself a macro command. However, its main application is in macro programming. When using 1-2-3 from Ready mode, you can simply look to see where the cellpointer is, so there is seldom any need to use the function. However, in a macro, the program itself often has to determine where the cellpointer is in order to decide what to do next.

Testing Noncurrent Cell Attributes

Less commonly, a macro needs to test the attributes of some cell other than the current cell. The function

    @CELL(LOCATION,"ATTRIBUTE")

is used for this purpose. LOCATION can be a cell address or a range name. If a range name is used, the ATTRIBUTE is returned only for the cell at the upper left corner of the range.

CONTROLLING USER INPUT

Perhaps the most basic of all macro jobs is getting input from the user in a controlled fashion. In a macro, you can pre-position the cellpointer, preselect the desired kind of input, and pause the program until the user provides the input. If you want to give someone else the repetitive task of entering new data into a worksheet that you have built—with certainty that the data will be put in the right cells—input commands are the answer to your problems.

Getting Numeric Input

The command

```
{GET-NUMBER "prompt",location}
```

displays a prompt of up to 511 characters and waits for the user to type a number. The number is stored in location. Location can be a cell address, a range name, or the current cell.

If the user presses ESC or clicks on Cancel, location is erased. If the user presses ↵, or clicks on OK, without typing a number, ERR would be stored in location. This is a common cause of corrupted input. Later we discuss how to force the user to provide valid numeric input.

These are examples of the three variants of the GET-NUMBER command:

- {GET-NUMBER "Type your birthday like 5/27/74:",B5} would pause the macro, display the prompt, wait for user input, and store the input in cell B5. As a rule, you should not use a literal cell location such as D7. Using literal cell references may cause you grief if you have to cut and paste the worksheet after finishing your macro.
- {GET-NUMBER "Type Number of Units Received: ",NUMGOT} would pause the macro, display the prompt, wait for user input, and store the input in the upper left cell of the range NUMGOTS.
- {GET-NUMBER "Type Dosage:",@CELLPOINTER("ADDRESS")} would pause the macro, display the prompt, wait for user input, and store the input in *the current cell*. This variant is particularly useful when the macro needs to walk down a column, pausing for data in each cell. There is no need to worry about where to store the input; it is automatically stored in the current cell, courtesy of the @CELLPOINTER function.

Getting Label Input

The command

```
{GET-LABEL "prompt",location}
```

displays a prompt of up to 511 characters and waits for the user to type a label. Even if the user types an otherwise invalid mixture such as 123 Oak St., the input is automatically given a label prefix and stored as a label.

The label is stored in location. Location can be a cell address, a range name, or the current cell. If the user hits ESC, ↵, or clicks on OK without typing anything, a label prefix is stored in the cell. As with GET-NUMBER, this is a common cause of corrupted input; later we discuss how to work around the problem. Otherwise, GET-LABEL works like GET-NUMBER. You can use the same three variants for specifying the location.

The GET-NUMBER and GET-LABEL commands have several optional parameters that are not present in this discussion.

Using GET-LABEL and GET-NUMBER

Close your file and set up the labels and macros shown in Figure 14.1.

FIGURE 14.1

Getting User Input

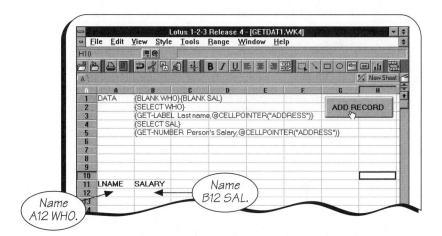

Invoke the macro by clicking on the button. The first line of the macro erases the WHO and SAL ranges. The second line moves the cellpointer to WHO. The third line displays the dialog box shown in Figure 14.2.

FIGURE 14.2

The Get-Label
Dialog Box

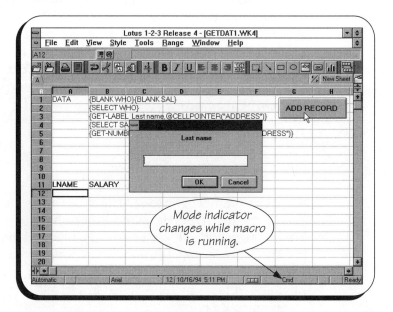

When the user types an entry and presses ↵ or clicks on OK, 1-2-3 places the entry in WHO. The cellpointer then moves to SAL, and a similar dialog box appears, requesting the user to enter the salary. Then the macro stops running because there is no more code.

We now have a macro-driven data-entry mechanism. Let's make the macro handle the job of appending the record onto a database. Copy the labels in A11..B11 to A14. Create the name AREC for A11..B12. Create the name EMPS for A14..B14. Add this line of macro code in B6:

```
{DATABASE-APPEND AREC;EMPS}
```

Your screen now should look like Figure 14.3.

FIGURE 14.3
A Macro-Driven
Database

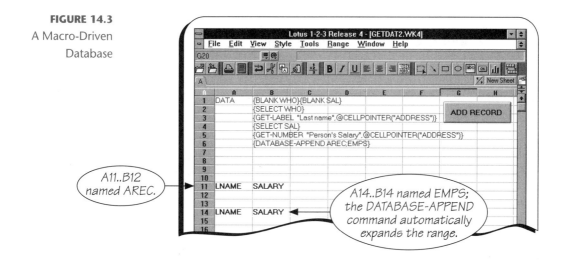

A11..B12 named AREC.

A14..B14 named EMPS; the DATABASE-APPEND command automatically expands the range.

When you run the macro, the final line automatically appends your new record onto the bottom of the database and expands the database range to include the new record. You may remember we did this process manually, with the Tools Database Append Records command in Chapter 10. In a real-world application, the macro works far better because it reduces the chances for operator error.

CONTROLLING PROGRAM FLOW

Controlling program flow means controlling "what happens next." Up to this point, our programs have resembled unguided missiles; we have had no control over what happens next. The macro interpreter has simply marched down the list of commands, quitting when it hit a blank cell.

For many programming jobs, you need more flexibility. Sometimes your program needs to execute a particular block of code and sometimes it needs to execute another. In other words, the program itself needs to decide what to do next based on your program flow instructions.

A program-driven worksheet can make decisions on an overall basis. For example, your worksheet can decide whether or not more input is needed, whether or not information should be extracted from another file on disk, whether or not the overall task is completed, and so forth.

The basic commands for controlling program flow are shown in Table 14.2. The two most fundamental programming commands are BRANCH and IF.

TABLE 14.2   Basic Macro Programming Commands

Command	Programming Function
{IF comparison}true task	Executes "true task" conditionally.
{MACRO RANGE NAME}	Runs the range name as a subroutine.
{RETURN}	Returns control to calling macro from subroutine, or to Ready mode from a startup macro.
{BRANCH location}	Unconditionally transfers program control to location.
{QUIT}	Halts the macro or the subroutine and returns to Ready mode.

Looping with {BRANCH Location}

{BRANCH location} is the 1-2-3 macro command for "quit reading macro instructions here and start reading macro instructions at the location specified." In formal notation, the form of the command is:

        {BRANCH location}

where "location" is the cell location or range name of the cell in which you want 1-2-3 to begin reading instructions. You can use a literal cell address rather than a range name, but with a literal cell address, your macro will crash if later you insert or delete rows or columns.

The {BRANCH location} command has two main uses. It allows you to set up a **loop** within a macro—forcing the repetition of an operation; and it allows you to transfer program control from one macro to another.

We could use {BRANCH location} to streamline our data entry process. Typically more than one record would be entered in a database at one sitting. Let's modify the macro so that, after the clerk enters one record, the macro automatically sets up for another record. Modify your macro as shown in Figure 14.4.

FIGURE 14.4

Endless Loop Macro

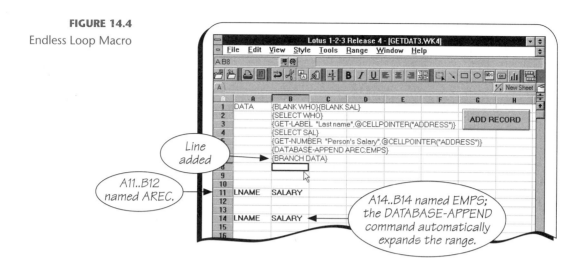

Once the user clicks on the ADD RECORD button, the macro repeats itself again and again. The preceding macro illustrates an **endless loop**. This sort of loop resembles a car without brakes. It runs and runs and runs, but it has no mechanism to bring it to a stop!

The ability to make a macro repeat itself, or loop, is a very useful programming tool. Normally, however, you want the looping to stop automatically when some condition occurs. The most common "stop" condition is based on the cellpointer address, or the characteristics of the current cell's contents. In our case, the macro should stop working if the user hits ESC, ↵, or clicks on Cancel without typing a last name. The {IF} command can make this happen.

Using {IF} to Control Program Flow

{IF} controls program flow. It is *not* the same as the plain-1-2-3 @IF function, which can only pick a value rule for a single cell. {IF} makes a comparison and decides what the *macro program* does next, based on the outcome of the comparison.

The general structure of {IF} is:

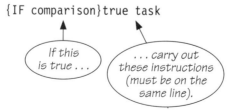

The comparison is some sort of relational expression—the same kind you already are familiar with. The true task is a set of macro instructions that are to be carried out if the comparison is true. If the comparison is false, the true task is ignored completely and 1-2-3 drops to the cell below the IF for more instructions.

An IF in 1-2-3 cannot take up more than one line. The true task can consist of several commands, but all must be on the same line as the {IF}. However, this is not as restrictive as it sounds; the true task can be a subroutine call (discussed later), and the subroutine can be as many lines as you wish.

IF is a perfect vehicle for determining whether or not we should enter another record. Select the range B4..B7 and move it to B5. Then, in B4, type {IF @LENGTH(@S(WHO))<2}{RETURN}. The @S(WHO) guarantees that WHO will contain a null string, even if the user hits ESC or ↵ with no input. If WHO contains fewer than two characters (determined by @LENGTH), WHO cannot be a valid employee name, so we RETURN.

Your worksheet should look like Figure 14.5. The inserted line of macro code is shown in boldface.

FIGURE 14.5

Controlling

Loop Repetition

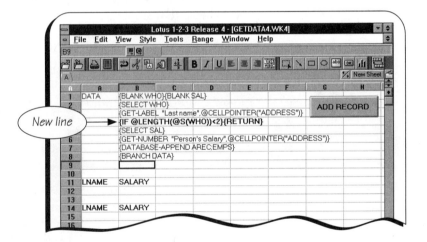

Run the macro. However, instead of entering a name at the prompt, simply press the ENTER key, or hit ESC, or click on the Control button in the dialog box. The new line of code tests to see if the length of the string in WHO is less than 2; it will be since you didn't type any characters. The {RETURN} command takes effect because it is the true task of the IF. The macro ceases working, and 1-2-3 returns you to Ready mode. The macro never gets to the {SELECT SAL} line; it simply stops cold.

Halting a Macro at a Specified Row

Now let's use the @CELLPOINTER function to halt a macro when the cellpointer reaches a specified row. Set up a macro like the one shown in Figure 14.6. Then run it. In the figure, the macro has executed. The fourth line of the macro creates a quarter-second delay, so you can see the cellpointer cycling down column E.

FIGURE 14.6

Checking for
Cellpointer's
Row Position

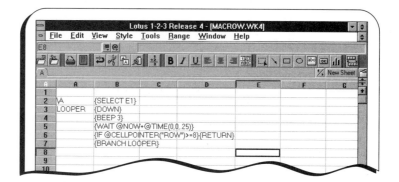

In the example, the macro quits running when the cellpointer reaches row 8. The IF tests to see what row the cellpointer is in; when the row value reaches or exceeds 8, the true task of the IF kicks in to RETURN the macro to whatever routine called it. In our case, it was called from Ready mode, so RETURN results in Ready mode.

How to Process a List

Another common use of the @CELLPOINTER function is in list processing. When doing some operation on a list of items, you need (or, rather, your macro needs) a way to determine when the end of the list is reached. An easy way to determine when the end of a list is reached is to test whether the cellpointer is on a blank cell. The example in Figure 14.7 shows how to do it.

FIGURE 14.7

A Rudimentary List
Processing Macro

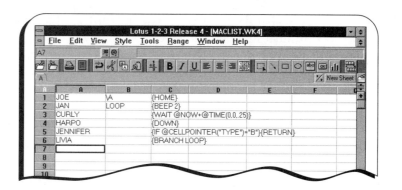

The macro in Figure 14.7 quits running when @CELLPOINTER("TYPE")="B" becomes true. In other words, it quits when the IF detects a blank cell. As it stands, the macro does nothing useful except illustrate the concept. To make it carry out some actual task for each item in the list, you could insert more code in place of line 3.

HOW TO SET UP A FOR LOOP

Lotus provides another way of looping: the FOR loop. It is useful if you know in advance, or can calculate, how many times a loop should execute. Figure 14.8 shows a simple example of a FOR loop:

FIGURE 14.8

A FOR Loop

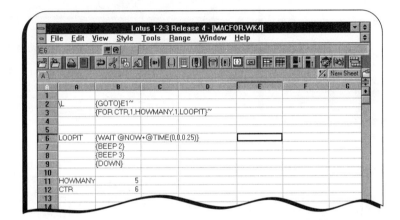

The general syntax of the FOR loop command (cell B3 of Figure 14.8) is:

```
{FOR countercell,begin#,end#,increment,subroutine-to-execute}
```

The countercell is where Lotus keeps the count of how many loop repetitions have been done. In other words, when you run the macro, Lotus uses the countercell as a scratchpad for storing the number of loop executions that have been done.

The begin# tells Lotus where to start counting; normally it is 1. Begin# can be a literal number like the "1" in the preceding example, or it can be the number in a designated cell.

The end# tells Lotus when to stop. It can be a literal number, but in the preceding example we named a cell HOWMANY and placed the number 5 in HOWMANY.

The increment is normally 1; it tells Lotus what value to add to the countercell after each loop. Like the other elements, the increment can be a literal number or can reference the value in a cell.

The final piece of information in the FOR command is the name of the macro you want executed. In the preceding example, LOOPIT is to be executed as many times as the value in HOWMANY.

SECRETS OF PROFESSIONAL PROGRAMMERS: SUBROUTINE USE

Many real-world Lotus macro programs are large and complex. To avoid drowning in detail under those circumstances, you have to break the programming job down into manageable chunks, complete and test each chunk, and then tie the chunks together.

To call a subroutine, all you have to do is tell Lotus the subroutine's name, like {subroutine-name}. For example, if you wanted to call a subroutine named DOG, you would say:

{DOG} or {dog}   Lotus isn't picky about capitalization.

When Lotus encountered the {DOG} subroutine call, it would search for a cell named DOG and begin treating the characters in DOG (and any occupied cells below) as macro instructions. When Lotus found a blank cell in DOG (or a conditional return), Lotus would return to the point at which it left off reading keystrokes in the main macro. This may seem complex and unnecessary at first. Actually it is the key to simple, easy-to-understand macro programming.

To see how subroutine calls work, set up the main macro and subroutines shown in Figure 14.9. Name all the macros at one time by selecting I1..I18 and using Range Name with the Use Labels to the right option.

FIGURE 14.9

A Main Macro with Subroutines

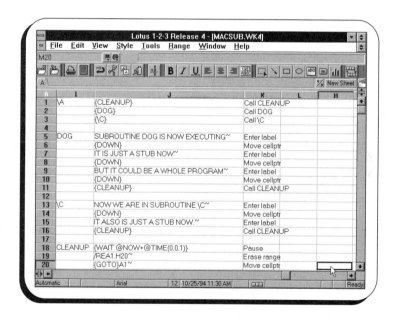

Select Tools Macro Single Step and Tools Macro Trace. Then invoke the main macro by typing CTRL A, and begin pressing ↵ to step through the program. Watch the transcript window as the program executes.

First, the main program calls the CLEANUP subprogram, which

1. Pauses for one second.
2. Erases the range A1 through H20.
3. Moves the cellpointer to cell A1.
4. Returns to the calling program at the next character after the subroutine call command.

The next command is another subroutine call, {DOG}. So, 1-2-3 executes the DOG subroutine, which does its thing. But notice that the DOG subroutine also calls the CLEANUP subroutine. This is perfectly legal. One subroutine can call another subroutine, and for that matter the sub-subroutine can call another subroutine, almost ad infinitum.

When 1-2-3 finds a blank cell in DOG, it returns to the main routine. The main routine (\A) transfers control to the \C subroutine. The \C subroutine executes and returns control to the calling macro, \A. Since there are no more characters in \A to be interpreted, \A ceases execution.

Do not use macro keywords as range names. For example QUIT, DOWN, and RETURN are illegal as subroutine names.

You probably remember that {IF comparison}true task~ must be a one-line statement. Yet sometimes the true task is too involved to place on a single line, or else you may need the same lengthy set of instructions for more than one IF. In that case, set the true task up as a macro subroutine. Then use {subroutine-name} to call the true task macro subroutine as needed.

USING {LET}~ TO AVOID CELLPOINTER MOVEMENT

Syntax of {LET} is:

```
{LET cell,value, exp, or label}~
```

The tilde is more or less optional. I suggest that you always follow a {LET} with the tilde—it guarantees that the target cell will be updated with the {LET} value in timely fashion.

The {LET} macro command lets you place literal values, the results of expressions, or labels in cells *without* necessarily moving the cellpointer. For example, if you wanted a macro to place the number 56 in cell R22, you could say:

```
{LET R22,56}~
```

If you wanted to place the product of A1 times B1 in R22, you could say:

```
{LET R22,A1*B1}~
```

An important point is that only the *result* of the expression—not the formula itself—is placed in R22. For example, if A1 held the number 5 and B1 held 6, the LET macro would put only the number 30 in R22. The formula A1*B1 would *not* be placed in R22. In this sense {LET} works sort of like Edit Paste Special in nonmacro Lotus. If you actually want the *formula* copied into the target cell, {LET} will not serve your needs.

One of the big advantages of {LET} is speedy execution. Moving the cellpointer around the worksheet drastically slows down the execution of a macro. The slowdown is not important in small worksheets, but in bear in mind that some real-world worksheets are huge and take many minutes or even hours to run, even when optimally designed. Unnecessary cellpointer movement can take lots of time under those circumstances.

TARGET RANGE NAMES IN MACROS

In a macro, there are two ways to refer to a target cell. You can do it by a literal cell reference, such as {GOTO}C3~, or you can assign a range name to the cell and reference the range name. For example, if cell C3 contains a sales figure, you could use Range Name to name the cell "SALES." Then you could refer to the target cell by the range name: {GOTO}SALES~.

Either method works, *so long as you do not insert or delete any rows or columns after you build your macro.* If you insert or delete rows or columns, a literal cell reference such as {GOTO}C3~ may or may not put the cellpointer where you wanted it. For example, if you insert three rows above C3, the contents of C3 move down to C6, but your cell reference still says {GOTO}C3~. There is no way your macro can automatically adjust to any shifts in the position of the referenced cell. After all, the macro is just a text entry. To correct the problem, you would have to edit the macro and change your literal cell reference to {GOTO}C6~.

This is no great job for a single cell reference, but a large macro may have many cell references. Worse yet, you may forget to change some of your literal references and blow up your model.

You can avoid these problems by assigning a range name to each cell you need to {GOTO} or otherwise manipulate. The great virtue of range names is that they are *sticky*. Range names go where the named cell goes. Adding or deleting rows and columns has no effect on the validity of a range name reference, so long as you do not delete the cell that holds the range name. A macro command such as {GOTO}SALES~ will go to the cell you named SALES, wherever it be, insertions and deletions notwithstanding.

Write a macro program that:

1. Sets up a counter cell in D10.
2. Sends the cellpointer to A1, beeps, and enters the message HELLO.
3. Erases A1.
4. Sends the cellpointer to G1, beeps, and enters the message HELLO.
5. Erases G1.
6. Sends the cellpointer to A15, beeps, and enters the message HELLO.
7. Erases A15.

Repeat the preceding actions 10 times.

Use a subroutine call for the message entry and cell erasures.

None for this chapter.

Menu-Driven Macros

OBJECTIVES   After studying this chapter, you should know how to:

- Create simple menu-driven macros.
- Create multi-level menu-driven macros.
- Create auto-executing macros.

By setting up menu-driven macros, you can leverage the capabilities of users with minimal Lotus skills. Menu-driven macros provide the basis for total "turnkey" programs that require almost no user skills to run productively.

Menus also can give you complete control over what the users of a worksheet can and cannot do. For example, you can create a customized menu that automatically pops up whenever a particular worksheet is retrieved from disk and that bars the user from doing anything that isn't on the menu you create.

THE MENUBRANCH AND MENUCALL COMMANDS

1-2-3 has two macro commands for building menus, MENUBRANCH and MENUCALL, which create a dialog box from which the user can choose an action. The syntax of these commands is

```
{MENUBRANCH location} or {MENUCALL location}
```

where location is the cell address or range name of the upper left corner of a custom menu layout.

The difference between MENUBRANCH and MENUCALL is the same as the difference between a plain branch such as {BRANCH LOOPER} and a plain subroutine call such as {PRINTIT}. MENUBRANCH is a "go and don't bother coming back" command, whereas MENUCALL is a "go but come back here when you finish" command.

For maximum control over the user's actions, you normally want to lock the user into a menu, so that when one menu choice is finished, the menu automatically reappears. If you use MENUBRANCH, the menu does *not* automatically reappear after the user gets through with a particular choice, unless you add branching code to each macro called by the menu.

In most programming situations, MENUCALL is the more useful form because it makes it easy to lock the user into a menu. Our discussion concentrates on using MENUCALL.

Menu-building is a fairly complex subject, so let's approach it one step at a time and by way of an example. Open the CARPMT file that we used in Chapter 7. Widen column C to 3 characters. Then add the labels shown in the range D1..G5. Your worksheet should look like Figure 15.1.

FIGURE 15.1

First Stage of
Menu Creation

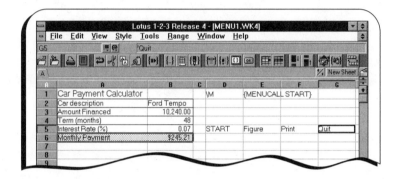

In a real-world application, you probably would not bother to drive this simple worksheet with a menu if you were going to be the one who actually used it from day to day. However, if less-skilled 1-2-3 users would use it, a menu-driven approach would reduce their frustration and errors.

Menus can drive much more sophisticated applications such as integrated pro forma financial planning models, but for illustrative purposes, the simplicity of the loan payment calculator is an advantage in understanding how menus work. Once you understand the principles, you can expand to more ambitious applications. For now, let's assume you want to turn the payment calculator into as nearly foolproof a program as possible, so your non-computer-literate clerk can use it without messing anything up.

You want your clerk to be able to do three things:

1. Input the data for car description, amount financed, term, and interest rate.

2. Print a copy of the results in A1..B6.

3. Quit to Ready mode.

We are going to set up a menu-driven macro to do these three things. Normally your macro would be off the home screen area, but for illustration we have placed it beside the data area.

After you have made the entries in D1..G5, select D1..D5 and select Range Name Use Labels To the Right to name cells E1 and E5.

Press CTRL+M to run your macro. You should see the 1-2-3 menu dialog box shown in Figure 15.2.

FIGURE 15.2

The Macro Menu
Dialog Box

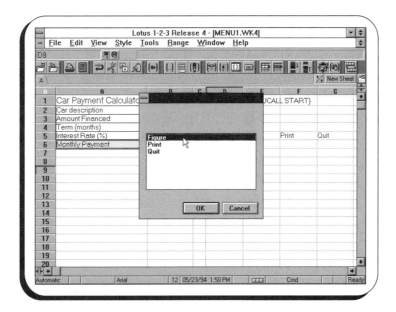

True to your macro instructions, the {MENUCALL location} command executed; your custom menu appears in the dialog box. The highlight will be on the first menu choice, Figure.

The CMD indicator appears in the status bar. That informs you that 1-2-3 is running under macro control

Move the highlight bar from choice to choice. Of course, the menu doesn't do anything yet. There is not even a submenu of explanatory text. Just for fun, however, put your cursor on whichever menu choice appeals to you and press ENTER. The menu disappears and you are back in Ready mode.

Why? Because we didn't include any instructions about what to do when a choice was selected. 1-2-3 did everything we told it to do—it displayed the first line of the menu beginning in START and waited for you to make a selection. You made a selection, but when 1-2-3 went to look for instructions to match the selection, there were only blank cells. By now you know what 1-2-3 does when it hits a blank cell in a macro; it stops executing.

Let's add some more instructions to our macro. Move your cellpointer to cell E6, just below the Figure item in the menu choices. Add the line of explanatory text in E6, as shown in Figure 15.3.

FIGURE 15.3

Explanatory Text
for the Menu

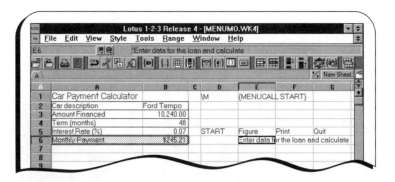

FIGURE 15.3

Explanatory Text
for the Menu

Now run the menu macro again, with CTRL+M. Your dialog box should look like Figure 15.4.

FIGURE 15.4

Dialog Box Shows
Explanatory Message

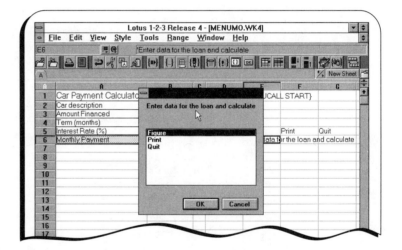

We also will have to put explanatory lines under Print and Quit, but for now let's continue with the Figure menu choice. If you take the Figure choice at this point, nothing happens because there still are no instructions associated with it except to display the explanatory text line. Click on OK (or Cancel) to return to Ready mode. Now we need to get user input. Add the macro code shown in Figure 15.5.

FIGURE 15.5
FIG Code Treated
as a Subroutine

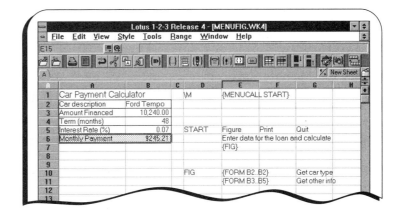

We could have inserted the code in E7 and downward, directly under the Figure menu choice. However, it is better form to call the menu actions as a subroutine. We also have to place code under the Print and Quit choices, and we cannot use the adjacent columns for documentation if we write the code directly under the menu choices. By using subroutine calls to activate the menu choices, we have lots of elbow room for writing and documenting the code. The code is much easier to read when you are examining or debugging it.

Run the macro with CTRL+M. You can input data in the specified cells (which must be unprotected), but you cannot move the cellpointer outside the ranges specified in the FORM commands. This makes it more difficult for a user to mess up; the cellpointer is guided to the proper locations for data input. When the Figure menu choice finishes running, 1-2-3 drops to Ready mode. Add the code shown in Figure 15.6 for the Print and Quit choices.

FIGURE 15.6
The Completed
Macro Menu

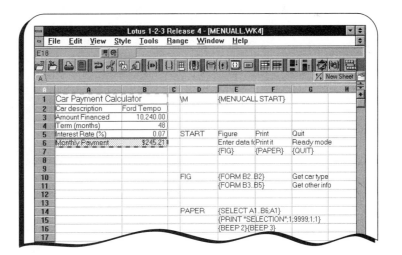

{QUIT} in G7 is not a subroutine call. It is a native 1-2-3 macro keyword that stops a macro and drops to Ready mode.

Looping the Menu

Usually you want a menu to redisplay after an action is completed. To make this happen, add the line of code shown in cell E2 of Figure 15.7.

FIGURE 15.7

Making the
Menu Loop

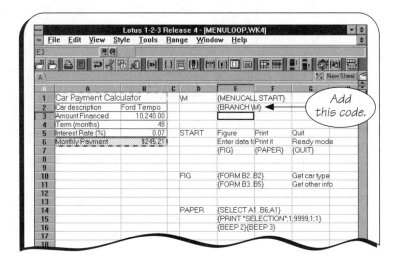

Now run the macro. Select Figure. When you finish, the menu is redisplayed in the control panel. To understand how this works, trace through the sequence of actions when you run the \M macro. {MENUCALL START} treats START as a menu subroutine, so when the code under a single menu choice such as Figure (in our example) is completed, control returns to \M and the \M macro resumes reading instructions on the second line. The second line of \M, {BRANCH \M}, tells 1-2-3 to begin reading macro instructions in the cell named \M, which simply reruns the \M macro!

And there you have it: a menu-driven macro that permits your clerk to generate loan payments and print the results, without any real knowledge of how Lotus works. The only skills needed are the ability to take menu choices and type in the requested information.

Multilevel Menus

Custom menus are not restricted to one level. You can create menus that call other menus, nesting many layers deep if necessary.

CREATING AUTO-EXECUTING MACROS

The macros we have examined up to this point require the operator to invoke them with CTRL+letter. With some slight modifications, you can turn any of these plain macros into auto-executing macros—macros that begin running without the need for invoking with CTRL+letter. There are two forms of auto-execute macros. One form automatically runs a macro when you open the file that contains it. The other form is not only auto-executing, it is also auto-loading.

It automatically loads itself into memory and begins executing as soon as you launch 1-2-3.

To create a simple auto-executing macro, all you have to do is assign the special name \0 (backslash zero) to the macro's top cell. For example, if you want to fix the payment calculator macro so that it begins executing as soon as you retrieve it from disk, name cell E1 \0. The fact that E1 already has some other macro name does not matter. A cell can have two names. If you save the file and then open it, you will find that the menu appears without your having to invoke it. If thereafter you want to run it again, you can manually invoke it using the ordinary macro letter-name, for example, CTRL+M. In fact, you always should assign an ordinary macro name to your auto-execute macros. Once a \0 macro loads and runs, you cannot invoke it again by using CTRL+0. To invoke it again, you must use its ordinary letter-name.

To make a file auto-load, all you have to do is name the file AUTO123. For example, you could select File Save As and save the payment calculator as AUTO123. Thereafter, any time you booted up Lotus with the mortgage amortization file on the default drive, it would automatically load into memory. If the mortgage amortization file had the name \0, it would then immediately begin running.

The auto-execute features are widely applied by 1-2-3 gurus such as yourself, who write macro programs for less skilled people to use. If a worksheet autoloads and autoexecutes and uses the other user-friendly tools such as macro buttons and menus, a person with very little knowledge of 1-2-3 can use it productively.

CASE

Ace Castings, Inc.

Congratulations. Word of your Lotus guru-hood has spread far and wide. Based on your enviable reputation, Ace Castings, Inc., (a foundry; they cast bronze propellers for ships) has offered you a consulting job.

For $15,000, they want you to develop and test a macro program for recording and analyzing the starting and ending dates/times of all their propeller-casting jobs. Most jobs take 7 to 10 days; some take considerably longer.

Name your worksheet CASTINGS.

1. Create a database with these fields:

   WK_ORDNUM STARDATE ENDDATE ELAPSED

2. Create a menu macro. The menu choices are:

   JOB LOGIN   JOB LOGOUT   EXTRACT RECORDS   Print_X   QUIT

For each menu choice, your macro should execute these actions:

JOB LOGIN—asks for work order number; searches database for duplicate; if no duplicate, create a new record—enter the work order number; automatically enter starting time and date using @NOW and Edit Calc.

JOB LOGOUT—used when a job is finished. Asks user for a work order number; search for it; if found, automatically enter ending time and compute elapsed time (days) for the job.

EXTRACT RECORDS—allows user to enter extract criteria; extracts the hits. For example, the user might want to extract all jobs that took 12 or more days.

Print_X—automatically establishes print range and prints the extract range if any records present.

QUIT

3. When a menu choice is completed, give the user the main menu again. The following is an example of a record:

```
WK_ORDNUM    STARDATE    ENDDATE    ELAPSED
19901021_1   19-SEP-90
```

Set up a macro-controlled database that your Lotus-ignorant clerical personnel can use for data entry. Set up one that relates to your business or profession.

None for this chapter.

A Primer on Modular Macro Programming

OBJECTIVES   After studying this chapter, you should know how to:

- Use the MACTOOLS macro subroutine library.
- Create subroutine-based macro programs.
- Generate macro-driven picklists.
- Set up macro-driven databases.
- Create macro-driven sort routines.

Now that you are equipped with basic macro skills, it is time to look at a labor-saving technique used by advanced macro writers: modular macro programming.

The modular approach works by calling flexible prewritten programs (subroutines) to do the common jobs involved in creating new macro applications. With a good set of subroutines, you can create sophisticated macro programs without writing much, if any, of the detailed code we have discussed earlier. You can, of course, create your own subroutines. However, that is beyond our scope in this book. We will simply use the author's set, in MACTOOLS.wk4 on your SMART disk.

BRINGING MACTOOLS INTO A NEW WORKSHEET   Most of the tools you will use to create modular programs are not a built-in part of Lotus. They are in the MACTOOLS worksheet on the accompanying disk. You have to get them into each new worksheet you create before you can use them.

There are actually two different ways to make modular routines available to your worksheet—one simple and one somewhat more complicated. For our purposes, we will look at the simpler way. To set up a new modular worksheet (basic method), always follow this procedure:

1. File Open the MACTOOLS worksheet MACTOOLS.wk4 from disk.
2. Immediately File Save As the worksheet under whatever new filename you wish. By doing this you incorporate the various modular routines contained in MACTOOLS.wk4, into your new worksheet.

This procedure is not simply a learning technique. Any time you want to set up a new macro worksheet, you should begin by opening MACTOOLS and saving as your desired worksheet name.

CREATING A MODULAR MACRO APPLICATION

Without any further ado, let's create a modular macro application. Assume you are working for a long-distance trucking firm and you need a worksheet that logs three pieces of information: drivers' names, the date they left your loading dock with a load, and the time they left.

The name of the worksheet is going to be TRUCKS. To begin, follow the standard procedure: File Open MACTOOLS, and then File Save As under the filename TRUCKS. At this point, the TRUCKS worksheet is an exact duplicate of MACTOOLS, so it contains all the MACTOOLS subroutine modules.

Now set up the worksheet shown in Figure 16.1. Put the label DRIVER in A8; the label DATE in B8; and the label TIME in C8. Then enter the macro code in column D. Note that all MACTOOLS subroutine range names begin with an underscore character. The purpose of the beginning underscore is to keep anyone from confusing MACTOOLS subroutines with native 1-2-3 macro commands.

FIGURE 16.1

Macro-Driven Trucking Log

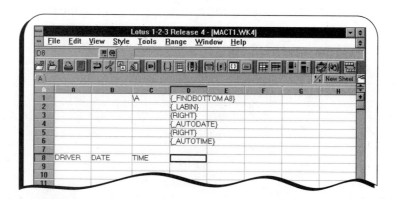

Use Range Name to name cell D1. The label in D1 is a call to a subroutine named _FINDBOTTOM, which handles the cellpointer-positioning job. There is a space between _FINDBOTTOM and A8. The A8 is additional information needed by _FINDBOTTOM.

For now, don't worry about how anything works—just type in what you see, exactly as you see it. After typing in your new macro lines, run the macro with CTRL+A. If you correctly entered all the labels, you should see this on the screen:

FIGURE 16.2

Macro Pauses
for Label Input

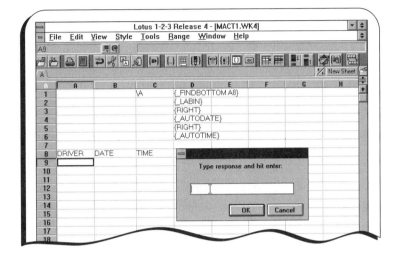

The {_FINDBOTTOM A8} command sends the cellpointer to the first blank cell below A8. Then the second line calls up a subroutine called _LABIN, which displays a standard prompt message and waits for the user to type some sort of label. The name _LABIN helps you remember the purpose of the routine—to get LABel INput. _LABIN does not allow the cellpointer to move until the user types some characters. In other words, the user cannot intentionally or accidentally skip over the field by hitting the ESC key or by hitting ↵ before typing in some characters.

Assuming you type in the response SMITH, the _LABIN routine goes back to sleep, so to speak. The next line of the macro, {RIGHT}, moves the cellpointer rightward (to cell B9). As you probably remember, {RIGHT} is a built-in native Lotus macro command; it is not a modular routine. {RIGHT} is the only native Lotus macro command in the entire program. The next line of the macro, {_AUTODATE}, calls the _AUTODATE subroutine. _AUTODATE makes your screen look like Figure 16.3.

FIGURE 16.3

Macro Pauses
for Date Input

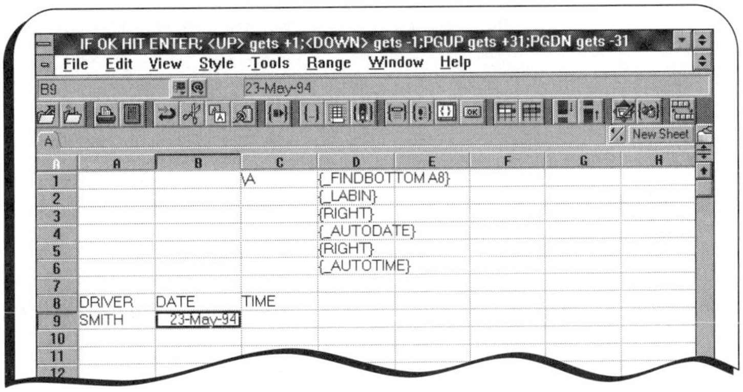

When _AUTODATE is working, you will see the instruction bar in the control panel; the cellpointer will be on cell B9, which suddenly will contain a date. If your system clock is giving the correct date, cell B9 will show today's date, which we are assuming is May 23, 1994. The user (in this case, you) can kick the date forward or backward one day by hitting the up arrow or the down arrow. You can kick the date forward or backward 31 days at a time by hitting the PageUp or PageDown key. When you are satisfied with the date, hit the ↵ key and the macro will continue running.

After you select a date and hit ↵, the cellpointer pops right to cell C9 and the _AUTOTIME routine begins running. The prompt will be similar to that shown for _AUTODATE. After you supply a time by using the arrow keys, the _AUTODATE returns control to the macro. There are no more instructions—cell D7 is blank—so the \A macro quits running and you are back in Ready mode.

The detailed code to do the _AUTOTIME job is similar to that needed for _AUTODATE—complex, lengthy, and the author already did it for you, so just use and enjoy. After the program finished running, your line of data would look something like Figure 16.4.

FIGURE 16.4
Complete Record
Generated by Macro

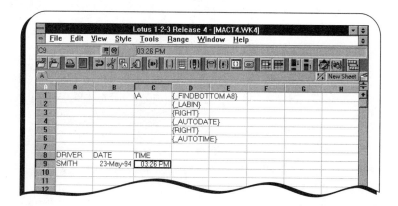

Bear in mind that the _LABIN, _AUTODATE, and _AUTOTIME lines in your macro do not in themselves carry out all the complex programming actions needed to get the user input. They simply call preexisting modular routines named _LABIN, _AUTODATE and _AUTOTIME, which step in to handle the details.

The preceding program illustrates the goal in intelligent macro programming: Don't write low-level, detailed macro code except as a last resort. Whenever possible—which is almost all the time—use a modular routine.

A SECOND MODULAR APPLICATION

Let's do another modular macro. Assume we need to develop a worksheet that allows us to input personal data for all 1750 employees of Blatz Pickle, Inc. To begin the new project using MACTOOLS subroutines, follow this procedure:

1. Close any files currently open and File Open MACTOOLS.

2. Immediately File Save As it under a *different filename* (we will use PICKLE as the filename).

3. Begin setting up your new project in the PICKLE worksheet, which of course contains all the handy subroutines that were in MACTOOLS.

We assume you have taken these three steps. In the PICKLE screen in Figure 16.5, we have set up field names to indicate what each column will contain. Columns A, B, and C will hold lastname, firstname, and middlename, respectively. Column D will hold the employee social security number. Column E will hold a number (a Lotus date-number) specifying the year, month, and day the particular employee was hired.

FIGURE 16.5

Employee
Information Table

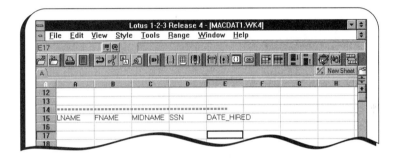

If we plan to use the data later to generate reports, it would behoove us to be sure the information is input with as few errors as possible. Simply turning someone loose to fill in the data from Ready-mode Lotus would be a recipe for all sorts of future headaches.

What could go wrong with such a simple process as filling in a row with a few pieces of information? Lots of things. The person inputting the data could leave a row entirely blank, which could mess up later macro report-generating operations. Or the inputter could fail to fill out a field. Or the inputter could fail to input a valid date. Or . . . you get the idea.

If you have had experiences of this sort, you know that expecting non-Lotus experts to consistently get everything right using Ready-mode Lotus is like expecting the Tooth Fairy to pay regular visits.

The only way to be reasonably sure that the data is entered consistently is to set up a macro to guide the people who punch in the data. The modular macro in Figure 16.6 would do the job admirably. For easy reading, we have placed both the macro code and the database in the home screen area.

FIGURE 16.6

Data Input Macro

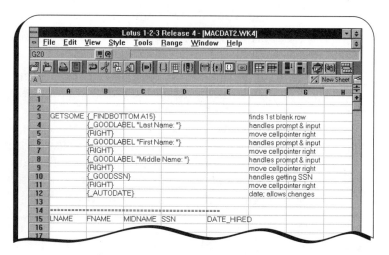

The preceding macro easily could be included as a choice from a menu. Each time the user invokes it, the macro automatically finds the first blank row below A15 and moves the cellpointer from column to column as the user inputs data.

Notice that the entire program, except for {RIGHT}, consists of calls to "canned" MACTOOLS subroutines. The second line, {_GOODLABEL "Last Name: "}, calls a program called _GOODLABEL and tells it what prompt to display in the control panel while it waits for the user to type something. _GOODLABEL does not allow the cellpointer to move until the user types some characters. In other words, the user cannot intentionally or accidentally skip over the field by hitting ESC or by just hitting ↵ before typing in some characters. Also, _GOODLABEL chops off any leading or trailing spacebar characters in case the user accidentally hit the spacebar instead of a character. Finally, _GOODLABEL converts the user's input to uppercase characters, regardless of how the user typed them in.

After calling the _GOODLABEL subroutine and moving the cellpointer with {RIGHT} until the employee's last, first, and middle names are input, the program pops into column D and calls the _GOODSSN subroutine. Then the cellpointer moves to column E and the macro calls the _AUTODATE subroutine to get the date.

After GETSOME finishes getting the first record, the database might look like Figure 16.7. Save your PICKLE worksheet.

FIGURE 16.7

Record Created
by Macro

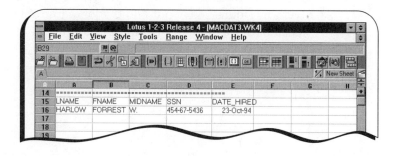

The MACTOOLS worksheet has several other input-getting subroutines, such as _BLANKLABEL, _YESNO, _GOODNUMBER, _MINMAXNUM, and _PICKLIST. We will discuss them in due time.

Getting Numeric Input

If you want to force the user to provide a valid number, but you don't need a specialized prompt, use the {_NUMIN} subroutine. If you want a specialized prompt to be displayed, use the _GOODNUMBER subroutine.

_NUMIN and _GOODNUMBER are very useful in "idiot-proofing" a macro worksheet against common numeric-input errors. Not only does it provide a prompting message to the user, it locks up the worksheet until valid numeric input is provided. The cellpointer does not move until a numeric entry is typed in and the ↵ key is pressed.

To see how _GOODNUMBER works, File Open MACTOOLS; then immediately File Save As PERNELL; and set up the worksheet shown in Figure 16.8. It gets both label and numeric input.

FIGURE 16.8
Macro for Label
and Numeric Input

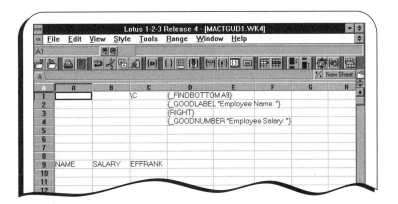

After setting up the preceding worksheet, invoke the macro and type Smith when the macro asks for an employee name. The cellpointer pops rightward to B10 and asks you for the employee salary. Try to move your cellpointer before typing anything. It can't be done. Then try to bluff _GOODNUMBER by merely pressing the ↵ key. That won't work, either; nor will typing in some text.

FIGURE 16.9

The _GOODNUMBER
Routine in Action

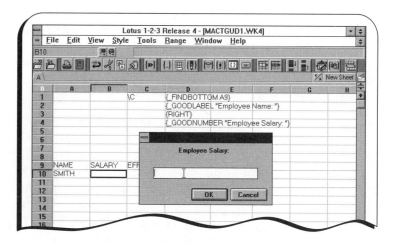

FIGURE 16.9

The _GOODNUMBER
Routine in Action

The only way to get free is to provide a number and press ↵. For the example, we are inputting a salary of $50,000. _GOODNUMBER will be one of your bread-and-butter subroutines from this point on. The ability to force good numeric input is crucial to most macro applications.

Sometimes you need to go beyond simply getting good numeric input and control the acceptable range of the input. For example, if you wanted the user to input data on an efficiency ranking (EFFRANK, in our example) the only possible rankings might be between, say, 1 and 10, where 1 represents rotten and 10 represents the absolute best. If that is the applicable numeric scaling, any number outside the range 1 through 10 would be due to user error. Out-of-range numbers would mess up the validity of the data. For example, if a clerk accidentally input an EFFRANK of 100 for someone, the 100 would skew any average we computed from the data.

Erase the range A10..C10. If you want to control the user's response within a range, use the _MINMAXNUM subroutine. To see how _MINMAXNUM works, add the code shown in Figure 16.10. Then run the macro. When you run the macro and supply data for the NAME and SALARY fields, your screen should look like the example in Figure 16.10.

FIGURE 16.10

The _MINMAXNUM
Routine in Action

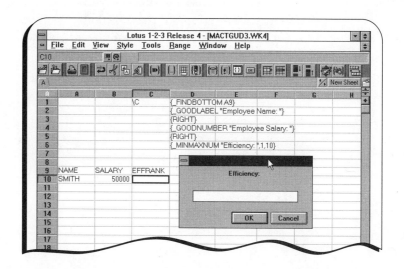

Notice that _MINMAXNUM requires three pieces of information: the prompt, the minimum allowable number, and the maximum allowable number:

```
{_MINMAXNUM "Efficiency:",1,10}
```

Prompt   Minimum   Maximum

Waiting for the User to Hit a Key

If your macro needs to pause without getting actual data input, use _PAUSIT, like this:

```
{_PAUSIT "Hit a key to continue"}
```

_PAUSIT displays in the control panel whatever message you specify. As this _PAUSIT is set up, the message would be "Hit a key to continue."

Displaying Messages in the Title Bar

Frequently your macro will need to show some general message to the user. One way to show a message is to use the 1-2-3 {ALERT message} macro command, which places the message in a dialog box and pauses the macro.

1-2-3 also has a native macro command {INDICATE "message"} that lets your macro place a customized message in the title bar. The MACTOOLS {_LITEBAR "message"} routine uses the INDICATE command to space the message in the title bar. The {_LITEBAR "You messed up."} command would display the message roughly centered on the top line of the control panel, and it would blank out everything else except the control buttons, as Figure 16.11 shows.

FIGURE 16.11

Using the Title Bar for a Message

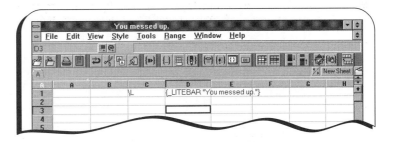

However, the message in itself does not make the macro pause. If you want to be sure the user reads a message before the macro continues, you could use _PAUSIT instead of _LITEBAR.

```
{_PAUSIT "Hit a key when you finish reading."}
{_LITEBAR "Now continuing"}
{_ALARM 6}
{INDICATE}
```

This code would display the message centered on the top line of the control panel; when the user hit a key, the "Now continuing" message would appear; the alarm would sound; and the Mode indicator would be returned to its native state.

Close your file. Next we will examine a routine for getting input from the user, via picklist.

SUPER-SOPHISTICATED INPUT USING THE _PICKLIST SUBROUTINE

Some data input jobs are so complex they tend to make ordinary macro programmers throw up their hands in surrender. The following case is one of those. But take heart—armed with the MACTOOLS subroutines, you are no ordinary macro programmer.

Let's assume Blatz Pickle, Inc., now needs a more sophisticated database like the one shown in Figure 16.12. To begin the new project, close any open files; then open MACTOOLS and save under the filename PERSDATA. For variety we are going to set it up starting in A1010.

FIGURE 16.12
A More
Complex Employee
Information Table

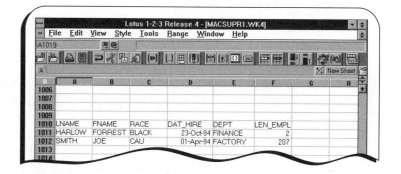

Most of the field names are self-explanatory. DAT_HIRE is the date the employee was first hired. LEN_EMPL is a computed field based on today's date minus the date-number in DAT_HIRE.

The basic idea is to get input into each field, but we cannot afford any mess-ups, particularly in the RACE and DEPT fields. To avoid mess-ups, we need a complete list of all of Blatz's departments and another list of the various human races.

The data needs to be good because we will be using the database to generate various internal and external reports based on RACE, DEPT, and so forth. If one of our departments is called FINANCE, but the data-inputter abbreviates it to FIN, or spells it FINENCE in a few records, or decides that MONEY would do just as well in the DEPT field, we will not get a true report based on records where the DEPT field is FINANCE.

The only way to get total consistency is to let the data-inputter select from a picklist instead of manually typing in the data. Create the two picklists shown in Figure 16.13.

FIGURE 16.13

Two Picklists Created

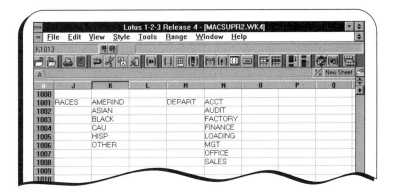

Use Range Name to name cell K1001; call it RACES. Likewise name cell N1001; call it DEPART.

Now that we have the picklists set up, we need to create a program to use them. The program shown in Figure 16.14 has an unfamiliar line at the top. {PANELOFF} simply shuts off the screen updates of the control panel while Lotus is running the macro. The macro would work fine without {PANELOFF}, but it looks neater and runs somewhat faster if Lotus doesn't have to spend CPU time updating the control panel.

The second line, {_LITEBAR "GETTING DATA"}, is a MACTOOLS routine with which you already are familiar. You already know how to write the macro code to get the two name fields. However, the _VWINDOW routine, also from MACTOOLS, is worth a comment. As you may know, there is a 1-2-3 command sequence for creating a vertical split screen (View Split) and a command to "unsynchronize" the two screens so they can scroll independently. _VWINDOW uses those commands to automatically set up an unsynchronized vertical window, a specified number of columns to the right of the cellpointer location. For example, {_VWINDOW 4} creates a vertical window 4 columns right of the current cellpointer location, which would be somewhere in row C just before _VWINDOW was called.

The _PICKLIST routine automatically changes the indicator bar to show:

```
Highlight your choice with down arrow or up arrow; then hit
ENTER.
```

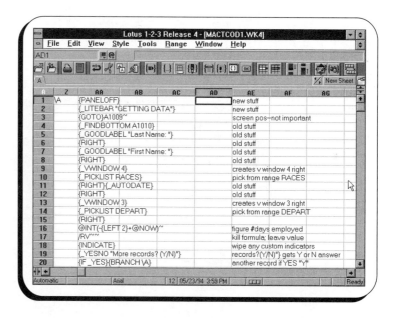

After {_VWINDOW 4} and the next line, {_PICKLIST RACES}, ran, the screen would look like Figure 16.15.

The screen is split into two windows, and the cellpointer has popped into the right window, in cell K1001. The Mode indicator is now saying

```
Use <up> and <down> arrows to highlight your choice and hit
ENTER.
```

The user has no choice but to follow the instructions, because no keys work except the up arrow, the down arrow, and ENTER. When the user makes a choice, the split screen disappears and the selected RACE is automatically placed in the correct cell in the database area (C1013, in the example).

The same basic thing happens when the macro gets to the line {_PICKLIST DEPART}, except that the split screen lets the user point to a choice in the range named DEPART. The line {_YESNO "More records?(Y/N)"} pauses the macro until the user types either Y or N, with the user's response stored in a cell named _YES. The final line {IF _YES}{BRANCH \A} reruns the macro if the user typed Y—in other words, it sets up for entry of another record.

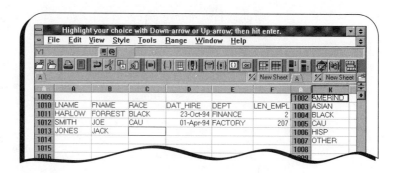

MACRO-DRIVEN DATABASES

Some people try to do database operations manually, but the results often are unhappy. Lotus database operations require a fairly complex set of procedures to set up a database and to use the database once it is set up. The probability of ordinary users getting manual database operations right every time is not high.

A database needs a menu-driven front end if anyone but a Lotus guru will be using it, and low-level database macros are tedious and complex to create. As usual, the solution is a MACTOOLS subroutine.

RAPID-PROTOTYPING THE DATABASE PROJECT: {_MAKEDATABASE}

When you first begin putting together a new database worksheet, the best idea is to knock out a **rapid prototype**—a rough working model of the project. MACTOOLS offers a unique tool for prototyping: the _MAKEDATABASE command. _MAKEDATABASE lets you do an hour's worth of database prototyping work in about 30 seconds. Definitely a bargain.

The _MAKEDATABASE command handles the details of database creation. _MAKEDATABASE automatically creates a blank database setup, with criterion, input, and output ranges, based on whatever field names you provide. It also provides a menu-driven front end to operate the database. The menu offers selections for inputting records, extracting records, sorting extracted records, and deleting records. What you get when you use _MAKEDATABASE is *not* likely to provide enough control over user input for the final, finished version of your project, but it instantly builds a robust working model.

To experiment with _MAKEDATABASE, first get a clear worksheet. Then File Open MACTOOLS.WK1, and immediately File Save As; call the new file EMPDATA. To invoke the _MAKEDATABASE subroutine, do an ALT+F3 and select _MAKEDATABASE. Figure 16.16 shows what you should see in the control panel.

FIGURE 16.16

Initial _MAKEDATABASE Screen

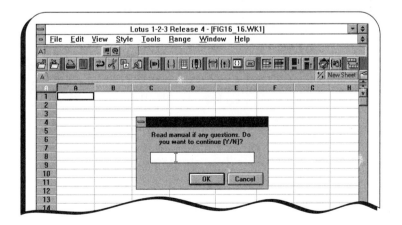

How "sizable" the blank area needs to be, depends on how many field names your database will have. _MAKEDATABASE writes header information into two columns for every field name you provide. The simplest way to be sure you have enough room is to begin with a copy of the MACTOOLS worksheet such as EMPDATA, and begin your database in the home area of the screen. If you have *not* picked out a large blank area in which to create your database, type N at the preceding screen. Otherwise, select Y to get the screen shown in Figure 16.17.

FIGURE 16.17

Selecting the Setup Location

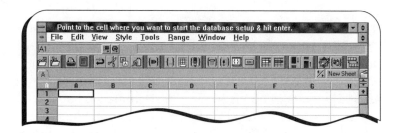

When you hit ENTER, you should see a control panel display like the one shown in Figure 16.18.

FIGURE 16.18

Field Name Input

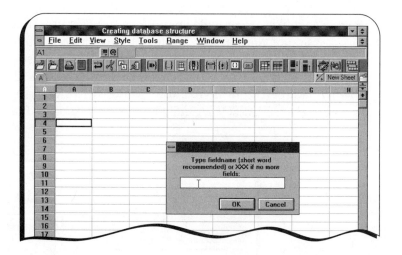

Begin typing your field names. The _MAKEDATABASE macro will automatically set up your fields in adjacent columns, as shown in Figure 16.19. In this example, we have provided the three field names shown, and then typed "XXX" to indicate we have no more field names.

FIGURE 16.19
Halting Field
Name Input

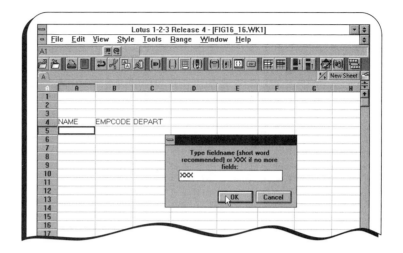

Next, the _MAKEDATABASE macro handles the details of copying your selected field names to the necessary ranges. Then it automatically attaches a generic, menu-driven front end for your new database, and pops the menu into the control panel as shown in Figure 16.20.

FIGURE 16.20
_MAKEDATABASE
Menu

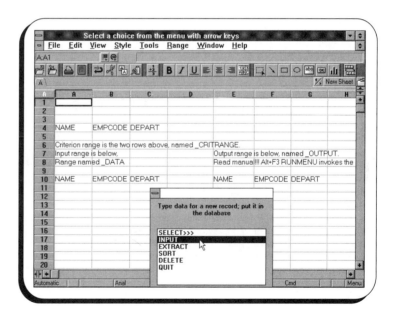

The menu macro created by _MAKEDATABASE is named _RUNMENU. _RUNMENU offers a quick-and-dirty way to handle data input, record extraction, sorting, and deleting. The QUIT choice drops you to Ready mode. If you select QUIT, you can run the menu again by pressing ALT+F3 and selecting _RUNMENU.

_RUNMENU provides a functional system, but remember it is only a starting place. You can customize its code any way you want to, for example, by changing the generic routines for input and so forth by plugging various subroutines into the menu subroutines. You also can customize the database by changing column widths and formats to meet your needs.

MACRO SORTING WITH THE { _SORT1KEY ... } SUBROUTINE

One of the subroutines in MACTOOLS is a generic single-key sort program, called _SORT1KEY. _SORT1KEY requires these parameters:

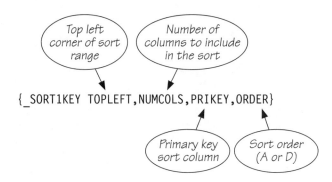

Writing a reliable macro sort program also is a fairly involved procedure. MACTOOLS subroutine sorting, on the other hand, is a snap. Consider the example shown in Figure 16.21.

FIGURE 16.21
Unsorted Data

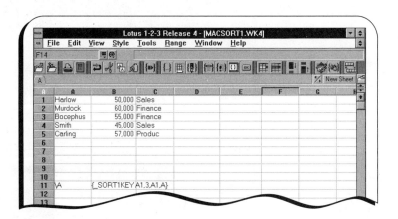

After you run the macro with CTRL+A, you should see the screen in Figure 16.22.

FIGURE 16.22

Data After
Macro Sort

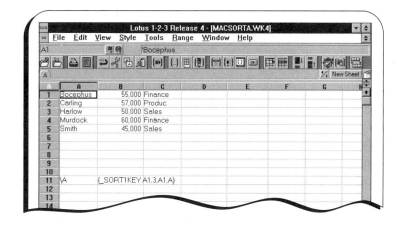

If you needed a macro that sorts on the second column, you could set up one like this:

\B   {_SORT1KEY A1,3,B1,A}

*Primary sort
key is B1.*

A TWO-KEY SORT   The MACTOOLS subroutine {_SORT2KEYS ...} automates the process of two-key "yellow page" sorting. The subroutine is invoked like this:

{_SORT2KEYS TOPLEFT,NUMCOLS,PRIKEY,ORDER1,SECKEY,ORDER2}

where

TOPLEFT is the upper left corner of the sort range.

NUMCOLS is the number of columns to be included.

PRIKEY is the primary sort key column.

ORDER1 is the primary sort key order (A or D).

SECKEY is the secondary sort key column.

ORDER2 is the secondary sort key order (A or D).

For example, consider the macro shown in Figure 16.23.

FIGURE 16.23
Macro for
Two-Key Sort

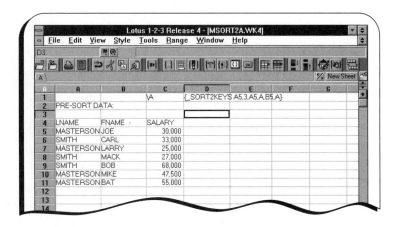

The parameters have this significance:

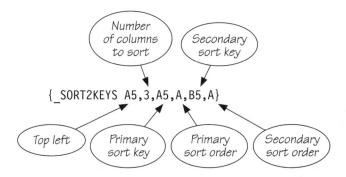

When the macro runs, notice the effect as shown in Figure 16.24.

FIGURE 16.24
Data After
Two-Key Macro Sort

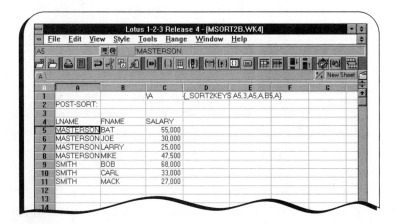

The primary sort key, column A, is sorted ascending. Note that all the MASTERSON records come before the SMITH records. The secondary sort key, column B, is also sorted ascending. You can see this because the order of FNAMEs for records with the same LNAMEs is also ordered. To change the sort order, all you need to do is modify the macro's parameters, as shown in Figure 16.25.

FIGURE 16.25
Sort Order Switched
to Descending

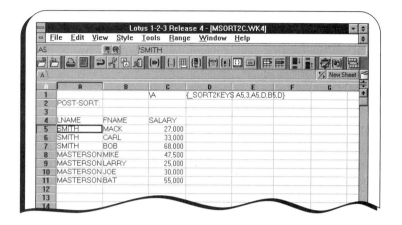

In the preceding sort, the primary and secondary sort orders have been switched to Descending.

OTHER MACTOOLS MODULAR ROUTINES

The MACTOOLS worksheet on your SMART diskette contains many other modular routines that we will not cover here. They are provided both for immediate use and as a guide to developing your own subroutines. You will find comments on how to use the routines in the MACTOOLS appendix, Appendix C.

Congratulations. Due to your 1-2-3 macro prowess, you have been hired as a consultant to the Laredo & Western Railroad (LWRR), a small common carrier. LWRR has 7 locomotive engines. Each engine *must* be inspected every 92 days, without fail, or federal inspectors will be all over LWRR like ugly on an ape.

Each time an engine is inspected, a document showing the engine serial number and the date of inspection goes to LWRR headquarters. For the inspectors, LWRR has to keep a complete historical log showing each engine number and each date of inspection.

Currently, clerical workers use 1-2-3 to input the data, but they make many errors. The engine serial numbers are hard to type correctly, and the dates also cause input trouble.

LWRR will pay you $5000 for a macro-driven worksheet that does the job. LWRR wants the most painless, and the most accurate, data input system you can develop. The clerks should *not* have to manually key in the engine serial numbers, for obvious reasons of data integrity. Likewise, the clerks should *not* have to key in the date. Your macro should generate data like this:

```
LWRR DATABASE

ENGINE     DATE_INSP
TXR45KZ1   15-Jul-95
BD21TX12   16-Jul-95
TXR45KZ1   15-Oct-95
```

Notice that a given locomotive will recur in the list; the list will get longer and longer as time passes. Normally the DATE_INSP will be the current date, but it might be plus or minus a few days. The serial numbers of the seven locomotives are:

```
TXR45KZ1
BD21TX12
R2D46W12
TXR45K4E
EE23QA33
KK3D3Z21
AB2CC34C
```

Write the macro using the appropriate MACTOOLS subroutines.

None for this chapter.

Using the SMART Auto-Checking Problem Set

Learning to use Lotus 1-2-3 is somewhat like learning to pilot an airplane. Studying printed material helps, but you will never master the art without lots of hands-on practice. That is where the disk in the back of this book comes in.

INTRODUCTION TO THE SMART PROBLEMS

The diskette contains a set of 39 1-2-3 exercises known as SMART problems. The SMART problems (short for Self-Marking, Auto-Recording Template) are coordinated with the chapters in the text. They can be used as homework assignments, as lab work, or, for that matter, as tests.

The big advantage of SMART problems is that you get instant feedback on your progress (and your mistakes). As you work through a SMART exercise, the SMART system checks your work at your command.

MAKE A BACKUP COPY OF YOUR SMART DISK

There are hundreds of ways to ruin a floppy diskette. To protect your investment in your SMART disk, make a backup copy before you begin using it. If you do not know how to copy a diskette, find someone who does and get them to make a backup for you. Put the backup disk in a safe place and use it if the original SMART disk goes bad.

If your SMART diskette goes bad and you do not have a backup disk, find a classmate who *did* make a backup, and ask or, if necessary, beg to make a copy of your prudent classmate's backup disk.

USING THE SMART DISKETTE

To work on a SMART problem, place your SMART diskette in the diskette drive and launch Lotus 1-2-3. Then follow these steps:

1. Select Tools User Setup and make A:\ the Worksheet directory. The programs inside SMART problems have to look on your diskettte for other files besides the problem you are working on; this step is important.

2. The first time you use the SMART disk, open the SID.WK4 file. It asks you for Student IDentification information (your name and class identifier such as MIS2323.010 for course and section). Your responses will be stored on disk in a text file named SID. In the future, you will not have to type the information again; SMART will look in the SID text file to determine who you are.

3. Open the SMART worksheet of your choice.

4. Leave your SMART diskette in the drive as you work. Do not remove it. Occasionally the SMART system writes information to the diskette. If it is not in the drive SMART cannot maintain its records.

When you open a SMART problem, you will see the introductory dialog box shown in Figure A.1.

FIGURE A.1
SMART Introductory
Dialog Box

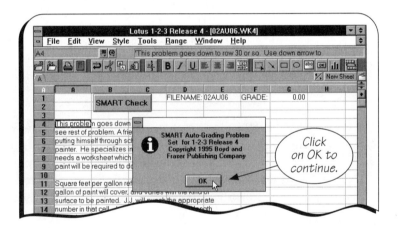

The introductory dialog box is just a reminder that the problems are copyrighted. Click on OK to continue.

USING THE SMART AUTO-CHECKER

Yellow cells are for your answers. To check your work in a SMART problem, either click on the SMART Check button or press CTRL+A. When you run the checker, SMART examines your answers. Correct answers are turned green; incorrect answers are turned red. On some large problems where you copy formulas to big ranges, SMART checks only some of the yellow cells. You can tell which cells SMART checks because they will either be green (correct) or red (incorrect).

After SMART finishes checking your problem, you should see the dialog box shown in Figure A.2.

FIGURE A.2
SMART Post-Check
Dialog Box

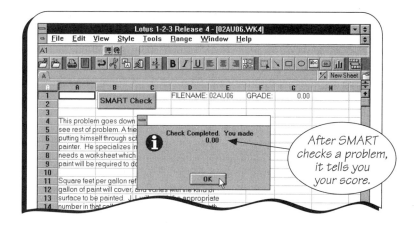

The dialog box tells you your current score on the problem. In the preceding example, some additional work would be in order!

You can run the SMART checker any time you see the Ready mode indicator in the status bar. You do not have to complete the entire problem before running the checker. If you are working on a complicated problem, you may want to run the checker frequently to determine whether you are on the right track. After you run the checker, fix your mistakes in the cells that SMART did not turn green. Keep working and running the checker until you have the maximum possible points.

In addition to flagging your mistakes, the SMART system also maintains an on-disk record of your progress. As you work through the exercises, a file called GRADES.PRN (on your diskette) gradually gets bigger and bigger. GRADES.PRN is a plain-text file that automatically receives a record each time you use the SMART checker on an exercise. Among other information, GRADES.PRN records what score you make each time you run the SMART checker.

You can look at GRADES.PRN at any time, by editing it with a word processor or by importing it into a 1-2-3 worksheet. Your instructor may take up your disk and examine your GRADES.PRN file. However, your instructor has other SMART-related tools besides GRADES.PRN if he or she wants to track your performance. It is not advisable to change anything in the GRADES.PRN file.

SMART FILENAME CONVENTIONS

The various SMART worksheets on your disk have filenames such as 01AU03. The first two digits tell what chapter the worksheet is geared to. For example, the filename **01**AU03 is geared to Chapter 1. The first letter (01**A**U03, in this case) tells you how hard the exercise is. A means easy; B means somewhat more challenging; and C means advanced. Most of your exercises will be "A" level. The second letter (01A**U**03, in this example) tells you whether the exercise is Untimed or Timed. U means you are not racing against the clock. T means SMART starts a clock as soon as you retrieve the exercise from disk, and you have only a set number of minutes to complete the exercise. The last two digits (01AU**03**, in this example) tell you the maximum point value of the exercise. 01AU**03** gives you 3 points if you do everything correctly.

As another example of how SMART filenames work, consider the filename **11CU18**. The first two digits, **11**, tell you it is designed to go with Chapter 11. The letter **C** tells you it is advanced. The letter **U** tells you it is Untimed. The last two digits, **18**, tell you it is worth 18 points.

SAVING YOUR SMART WORKSHEETS TO DISK

Treat your SMART problems like any other 1-2-3 worksheet: Get in the habit of saving them to disk every five or ten minutes. Doing frequent saves should become a kneejerk reflex as you use this book, and also for the rest of your career as a Lotus 1-2-3 user.

WHAT NOT TO DO ON SMART EXERCISES

The SMART system is easy to use. However, you can avoid difficulties if you follow these guidelines.

Do Not Copy Worksheets

Do not copy someone else's partially (or fully) completed SMART worksheet. SMART "stamps" all worksheets with your name and class. If it finds a conflict between the stamp and your own name and class, it displays the dialog box, as indicated in Figure A.3.

FIGURE A.3
SMART "Bad
SID" Screen

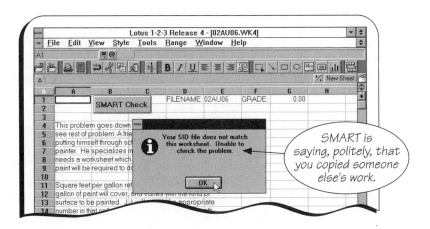

SMART will not check if it detects a SID problem. If that happens, you will have to start the exercise over, using an original, unchecked copy of the exercise.

Do Not Insert, Delete, or Move

Do not insert new rows or columns into a SMART worksheet. Do not delete existing rows or columns from a SMART worksheet. Do not move the material in a SMART worksheet from one place to another.

SMART has a built-in list of cell addresses to check on each exercise. If you insert or delete rows or columns, or move blocks of cells, SMART cannot check your work accurately. If you do insert, delete, or move within a problem, you will have to obtain an original copy of the problem and do it over.

Do Not Tamper with SMART Program Areas

Do not tamper with or erase anything in the top two rows of any SMART worksheet. These two top rows always contain SMART macro instructions. If you alter or erase them, SMART will not work. Sometimes SMART also will use cells in other (remote) parts of the worksheet. Do not alter or erase them. The SMART cells will not be in any part of the worksheet that will interfere with your work on the exercise.

Do Not Generate ERR or NA

The SMART checker will refuse to check a worksheet that contains any ERR cells (caused by invalid formulas like +A1/0) or NA cells (caused by placing @NA in a cell). If SMART detects any ERR or NA cells, it beeps and shows you a dialog box identifying the problem. For example, if you have ERR in a formula, you would see the screen in Figure A.4 when you run the checker.

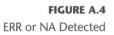

FIGURE A.4
ERR or NA Detected

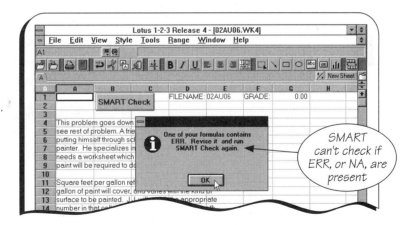

SMART cannot check your work when ERR or NA is present. The solution is to eliminate the offending ERR or NA cells, and then run the checker again.

Do Not Alter Range Names

The SMART checker makes use of many macro range names. Do not delete or change any of them or the checker will not work.

COPYING THE SMART DISKETTE TO A HARD DRIVE

If you copy your SMART disk to a subdirectory on a hard drive, be sure to copy the SID file into the subdirectory and the GRADES.PRN file into the root directory. SMART expects to find GRADES.PRN in the root, not in a subdirectory. If SMART cannot find GRADES.PRN in the root directory, it cannot update GRADES.PRN. Consequently GRADES.PRN will not fully reflect your progress through the SMART problem set.

TROUBLESHOOTING

SMART provides diagnostic dialog boxes for most problems. The following list discusses a few situations in which you don't get a dialog box.

Problem: Nothing happens when you click the Check Problem button.

Diagnosis and Solution: *You either deleted a range name, or inserted or deleted rows or columns. Don't save the worksheet to disk. Close the file without saving, and open it again. If you already have saved your file to disk before noticing the problem, the only solution is to get a fresh, unused copy of the file (you did make a backup copy, didn't you?).*

Problem: SMART checks your work, but it hits the wrong cells and you get a grade of zero.

Diagnosis and Solution: *You inserted or deleted rows or columns or moved data, changing some of the cell references that SMART is programmed to check. You may be able to mend the damage by inserting a row or column where you deleted one, or deleting a row or column where you inserted one. If that doesn't work, don't save your work to disk; close the file without saving it and open it again.*

If you already saved your file to disk before you noticed the problem, the only solution is to get a fresh, unused copy of the file.

Problem: Some of previously yellow cells are now red or green, but SMART is not checking them at all.

Diagnosis and Solution: *As noted earlier, SMART does not necessarily check every cell in larger problems. All the cells where you should put a formula start out yellow, but if you run the checker, get red or green cells, and then copy the red or green cell across a range, the color goes with the copy and replaces the cells' prior color. Since SMART pays no attention to cells it doesn't check, it will not recolor unchecked cells whose color you changed.*

SMART still works correctly; the color of unchecked cells does not matter. If you wish, you can use _Style _Lines & Color to restore the colors, but it is not necessary.

You cannot change your score by deliberately changing cell colors!

Problem: No cells are red when the check finishes, but SMART is not giving you full credit. (This is a problem you will not see until you begin working on the more advanced problems beginning with Chapter 7.)

Diagnosis and Solution: *Usually SMART enters different numbers into your data area and does multiple checks on your answer cells. On some of the more complex problems (such as those involving @IF statements), your answer can be correct with one set of data and incorrect with another. However, the change from red to green may be rather rapid.*

Watch carefully to see if a cell changes color repeatedly during the checking process.

Reference Guide to Selected 1-2-3 Functions

This appendix covers only the more common 1-2-3 functions. There are scores of specialized functions for mathematics, engineering, statistical analysis, financial analysis, and string manipulation. For a complete list of functions, browse the function index in Help.

@@(RANGE NAME OR ADDRESS)

Returns the *contents* of whatever cell you specified in the argument.

Example: If you placed **@@(B10)** in cell A1 and cell B10 contained the cell address C5, in cell A1 you would see the *contents* of cell C5.

@ABS(CELL REFERENCE OR PLAIN NUMBER)

Converts negatives to positives.

Example: @ABS(C4) with –5.5 in C4 gives 5.5; @ABS(C4) with 5.5 in C4 gives 5.5.

@ACOS(CELL REFERENCE OR PLAIN NUMBER)

Gives the arc cosine of the argument. The arc cosine is the angle in radians of the cosine argument. The argument has to be between –1 and +1; otherwise, you get an ERR.

@ASIN(CELL REFERENCE OR PLAIN NUMBER)

Gives the arc sine of the argument. The arc sine is the angle in radians of the sine in the argument.

@ATAN(CELL REFERENCE OR PLAIN NUMBER)

Gives the arc tangent of the argument. This is the angle in radians of the tangent used as the argument.

@AVG(RANGE)

Gives the arithmetic average of the values in the range, but any label cells in the range are evaluated like numeric zeros. *See also* @PUREAVG.

@CELL("ATTRIBUTE",RANGE)

Gives information about the characteristics of the cell specified as the range. The most commonly used attributes are "Contents" and "Type." Like the related function @CELLPOINTER, the @CELL function is used almost entirely in macro programming.

Example: @CELL("CONTENTS", A1..A1) would return the label "Hello" if cell A1 contained "Hello."

@CELLPOINTER("ATTRIBUTE")

Returns information about the current location of the cellpointer, such as whether the cellpointer location is blank. Seldom used except in advanced macros.

Example: @CELLPOINTER("TYPE") would return "b" if the current cellpointer location was blank.

@CHAR(CELL REFERENCE OR PLAIN NUMBER)

Gives the character equivalent of the integer number in the referenced cell (or the plain number). Since characters only go through 255, you will get an ERR if the cell ref or number is greater than 255 (or less than 1). This is a seldom-used function. *See also* @CODE.

@CHOOSE(KEY VALUE,LIST OF VALUES OR CELL REFERENCES TO CHOOSE FROM)

Selects an item from the list whose POSITION in the list corresponds to the key value. The key value can be a plain number, a formula, or a cell reference. @CHOOSE is somewhat tricky because the key value starts at zero, rather than one. That is, to pick the first item from the list of values, the key would have to be 0 rather than 1. To pick the last item, the key would have to be one less than the number of items in the list. The function @CHOOSE(0,43,55,67) gives 43 because the key—0—means take the *first* item in the list of choices; the *first* item is 43. @CHOOSE(3,43,55,67) gives ERR because the numbering for list items goes "0,1,2" instead of "1,2,3."

@CLEAN(CELL REFERENCE OR LITERAL STRING)

Removes special control characters from the argument. You will never need it unless you import word processor documents into 1-2-3.

@CODE(CELL REFERENCE OR LITERAL STUFF IN "")

Is the flip side of @CHAR. @CODE yields the numeric code of the first character in the referenced cell or literal.

@COLS(SOME RANGE)

Tells how many columns are in the specified range.

@COUNT(RANGE OF CELLS)

Returns the number of nonblank cells in the range. "Nonblank" means numeric or label. *See also* @PURECOUNT.

@CTERM(INTEREST RATE,FUTURE VALUE,PRESENT VALUE)

Gives the number of compounding periods for the specified present value to compound to the specified future value, at the specified interest rate per period.

@DATE(LAST 2 DIGITS OF YEAR,MONTH,DAY)

Gives the number of days since December 31, 1899. You cannot use the function for a date past December 31, 2099. You nearly always will want to format the cell containing the function to convert @DATE into familiar form.

@DATEVALUE(CELL REFERENCE OR PLAIN STRING)

Converts a character string (another word for "label") into a 1-2-3 date-number. You don't need it unless someone has entered labels instead of Lotus date-numbers.

Example: If you had the label '01/01/95 in cell B2 and you placed the function @DATEVALUE(B2) in cell A1, cell A1 would show a number representing the number of days since the turn of the century.

@DAY(CELL CONTAINING A DATE VALUE)

Pulls the day of the month from the specified date.

@DAVG(INPUT RANGE,FIELD,CRITERION RANGE)

Averages the specified field *only* of the records that meet the criterion provided in the criterion range.

@DCOUNT(INPUT RANGE,FIELD,CRITERION RANGE)

Counts the nonblank cells in *only* the records that meet the criterion specified in the criterion range.

@DMAX(INPUT RANGE,FIELD,CRITERION RANGE)

Finds largest value in *only* the records that meet the criterion specified in the criterion range.

@DMIN(INPUT RANGE,FIELD,CRITERION RANGE)

Finds smallest value in *only* the records that meet the criterion specified in the criterion range.

@DSTD(INPUT RANGE,FIELD,CRITERION RANGE)

Finds standard deviation of *only* the records that meet the criterion specified in the criterion range.

@DSUM(INPUT RANGE,FIELD,CRITERION RANGE)

Finds the sum of *only* the records that meet the criterion specified in the criterion range.

@DVAR(INPUT RANGE,FIELD,CRITERION RANGE)

Finds the variance of *only* the records that meet the criterion specified in the criterion range.

@ERR

Is a function you probably will never use. It is used inside @IF statements to place the value ERR in a cell. Since ERR has a ripple effect on formulas that reference it, you are likely to wind up with a spreadsheet full of @ERRs if you use this.

Example: @IF(A1>1000,@ERR,A1*B1)

@EXACT(LABEL1,LABEL2)

Gives 1 if both labels are exactly the same, including case and spaces; otherwise, it gives 0.

@EXP(NUMBER OR CELL REFERENCE)

Gives the value of *e* raised to the power found in the argument.

@FIND(SUBSTRING,STRING,STARTING POSITION)

Searches for and gives the numeric position where substring begins in string. The search of string starts at the starting position you specify.

@FV(PAYMENT,INTEREST RATE,TERM)

Gives the future value of an annuity of "payment" dollars per period, at the specified interest rate per period, for the specified number of periods (the "term").

@HLOOKUP(TEST VALUE,RANGE,ROW OFFSET)

Looks up the test value in the first row of the range. If the exact number is not found, Lotus locates the first one that is greater than the test value and then backs up to the previous value. The function returns whatever value is found the specified number of row offsets below.

@HOUR(TIMENUMBER)

Returns an hour between 0 and 23, from the number. The timenumber could be @NOW.

@IF(EXPRESSION,TRUE-VALUE-RULE,FALSE-VALUE-RULE)

Picks one of the two value rules based on whether the expression is true or false.

@INT(NUMBER OR CELL REFERENCE)

Gives the argument, stripped of decimal places.

Example: @INT(5.5) gives 5.

@IRR(DISCOUNT RATE GUESS,CASH FLOW RANGE)

Finds the discount rate that equates the value of a cash outflow with the present value of a set of cash inflows. The outflow is assumed to be immediate; the inflows occur at the end of each period. The discount rate guess is just a starting point.

@ISERR(COMPARISON)

Puts a 1 in the cell if the comparison generates a value of ERR; puts a 0 in the cell if the comparison does not result in an ERR. Normally used inside an IF function.

@ISNA(CELL REFERENCE)

Gives 1 if the cell reference contains the @NA function; otherwise, the function gives 0. Seldom used except in IF statements. If cell A1 contains NA, @ISNA(A1) would give 1.

@ISNUMBER(CELL REFERENCE)

Gives 1 if the cell reference contains a numeric value; otherwise, it gives a 0.

@ISSTRING(CELL REFERENCE)

Gives 1 if the cell reference contains character-type data; otherwise, it gives a 0.

@LEFT(CELL REFERENCE OR LITERAL STRING,NUMBER)

Starts at the left side of the argument and gives the specified number of characters. *See also* @RIGHT.

Example: @LEFT("Lotus",3) would give Lot.

@LENGTH(CELL REFERENCE OR LITERAL STRING)

Counts the number of characters in the character-type argument.

@LN(NUMBER OR CELL REFERENCE)

Gives the natural logarithm (base *e*) of the argument. If the argument is negative or zero, gives ERR.

Example: @LN(10) gives 2.302585.

@LOG(NUMBER OR CELL REFERENCE)

Gives the base 10 logarithm of the argument. If the argument is zero or negative, ERR results.

Example: @LOG(5) would give 0.698970. If cell A1 contained 10, @LOG(A1) would give 1.

@LOWER(CELL REFERENCE OR LITERAL STRING)

Converts the string data to lowercase if it was uppercase. *See also* @UPPER and @PROPER.

@MAX(RANGE)

Finds the largest value in the range. Labels are treated as zero. Consequently a range of only negative numbers, and labels, always will show 0 for the maximum. *See also* @PUREMAX.

@MIN(RANGE)

Finds the smallest number in the range. Labels are treated as zero. Consequently a range of positive numbers, and labels, always will show 0 for the minimum. *See also* @PUREMIN.

@MID(LABEL,STARTING POSITION,NUMBER OF CHARACTERS)

Returns a substring consisting of whatever characters are in the label, between the starting position and continuing the specified number of characters.

Example: If cell A1 contains the label Texas, @MID(A1,2,3) would return xas.

@MINUTE(TIMENUMBER)

Returns the minutes. Works on same principle as @HOUR.

@MOD(X,Y)

Gives the modulus of the first number or cell reference divided by the second. The modulus is the leftovers from the division process.

Example: @MOD(10,6) would give 4 because 6 goes into 10 once with a leftover of 4.

@MONTH(DATE-NUMBER)

Pulls the month number from the date-number.

@N(RANGE OR CELL ADDRESS)

Returns a 1 if the argument is numeric, or 0 if it is a label or blank. Used in macros.

@NA

Gives the value NA to the cell. Seldom used except inside an IF statement.

@NOW

Gives current date and time, and it gets updated during every recalc.

@NPV(DISCOUNT RATE,CASH FLOW RANGE)

Gives the present value of a series of cash flows at the specified discount rate. The discount rate can be either a plain decimal number or a cell reference.

@PI

Gives the value of pi.

@PMT(LOAN AMOUNT,INTEREST RATE PER PERIOD,NUMBER OF PERIODS)

Gives the periodic payment necessary to amortize a level-payment loan.

@PROPER(CELL REFERENCE OR LITERAL STRING)

Converts the string data so that the first letter in each word is uppercase.

@PUREAVG(RANGE)

Gives the arithmetic average of the values in the range, but any label cells in the range are ignored. *See also* @AVG.

@PURECOUNT(RANGE)

Returns the number of numeric cells in the range. Label cells in the range are ignored. *See also* @COUNT.

@PUREMAX(RANGE)

Finds the largest numeric value in the range. Labels are ignored. *See also* @MAX.

@PUREMIN(RANGE)

Finds the smallest numeric value in the range. Labels are ignored. *See also* @MIN.

@PV(PERIODIC PAYMENT,INTEREST RATE PER PERIOD,NUMBER OF PERIODS)

Gives the present value of an ordinary annuity.

Example: @PV(100,.12,4). Also works with cell references, of course.

@RAND

Generates a random number between 0 and 1.

@RATE(FUTURE VALUE,PRESENT VALUE,NUMBER OF PERIODS)

Gives the interest rate per period that will compound the PV to the FV in the specified number of periods.

@REPEAT(CELL REFERENCE OR LITERAL STRING,NUMBER)

Is mainly a fun-type function. It duplicates the string the number of times you specify.

Example: @REPEAT("JOE",4) gives JOEJOEJOEJOE.

@RIGHT(CELL REFERENCE OR LITERAL STRING,NUMBER)

Starts at the right end of the argument and picks off the specified number of characters. *See also* @LEFT.

@ROWS(RANGE)

Tells how many rows are in the specified range. Has its uses in macros.

@ROUND(NUMBER OR CELL REFERENCE,NUMBER OF DIGITS)

Gives a number rounded to the specified number of digits. This is not the same as using /Range Format to control how many decimal places are displayed on the screen. In fact, the main use of @ROUND is to make a formatted column of numbers seem to total properly.

Example: If you had a column of large numbers—say, from a financial statement— formatted in Comma format with no decimal places, the displayed total might not exactly agree with the sum of the actual numbers.

@SQRT(NUMBER OR CELL REFERENCE)

Gives the square root of the argument.

@STD(RANGE)

Gives the standard deviation of the numbers in the cell range.

@STRING(CELL REFERENCE OR LITERAL NUMBER,NUMBER)

Creates a string from the numeric argument. The string will have the specified number of places to the right of the decimal. Used to convert a number for use in string concatenation.

@SUM(RANGE)

Gives the sum of all the numbers in the specified range of cells. Blank cells and label cells are ignored.

@TERM(ANNUITY PAYMENT,INTEREST RATE,FUTURE VALUE)

Gives the number of periods for an ordinary annuity to compound to the specified future value at the specified interest rate per period.

@TIME(HOUR,MINUTE,SECOND)

Normally used with D6 format to give a human-readable display.

Example: @TIME(9,45,30) would give a strange fractional number unless you put it in D6 format to show 9:45:30.

@TIMEVALUE(LABEL)

Converts the label to a time value.

Example: @TIMEVALUE(A1) would return 0.50000 if A1 contained the label '12:00 PM.

@TODAY

Gives the date-number from the system clock.

@TRIM(CELL REFERENCE OR LITERAL STRING)

Chops out any leading and trailing spaces and puts only one space between words. This can be handy if you are using Lotus to print mailing labels from a database. It lets you make the labels neat.

Example: @TRIM("   555   Oak   ") gives 555 Oak.

@UPPER(CELL REFERENCE OR LITERAL STRING)

Converts the argument to all uppercase. *See also* @LOWER and @PROPER.

Example: @UPPER("doGgo") gives DOGGO.

@VALUE(LABEL)

Returns the numeric equivalent of the label.

Example: @VALUE(A1) would return the number 100, if cell A1 contained the label '100.00.

@VAR(RANGE)

Gives the variance of the numbers in the cell range.

@VLOOKUP(TEST VALUE,RANGE,OFFSET)

Does a vertical table lookup and gives the value of the cell at the offset position.

@YEAR(DATE NUMBER)

Pulls the year from the argument. The argument is @TODAY, @DATE(YY,MM,DD), or a reference to a cell containing @TODAY or @DATE.

Subroutines in the MACTOOLS Worksheet

{_ALARM n} *needs a numeric parameter*

> _ALARM provides a convenient way to sound an attention-getting warble-type sound. The bigger the parameter, the longer the sound goes on. Normally you would use ALARM if the user made some mistake or if some error condition is found in the worksheet.

> *Examples:*

{_ALARM 10}	sounds the warble for about 1/2 second.
{_ALARM 20}	sounds the warble for about 1 second.
{IF B100>65}{_ALARM 12}	when called as part of an IF.

{_AUTODATE} *needs no parameter*

> _AUTODATE puts the date from the system clock in the current cell, widens the column to a width of 10 if necessary to display the date properly, formats the cell, and then allows the user to kick the date up or down with the arrow keys. This is far easier and more foolproof than expecting the user to input a valid date by manually using the @DATE function.

> *Example:* Move the cellpointer to whatever cell you want, then call the AUTO-DATE routine:

```
{SELECT A20}     positions the cellpointer
{_AUTODATE}      calls the routine
```

{_AUTOTIME}   *needs no parameter*

_AUTOTIME allows user to increment or decrement the time number in the current cell by pressing the up arrow to kick the number up by 1 minute or the down arrow to decrease by 1; or the PageUp key to kick up 30 minutes; or the PageDown key to kick down by 30 minutes. This routine is great for getting times interactively from the user.

_AUTOTIME initially places the fractional part of @NOW in the current cell. For example, if the result of @NOW is 33456.50000, meaning it is 12 PM, _AUTOTIME places 0.500000 in the current cell.

Example: {SELECT A12}   send cellptr to A12
             {_AUTOTIME}   calls the routine

To set both the date and the time:

{SELECT A12}
{_AUTODATE}
{RIGHT}
{_AUTOTIME}

You can use two _AUTOTIMEs to compute the elapsed time between two events during the same day, just as you can use _AUTODATE to compute the elapsed days between two dates. You can also combine them to compute the elapsed days *and* fractions of a day.

{_BLANKLABEL prompt}   *where prompt is the desired user prompt*

_BLANKLABEL allows the user either to type some characters or to avoid typing characters by pressing ↵. Unlike simple GETLABEL, however, _BLANKLABEL does *not* put a label prefix in the current cell if the user presses ↵ or ESC. Instead it leaves the current cell entirely blank.

Example: {_BLANKLABEL "Type firmname or enter to quit "}

{_CRITDATES location}   *needs a parameter in the form of a cell address or range name; the parameter is the top cell in a database field of interest*

_CRITDATES is a specialized database search routine. It gives your macro a quick way to build a complex database date search criterion. For example, if you have a column of date fields and you need to place a formula in the Criterion range that will extract records whose date field falls between two dates, use _CRITDATES. The parameter you send to _CRITDATES is automatically built into the criterion formula.

Example: {_CRITDATES AX299}

{_CRITNUMBERS location}   *needs a parameter in the form of a cell address or range name; the parameter is the top cell in a database field of interest*

_CRITNUMBERS is a specialized routine designed to solve a rather complicated, but common, database problem. It automatically fetches a min and a max number for a field search, and then builds a search expression in the current cell location, which should be the appropriate cell in the Criterion range of the database you are working with. The parameter is the cell address or range name of the top cell in the search column.

Example: {_CRITNUMBERS OWES} top cell of search column is named OWES.

{_CHEKBLANK}   *needs no parameter; automatically sets _ONBLANK*

_CHEKBLANK checks to see if the current cell is blank. It will work for either row or column processing. Typically you would call _CHEKBLANK in a loop; then use {IF} to see if _ONBLANK is true. _CHEKBLANK puts a "false" in _ONBLANK if the current cell has something in it, that is, if the current cell is nonblank. _CHEKBLANK puts a "true" in _ONBLANK if the current cell is blank.

Example: \F
```
         {Your custom code might go here}
         {DOWN}
         {_CHEKBLANK}
         {IF _ONBLANK}{RETURN}
         {BRANCH \F}
```

{_CLEANMAC}   *needs no parameter*

The purpose of _CLEANMAC is to ferret out accidental leading or trailing blanks in your code, or a nonblank cell below a macro, or a numeric cell within a macro, all of which cause crashes, sudden terminations, or weird results. Trailing blanks in particular are a common culprit in buggy macros.

Tip: Always run _CLEANMAC on any macro that seems to do screwy things.

Typically you would put the cellpointer on the first cell of the macro and do an ALT+F3 to bring up the range name menu. Select _CLEANMAC. _CLEANMAC then boogies down your code column, looking for problems.

{_FILESAVE name,contingency-macro}   *needs 2 parameters*

_FILESAVE allows you to control what filename the users save under. _FILESAVE also avoids crashing your macro if there is a disk error (such as no disk in the data drive) during a file save.

Example: {_FILESAVE BUDGET,\A} means to save the current worksheet under the filename BUDGET, and if the operation causes a system error, branch to the macro named \A.

Typically \A would be a menu macro. The second parameter is necessary because the Lotus system error trapper operates like an unconditional BRANCH.

{_FINDBOTTOM location} *parameter is the starting address or range name*

The _FINDBOTTOM subroutine automatically finds the first blank cell in the column below location. It prevents disasters such as saying {END}{DOWN} {DOWN} when there is nothing to stop the cellpointer from shooting all the way to the bottom of the worksheet.

Example: {_FINDBOTTOM B100} searches for the first blank cell in the column beginning in B100 and puts the cellpointer on that cell.

If B100 were blank, the cellpointer would be placed on B100. If B100 were nonblank but B101 were blank, the cellpointer would be placed on B101. If B100..B200 were nonblank, the cellpointer would be placed on B201.

_FINDBOTTOM also works with range names. If cell K34 were named HORSES, you could use {_FINDBOTTOM HORSES} and get the same result as if you had used {_FINDBOTTOM K34}.

{_GOODLABEL prompt} *needs prompt string as parameter*

_GOODLABEL forces the user to type some characters, and it automatically stores the user's response in the current cell. The purpose of _GOODLABEL is to maintain data integrity; the user cannot bypass the required cell entry, and any leading or trailing blanks are automatically trimmed. If the user hit the spacebar and entered " Smith", the cell entry would contain the trimmed version, "Smith". This trimming process is important if you plan to sort the data or do database operations with it because " Smith " does not equal "Smith", or "Smith " either.

Example:
```
{_GOODLABEL "Type customer last name: "}
{_FINDBOTTOM A100}
{_GOODLABEL "Type customer last name: "}
{RIGHT}
{_GOODLABEL "Type customer I.D. number: "}
```

{_GOODNUMBER prompt} *needs prompt string as parameter*

_GOODNUMBER forces the user to type a valid number, and it automatically stores the number in the current cell. _GOODNUMBER does not return control to the calling program until the user types a good number—ESC or ↵ or any other nonnumeric entry such as "ABC" has no effect. If you use the built-in Lotus {GETNUMBER..} subroutine, the target cell will contain ERR if the user intentionally or accidentally hits ESC or ↵ with no input. The purpose of _GOODNUMBER is to maintain data integrity.

Example: First get the cellpointer to the desired input cell. Then if you want a "Please type the dollar amount: " prompt, you would use:

```
{_GOODNUMBER "Please type the dollar amount: "}
```

{_GOODSSN}   *needs no parameters*

_GOODSSN allows the user to type in a social security number (actually a label) in the format X99-99-9999. The user's input is placed in whatever cell the cellpointer is in when the subroutine is called. The dashes are supplied automatically. The first character can be a digit or an alpha because some SSNs begin with "N" instead of a digit. All the other characters must be digits. _GOODSSN enforces these rules and does not allow the user to type an invalid SSN such as "ABC-33-565T". The purpose of _GOODSSN is to maintain data integrity. If SSNs are not input consistently, any sorts or database operations you do on the data will not work correctly. For example, without such control, some users may type in social security numbers without dashes, and others may type them with dashes. If you then sort the data by the SSN column, the records will not be in the expected order.

Example: {_GOODSSN} allows the user to input something like 453-76-6598 or N54-67-8767.

{_HUGEMENU range}   *needs a range or range name parameter*

_HUGEMENU gets around the 9-menu-choice limitation of standard Lotus macro menus. With _HUGEMENU you can set up a very large, picklist-type menu, either in a column or a rectangular block.

_HUGEMENU lets the user point to any choice in a block of menu choices. The one selected is run as a subroutine out of _HUGEMENU. By using _HUGEMENU instead of the standard Lotus menu, you can have an unlimited number of menu choices rather than only 9. Each menu choice in the parameter supplied to _HUGEMENU must be the name of a macro. If the user selects a _HUGEMENU item that is not the name of a macro, _HUGEMENU crashes with the message {Unrecognized key/range name {...}

Example: For brevity, the following setup has actual menu choices only in A3..A7. The adjacent labels in column B serve the same purpose as the bottom line in a regular Lotus menu. Although the following example provides only 5 choices, you could have 50, or 500, if you wished. You also could omit the descriptors and fill a rectangular block of the screen such as C10..F50 with menu choices.

```
    ----A---- -----------B----------- -----C-----
  1                                   {_HUGEMENU A3..A7}
  2  SELECT A CHOICE FROM THIS MENU:
  3  SORTL    Sort by Lastname
  4  SORTSSN  Sort by SS Nunber
  5  PRINT1   Print balance sheet
  6  PRINT2   Print income statement
  7  \QUIT\   Consolidate
  8  any number of additional choices ...
  9
```

When the macro runs, the specified range (A3..A7 in this example) is automatically unprotected; the cellpointer pops to the top left cell of the range; and the user can use the pointer movement keys to move the cellpointer from choice to choice. When the user presses ↵, _HUGE-MENU treats the contents of the selected cell as the name of a macro and runs the macro as a subroutine.

When the called macro finishes, _HUGEMENU redisplays the menu—unless the called macro somehow broke the subroutine chain by issuing, say, a {QUIT} command.

For example, if the user selected cell A5, which contains the label PRINT1, _HUGEMENU would treat PRINT1 as a subroutine. If the user selected A7, _HUGEMENU would treat \QUIT\ as a subroutine. As you probably already know, you cannot use a reserved word such as QUIT as the name of a macro. That is why cell A7 contains the label \QUIT\ rather than simply QUIT.

If the user selects a blank cell within the range, _HUGEMENU ignores that choice and waits for another. Of course, you normally would not leave any blank cells in your menu range.

{_INPUTBOX range,datatype} *needs two parameters; the range is the allowable input area and the data type is ANYTHING or NUMBERS*

_INPUTBOX is based on the native Lotus {FORM} command, but is considerably easier to use.

_INPUTBOX allows data entry in a range with either no control over the kind of input, or with input limited to numbers only. If you do not need the tight control of MINMAXNUM and you do not want to bother with repeated {NUMIN} commands, use _INPUTBOX.

Example: If you want to let the user move the cellpointer to any one of the cells in the range B50..B80, but you want to be sure the user inputs only numbers, use

```
{_INPUTBOX B50..B80,NUMBERS}
```

The user then could put numbers into any one or all of the cells in that range. Input stops when the user presses ↵ twice, or uses the arrow keys to go to a new cell and presses ↵ with no input.

To allow any sort of input—labels or numbers—in a range, use

```
{_INPUTBOX B50..B80,ANYTHING}
```

{_KILLFORMULA} *needs no parameter*

_KILLFORMULA is a very simple routine; its only purpose is to strip the formula out of a cell and leave the numeric (or string) result. You need to do this if the formula's result will change as the macro continues.

Example: In the following example, the formula +B45*_TARGET will change if the macro moves the range name _TARGET. To stabilize the value in the cell, we use _KILLFORMULA.

```
\H        {GOTO}C200~          cellptr to C200
          +B45*_TARGET~        enter a formula in the cell;
          {_KILLFORMULA}       kill formula; leave only the result
```

{_LABIN}   *needs no parameter*

The _LABIN macro gets LABel INput into the current cell. It does not allow the user to short-circuit by pressing ESC or ↵; the cellpointer remains on the current cell until some sort of label input is typed. LABIN also trims any leading or trailing blanks. The built-in prompt is: "Type response and hit enter: ". *Note:* If you need to supply a customized prompt, use GOODLABEL.

Example: `{_FINDBOTTOM B200}`
             `{LABIN}`

{_LASTCOL n}   *needs numeric parameter representing rightmost column—the rightward boundary*

_LASTCOL tests the current cellpointer position to see if the cellpointer is on the specified "last" column specified by the parameter. The parameter for _LASTCOL has to be a value—it cannot be a range name. _LASTCOL puts a "false" in the range name _ONLASTCOL unless the cellpointer has reached the designated column (A is 1; B is 2, and so on); then _LASTCOL changes _ONLASTCOL to "true." Basically, _LASTCOL allows a list-processing macro (moving column to column) to know when to quit.

Example:

```
\A        {SELECT A40}
CONTIN    {RIGHT}
          {WHATEVER CODE YOU NEED GOES HERE}
          {_LASTCOL 4}                           Check to see if in col D
          {IF #NOT#_ONLASTCOL}{BRANCH CONTIN}    Will stop in col D
```

{_LASTROW n}   *needs a numeric parameter*

_LASTROW puts a "false" in the range name _ONLASTROW unless the cellpointer has reached the designated row; then _LASTROW changes _ONLASTROW to "true." Basically, _LASTROW allows a list-processing macro (moving down a column) to know when to quit.

Example:
```
\A        {SELECT A40}
CONTIN    {DOWN}
          {WHATEVER CODE YOU NEED GOES HERE}
          {_LASTROW 60}
          {IF #NOT#_ONLASTROW}{BRANCH CONTIN}
```

{_LITEBAR prompt} *needs label-type parameter max 76 chars*

The _LITEBAR routine places a message in the title bar.

Example: {_LITEBAR "HOW DOES IT WORK"} places the message "HOW DOES IT WORK" in the title bar.

{_LOOKTO location} *requires a range such as A40..B50 or the range name of a range*

_LOOKTO gives you a way to allow the user to browse around in a specified range within the worksheet without being able to change anything in that range. As an added bonus, _LOOKTO records in a cell named _LOOKRESULT what the cellpointer contents was when the user pressed ↵. It also records the address of the cell in a cell named _LOOKADDR. Consequently you can use _LOOKTO as a sort of picklist that saves the picked cell address *and* picked cell contents. However, unlike _PICKLIST, this subroutine does not automatically place the picked cell contents in the original cell location.

Example: If you want the user to be able to look around in the range A100..D110, use:

```
{SELECT A100}     send cellptr to upper left corner of the area
{_LOOKTO A100..D110}     i.e., the range to allow browsing in
```

The user then could move the cellpointer to any cell in that range, but could *not* change any of the data. Whatever cell address and cell contents the pointer was on when the user pressed ↵ would be recorded in _LOOKADDR and _LOOKRESULT, respectively.

{_MAKEDATABASE} *needs no parameters, but needs lots of room!*

The _MAKEDATABASE command handles the details of database creation. _MAKEDATABASE automatically creates a 1-2-3 classic database setup, with Criterion, Input, and Output ranges, to your specifications. It also provides a menu to operate the database. The menu offers selections for inputting records, extracting records, sorting extracted records, and deleting records.

To invoke the _MAKEDATABASE supermacro from Ready mode, do an ALT+F3 and select _MAKEDATABASE. It is doubtful you would want to place the command within a macro, but that can be done simply by the command {_MAKEDATABASE}.

{_MARKTIME n} *needs a numeric parameter*

The purpose of _MARKTIME is to provide an easy way to pause a macro for a specified number of seconds.

Example: {_MARKTIME 3} pauses the macro for 3 seconds before continuing.

If we wanted to display a message in the control panel for 4 seconds before continuing the macro, we could use:

```
{_LITEBAR "This program was written by A. Bocephus"}
{_MARKTIME 4}
{INDICATE}
{MENUCALL BUDGET}
```

The message "This program was written by A. Bocephus" would be frozen in the control panel for 4 seconds before the next line, {INDICATE}, wiped it out. Then the menu would appear.

{_MINMAXNUM prompt,nlow,nhigh}   *needs 3 parameters, in this order: promptstring, low boundary number, high boundary number*

_MINMAXNUM forces the user to type a valid number within the range specified by a Lownum and a Hinum, and then automatically stores the valid number in the current cell. _MINMAXNUM works similarly to _GOODNUMBER; otherwise, its purpose is to maintain data integrity.

Example: {_MINMAXNUM "Type a # between 1 and 100: ",1,100}

In the above example, _MINMAXNUM would not return control to the calling routine until the user types a number between 1 and 100. If the user types anything else, like 0, or 101, or "HI", _MINMAXNUM will simply loop and demand another input.

Notice that _MINMAXNUM demands three parameters—a prompt string, minimum value, and a maximum value.

{_NAME rname}   *where rname is the desired range name*

_NAME attaches a range name to the cellpointer location. If the chosen range name already exists in the worksheet, it is removed and reassigned to the cellpointer location.

The effect is the same as /RNCname~~/RNDname~/RNCname~~

Example: Assume the cellpointer is on A100 and your macro gives this command:

{_NAME DOGDOG}

Cell A100 now has the range name DOGDOG. If the range name DOGDOG existed prior to the {_NAME DOGDOG} command, it got deleted from its prior location and is now attached to cell A100.

{_NAMETARGET}   *needs no parameter*

_NAMETARGET makes sure the range name TARGET is properly applied to the current cell. _NAMETARGET is most often used in complex list processing, in conjunction with _TARGETDOWN. _NAMETARGET simply established the initial name. _NAMETARGET can be used without later using _TARGETDOWN, if you need to.

Example: Assume cellpointer is working down a list, but you need to move the cellpointer to some other area each time the cellpointer finds a new item in the list:

```
     {GOTO}B100~            cellptr to start of list
     {_NAMETARGET}          name the current cell (always named _TARGET)
LOOP {YOUR CUSTOM CODE}     usually move cellptr and do something else.
     {_TARGETDOWN}          cellptr to _TARGET; drops cellptr;names _TARGET
     {_CHEKBLANK}           see if the cell to which you moved is blank
     {IF _ONBLANK}{RETURN}  if blank, we are through with this routine
     {BRANCH LOOP}          if not blank, begin reading code at LOOP
```

{_NUMIN}   *needs no parameter*

_NUMIN works like _GOODNUMBER, except it requires no prompt string.

Example: {SELECT A50}
             {NUMIN}

The prompt "Type the number: " is automatically supplied. If you need a customized prompt, use _GOODNUMBER.

{_PAUSIT prompt}   *needs parameter prompt-string*

The _PAUSIT routine is used for only one purpose: It suspends operations until the user hits a key.

Example: {_PAUSIT "Hit a key after you finish looking"}

You can use the native 1-2-3 command, {ALERT Prompt}, for the same purpose.

{_PICKBLOCK range}   *needs range as parameter*

_PICKBLOCK works like _PICKLIST except it allows the user to move the cellpointer anywhere within a multicolumn, multirow area, and select a desired cell anywhere within the range by pressing ↵. The contents of the selected cell are copied to the cell where the cellpointer was, before _PICKBLOCK was invoked. The copy is of the /Range Value type—the result, rather than any formula.

Example: {SELECT A10}
             {_PICKBLOCK B15..D25}

After the macro executes, cell A10 will contain a copy of the contents of whatever cell the user selected in the range B15..D25.

{_PICKLIST location}   *needs cell address or range name as parameter*

Range names automatically created: _PICKLOC which contains the address of the cell which the user selects.

_PICKLIST pops the cellpointer to the top of a column of items and allows the user to point to the desired item. The cellpointer cannot move outside the target column until the user hits ENTER. The chosen item is automatically put into the current cell—voila—a picklist. The purpose is to make data entry easy, and also to maintain data integrity by eliminating misspellings and similar errors.

For example, {_PICKLIST EMPLOYEES} would begin the picklist in the cell named EMPLOYEES and allow picking from there to the end of EMPLOYEES list. The picklist cannot have any blank cells, or _PICKLIST will not detect all the items. It stops when it hits a blank cell. Normally you would use {_VWINDOW n} to set up a vertical window first. *See also* _VWINDOW routine for details.

Example: (used with _VWINDOW):

```
{GOTO}A200~
{_VWINDOW 6}
{_PICKLIST EMPLOYEES}
```

{_SORT1KEY topleftcorner,numrows,keycol,sortorder}

_SORT1KEY provides an easy way to sort any number of contiguous rows and columns. It automatically detects how many contiguous rows there are by looking downward for the first blank row.

Example: {_SORT1KEY TOPLEFT,3,TOPLEFT,A}

Means start the sort in the cell with the range name TOPLEFT; sort 3 columns; primary key is the cell named TOPLEFT; the "A" means do an ASCENDING sort. "D" would specify a DESCENDING sort.

_SORT1KEY also works like {_SORT1KEY A100,3,A100,A}—i.e. addresses instead of range names. If you wanted the sort key to be some other column besides the leftmost, you might say: {_SORT1KEY A100,3,B100,D}—meaning sort all contiguous rows from A100 downward; include columns A, B, and C in the sort (the 3 says sort 3 columns); use column B as the sort key; do a DESCENDING sort.

{_SORT2KEYS topleft,numcols,prikey,primorder,seckey,secorder}

_SORT2KEYS works like _SORT1KEY with the addition of a secondary sort key and secondary sort order. This is an example of using _SORT2KEYS: {_SORT2KEYS A3,2,A3,A,B3,A} starts the sort in A3; sorts two columns, uses column A as the primary key with ascending order; uses column B as the secondary key with ascending order.

{_TARGETDOWN}   *needs no parameter*

_TARGETDOWN flips the cellpointer from wherever it is, to a cell named _TAR-GET, then moves the cellpointer down one row, and then names the new cellpointer position with the range name _TARGET. _TARGETDOWN is always used after an initial call to _NAMETARGET. Before you can use the _TARGET-DOWN routine, some cell has to be named _TARGET. The initial creation of the name _TARGET is done with the _NAMETARGET routine. Look at the example in _NAMETARGET for an example.

```
_TARGETDOWN {GOTO}_TARGET~
            {DOWN}
            {_NAMETARGET}
```

The main use of _TARGETDOWN is in complex list processing, where you need to flip the cellpointer from its position in a list, to some other location in the worksheet, then return to the original position, and move down the list.

{_UPDOWNUM}   *needs no parameter*

_UPDOWNUM allows user to increment or decrement the number in the current cell by pressing up arrow to kick the number up by 1 or down arrow to decrease by 1; or the PageUp key to kick up by 31; or the PageDown key to kick down by 31. It is great for getting various sorts of numeric data from the user. The purpose is to provide a fast, user-friendly way to change the value in a cell.

Example: {SELECT A1}   send cellptr to A1;
              {_UPDOWNUM}   allow user to change whatever # is in A1 with
                             arrow keys

{_VWINDOW n}   *needs numeric parameter*

_VWINDOW creates a vertical split screen with the specified number of columns to the right of the cellpointer location, and unsynchronizes the two screens so that the cellpointer can move independently in either.

Example: {_VWINDOW 4}

Would create a vertical split screen 4 columns to the right of wherever the cellpointer is when the subroutine is called. You may have to experiment to get the split just like you want it. After you are through with the window, use /WWC to get rid of it. To understand how it works, try this macro:

```
{_VWINDOW 3}
{_PAUSIT HI}
/WWC
```

Normally you would use _VWINDOW to set up a split screen for _PICKLIST.

The SmartIcons

SmartIcons are short cuts for certain 1-2-3 menu commands. There are seven separate icon palettes, identified by the number beneath the icons. This appendix shows each palette and discusses SmartIcon usage.

To change icon palettes, click on the icon selector in the status bar. You should see a display like Figure D.1.

FIGURE D.1

The Icon Palette List

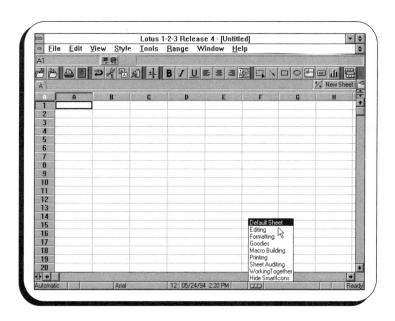

To switch from one palette to another, click on the desired palette name. You also can hide the icons by clicking on Hide SmartIcons.

If you point to an icon and press the *right* mouse button, a brief description of its purpose appears in the title bar (the top line of the screen).

PRESELECTING RANGES FOR ICONS

Many of the SmartIcons operate on whatever cell, or range, you have selected prior to clicking on the icon. For example, if you move the cellpointer to A3 and then click on the Boldface icon, the contents of A3 appears in boldface. If you select the range A3..B10 and then activate the Boldface icon, the contents of the entire range is boldfaced.

To preselect a range from the keyboard, press F4. Then use the cellpointer movement keys to highlight the desired range. Then press ENTER. Finally, activate the icon palette and select the icon you want to operate on the selected range.

To preselect a range with the mouse, click on a cell and drag the cellpointer. Then click on the icon you want to operate on the selected range.

ICON PALETTES

The following sections display all of the icons that appear when the given palette is selected. There is some redundancy because some icons appear in more than one palette.

The Default Palette

1 2 3 4 5 6 7 8 9 10 11 12 13 14 15 16 17 18 19 20 21 22 23 24

1. Opens another file without closing the current file.
2. Saves file to disk.
3. Prints the range you have selected.
4. Previews the current range you have selected for printing.
5. Undo last command or action, if UNDO is enabled.
6. Cut the selected range to the clipboard.
7. Copy the selected range to the clipboard.
8. Paste the clipboard contents to the currently selected range.
9. Builds @SUM function for cells above or to left of cellpointer.
10. Applies or removes boldface from the currently selected range.
11. Applies or removes italics from the currently selected range.
12. Underlines or removes existing underlines from range.
13. Left-aligns data in the currently selected range.
14. Center-aligns data in the currently selected range.
15. Right-aligns data in the currently selected range.
16. Fills the currently selected range with a sequence.
17. Selects multiple objects.
18. Draws an arrow.

19. Draws a rectangle or square.

20. Draws an oval.

21. Draws a text block.

22. Draws a macro button.

23. Charts data in the currently selected range.

24. Selects the next set of icons.

The Editing Palette

1 2   3   4   5 6   7   8   9   10   11 12 13 14   15 16 17 18 19 20 21 22 23   24

1. Opens another file without closing the current file.

2. Saves your file to disk.

3. Prints the range you have selected.

4. Previews the current range you have selected for printing.

5. Undoes last command or action, if UNDO is enabled.

6. Cuts the selected range to the clipboard.

7. Copies the selected range to the clipboard.

8. Pastes the clipboard contents to the currently selected range.

9. Deletes the current selection.

10. Deletes styles from the currently selected range.

11. Pastes cell contents.

12. Pastes cell styles.

13. Pastes a link.

14. Pastes formulas as values (destroys formulas).

15. Fills the currently selected range with a sequence.

16. Copies the left column in a range to other columns in range.

17. Copies the top row in a range to other rows in the range.

18. Transposes a selected row to a column, or vice versa.

19. Inserts rows.

20. Inserts columns.

21. Deletes rows.

22. Deletes columns.

23. Deletes worksheets.

24. Selects the next set of icons.

The Formatting Palette

1 2   3   4   5   6   7   8   9   10 11 12 13 14 15 16 17   18 19 20 21 22 23   24

1. Opens another file without closing the current file.
2. Saves your file to disk.
3. Prints the range you have selected.
4. Previews the current range you have selected for printing.
5. Undoes last command or action, if UNDO is enabled.
6. Cuts the selected range to the clipboard.
7. Copies the selected range to the clipboard.
8. Pastes the clipboard contents to the currently selected range.
9. Deletes styles from the currently selected range.
10. Applies or removes boldface from the currently selected range.
11. Applies or removes italics from the currently selected range.
12. Underlines or removes existing underlines from range.
13. Left-aligns data in the currently selected range.
14. Center-aligns data in the currently selected range.
15. Right-aligns data in the currently selected range.
16. Aligns data evenly in the selected range.
17. Rotates data in the currently selected range.
18. Adds or removes a border and drop shadow to the range.
19. Displays style templates for your selection.
20. Changes fonts and attributes.
21. Sets colors, patterns, borders, and frames.
22. Widens columns in selected range to fit the widest entries.
23. Copies styles to another range.
24. Selects the next set of icons.

The Goodies Palette

```
 1  2   3  4   5  6  7  8   9   10 11 12 13  14 15 16 17 18 19 20 21 22 23  24
```

1. Opens another file without closing the current file.
2. Saves your file to disk.
3. Prints the range you have selected.
4. Previews the current range you have selected for printing.
5. Undoes last command or action, if UNDO is enabled.
6. Cuts the selected range to the clipboard.
7. Copies the selected range to the clipboard.
8. Pastes the clipboard contents to the currently selected range.
9. Invokes versions and scenarios manager.
10. Hides or shows currently selected range.
11. Zooms in to increase size of cells.
12. Zoom out to decrease size of cells.
13. Cancels zoom in or zoom out; returns to default size.
14. Fills the currently selected range with a sequence.
15. Displays style templates for your selection.
16. Widens columns in selected range to fit widest entries.
17. Copies styles to another range.
18. Charts data in the currently selected range.
19. Creates a query table.
20. Crosstabs values from a database.
21. Audits cells.
22. Checks spelling.
23. Customizes icons.
24. Selects the next set of icons.

The Macro Building Palette

1 2 3 4 5 6 7 8 9 10 11 12 13 14 15 16 17 18 19 20 21 22 23

1. Opens another file without closing the current file.
2. Saves your file to disk.
3. Prints the range you have selected.
4. Previews the current range you have selected for printing.
5. Undoes last command or action, if UNDO is enabled.
6. Cuts the selected range to the clipboard.
7. Copies the selected range to the clipboard.
8. Pastes the clipboard contents to the currently selected range.
9. Toggles macro recording on or off.
10. Selects a macro to run.
11. Creates or deletes range names.
12. Runs the selected macro.
13. Toggles macro Trace mode on or off.
14. Toggles macro Step mode on or off.
15. Toggles macro Transcript window on or off.
16. Draws a macro button.
17. Inserts a range.
18. Deletes a range.
19. Moves cellpointer to nonblank/blank boundary downwards.
20. Moves cellpointer to nonblank/blank boundary upwards.
21. Invokes Dialog editor (create custom dialog box).
22. Starts macro translator (to translate Windows Release 1 to 4).
23. Selects the next set of icons.

The Printing Palette

1. Opens another file without closing the current file.
2. Saves your file to disk.
3. Prints the range you have selected.
4. Previews the current range you have selected for printing.
5. Undoes last command or action, if UNDO is enabled.
6. Cuts the selected range to the clipboard.
7. Copies the selected range to the clipboard.
8. Pastes the clipboard contents to the currently selected range.
9. Sets page layout for print job.
10. Selects range to print.
11. Sets columns to act as titles in print job.
12. Sets rows to act as titles in print job.
13. Sets portrait orientation for print job (standard).
14. Sets landscape orientation for print job (sideways).
15. Squeezes rows in print range to fit page.
16. Squeezes columns in print range to fit page.
17. Squeezes all rows and columns in print range to fit page.
18. Creates horizontal page break.
19. Creates vertical page break.
20. Zooms out (decrease size of display).
21. Discards zoom out effect.
22. Checks spelling.
23. Selects the next set of icons.

The Sheet Auditing Palette

1   2   3   4   5   6   7   8   9   10   11   12   13   14   15   16   17   18   19   20   21   22   23   24

1. Opens another file without closing the current file.
2. Saves your file to disk.
3. Prints the range you have selected.
4. Previews the current range you have selected for printing.
5. Undoes last command or action, if UNDO is enabled.
6. Cuts the selected range to the clipboard.
7. Copies the selected range to the clipboard.
8. Pastes the clipboard contents to the currently selected range.
9. Recalculates all formulas in the file.
10. Finds formulas in the worksheet.
11. Finds precedents for formulas.
12. Finds dependent cells for formulas.
13. Finds linking cells.
14. Finds DDE links.
15. Zooms out.
16. Zooms in.
17. Moves cellpointer to first cell in next range.
18. Moves cellpointer to first cell in previous range.
19. Moves cellpointer to HOME (A1).
20. Moves cellpointer to nonblank/blank boundary downwards.
21. Moves cellpointer to nonblank/blank boundary rightwards.
22. Moves cellpointer to nonblank/blank boundary upwards.
23. Moves cellpointer to nonblank/blank boundary leftwards.
24. Selects the next set of icons.

The Working Together Palette

1 2   3   4   5   6   7   8   9   10 11 12 13 14 15 16   17 18 19 20 21 22 23   24

1. Opens another file without closing the current file.
2. Saves your file to disk.
3. Prints the range you have selected.
4. Previews the current range you have selected for printing.
5. Undoes last command or action, if UNDO is enabled.
6. Cuts the selected range to the clipboard.
7. Copies the selected range to the clipboard.
8. Pastes the clipboard contents to the currently selected range.
9. Embeds data in the worksheet.
10. Applies or removes boldface from the currently selected range.
11. Applies or removes italics from the currently selected range.
12. Underlines or removes existing underlines from range.
13. Left-aligns data in the currently selected range.
14. Center-aligns data in the currently selected range.
15. Right-aligns data in the currently selected range.
16. Fills the currently selected range with a sequence.
17. Launches the Ami Pro word processor (not part of 1-2-3).
18. Starts Dialog editor.
19. Launches the Freelance graphics program (not part of 1-2-3).
20. Launches the Organizer program (not part of 1-2-3).
21. Launches the Improv program (not part of 1-2-3).
22. Launches Lotus Notes program (not part of 1-2-3).
23. Launches Lotus CC:Mail program (not part of 1-2-3).
24. Selects the next set of icons.

Indicators and Keyboard Shortcuts

TABLE E.1   Status Indicators

Status Indicator	Meaning
Calc	1-2-3 is in manual recalculation mode; formulas may not be showing current results. You should press F9 or click on the Calc indicator in the status bar before relying on the displayed values.
Caps	Caps Lock is active. All alphabetic characters you type will be uppercased.
Circ	You entered a formula containing a circular reference. For example, you entered +A1+1 *in* cell A1. You should click on the Circ indicator to find the circular reference unless you really intended to create it (you very seldom do).
Cmd	1-2-3 is in the middle of running a macro; the macro is in control of events.
End	You pressed the END key. 1-2-3 is waiting for you to follow up by pressing an arrow key. If you have changed your mind, you can toggle End by pressing it again.
File	You pressed CTRL+END. 1-2-3 thinks you want to move between active files.
Group	The current file is in Group mode; actions such as inserting or deleting rows will affect all worksheets in the group.
Mem	You are getting low on available memory. Less than 32 kilobytes remain available. If UNDO is active, you can free some memory by turning UNDO off.
Num	NumLock is active. The numeric keypad is ready for use and its direction keys will no longer work.

TABLE E.1 Continued

Status Indicator	Meaning
Pr	The current file is protected. You cannot save any changes you make unless you get the file reservation.
Scroll	Scroll lock is active. The arrow keys now will move the worksheet as well as the cellpointer.
Step	You have activated Step mode. This is used only for debugging macros.
Sst	You are executing a macro in Step mode.
Zoom	You pressed Alt+F6 to zoom the current pane to full-screen size (previously you created panes with View Split).

TABLE E.2 Mode Indicators

Mode	Meaning
Edit	You pressed F2 (the EDIT key), or else you are attempting to make an invalid entry (such as a formula with unbalanced parentheses).
Error	You have attempted some action that 1-2-3 cannot carry out, such as attempting to use a non-existent range name. You can press ESC to return to Ready mode.
Find	You are using the Tools Database Find-Records command to find records in a database. You can press F7 to break out of Find mode and return to Ready mode.
Label	You are entering a label into the current cell.
Menu	You have invoked one of the 1-2-3 menus; 1-2-3 is waiting for you to select a menu command.
Names	1-2-3 is displaying a list of names, such as range names, graph names, macro commands, or functions.
Point	1-2-3 is waiting for you to highlight a range.
Ready	1-2-3 is "idling" and is ready for any action you choose.
Value	You are entering a value (a number, function, or formula) into the current cell.
Wait	You cannot do anything until 1-2-3 completes the task currently underway, such as saving a file.

Each 1-2-3 function key is dedicated to a single task. Table E.3 shows each key and what task it carries out.

TABLE E.3   The Function Keys

Key	Function
F1 (HELP)	Opens the Help window and displays context-sensitive help for your current operation.
F2 (EDIT)	Puts 1-2-3 in Edit mode so that you can edit the current cell's contents.
F3 (NAME)	Displays a list of names related to the command you chose or range names for use in the formula you are creating.
F4	Used from Ready mode, F4 anchors the cellpointer so you can mark a range with the direction keys (rather than the mouse).
F4 (ABS)	Used from Edit, Point, or Value modes to change a formula reference from relative to absolute to mixed, depending on how many times you press the key.
F5 (GOTO)	Sends the cellpointer to the cell, named range, or named object. Works in the current worksheet by default; also can be used to go to a cell in another worksheet, or in another active file.
F6 (PANE)	Moves the cellpointer among horizontal, vertical, or perspective panes.
F7 (QUERY)	Updates data in a query table. Keyboard equivalent is Query Refresh Now.
F8 (TABLE)	Repeats last Range Analyze What-if Table command.
F9 (CALC)	From Ready mode, recalculates all formulas in all active files. From Edit mode (F2 followed by F9), strips away a formula value rule, leaving only the computed value in the cell.
F10 (MENU)	Activates the menu from the keyboard. Same effect as pressing ALT to activate the menu.

If you hold down the ALT key while pressing a function key, you get a different set of actions. Table E.4 shows each key and what task it carries out.

TABLE E.4   The ALT-C Function Key Combinations

Key Combination	Function
ALT+F1 (COMPOSE)	Creates nonstandard characters.
ALT+F2 (STEP)	Switches Step mode on and off for debugging macros.
ALT+F3 (RUN)	Displays a list of macros to run.
ALT+F4 (QUIT)	Same as File Quit
ALT+F6 (ZOOM PANE)	Enlarges the current pane to the full size of the window, or shrinks it to its original size.
ALT+F7 (ADD-IN 1) ALT+F8 (ADD-IN 2) ALT+F9 (ADD-IN 3)	Starts whatever 1-2-3 add-in you have assigned to the key.

Table E.5 explains key combinations for moving the cellpointer between worksheets in the current file. The key descriptions, in the form A+B, mean "press the first key and release it; then press the second key."

TABLE E.5 Moving Between Worksheets

Key Combination	Action
CTRL+HOME	Moves the cellpointer to cell A1 of the top sheet in the current file. Won't work if column A is hidden or if worksheet titles are set.
CTRL+PGDN	Moves cellpointer to the previous worksheet in the current file. Used to move quickly from sheet to sheet.
CTRL+PGUP	Moves the cellpointer to the next worksheet in the current file. Mirror image of CTRL+PGDN.
END CTRL+HOME	Moves the cellpointer to bottom right corner of the last sheet in the current file.
END CTRL+PGDN	Moves the cellpointer up through worksheets in the current file, placing the cellpointer in the END HOME position in each worksheet.
END CTRL+PGUP	Mirror image of END CTRL+PGDN.
CTRL+END HOME	Moves the cellpointer to the current cell in the first active file.
CTRL+END END	Moves the cellpointer to the current cell in the last active file.

1-2-3 has a set of keyboard shortcuts for performing common actions, as listed in Table E.6. You can accomplish the same things from the menu or from the icon palettes, but often the keyboard shortcuts are faster. Many of these keyboard shortcuts also appear on the menu, as a reminder of their existence.

TABLE E.6 Keyboard Shortcuts and Menu Equivalents

Key	Action
ALT+F4	Ends the 1-2-3 session, prompting you to save your work; same as File Exit.
CTRL+letter	Runs a backslash macro, such as \A. Same as Tools Macro Run, but faster.
	Note about CTRL+letter: Do not name backslash macros with letters that correspond to keyboard shortcut letters or the keyboard shortcuts will be disabled. For example, if you name a cell \B, CTRL+B will be assigned to the macro rather than to the keyboard shortcut.
CTRL+B	Boldfaces the currently selected range. If the range is already boldface, removes the boldface.

TABLE E.6 Continued

Key	Action
CTRL+C or CTRL+INS	Copies both contents and styles from the selected range to the Clipboard; same as Edit Copy.
CTRL+DEL	Deletes both contents and styles from the selected range.
CTRL+E	Center-aligns data in the selected range.
CTRL+F4	Closes the current file; same as File Close.
CTRL+GRAY MINUS	Deletes columns, rows, or worksheets; same as Edit Delete.
CTRL+GRAY PLUS	Inserts columns, rows, or worksheets; same as Edit Insert.
CTRL+I	Italicizes the selected range, or removes italics from the selected range.
CTRL+L	Left-aligns contents of the selected range.
CTRL+N	Removes bold, italic, and underlining from the selected range.
CTRL+O	Displays the File Open dialog box; same as File Open.
CTRL+P	Displays the File Print dialog box; same as File Print.
CTRL+R	Right-aligns contents of the selected range.
CTRL+S	Saves the current file; same as File Save.
CTRL+U	Underlines contents of the selected range, or removes existing underlining.
CTRL+V or SHIFT+INS	Pastes styles from the clipboard to selected range; same as Edit Paste.
CTRL+X or SHIFT+DEL	Cuts contents and styles from the selected range to the clipboard; same as Edit Cut.
CTRL+Z or ALT+BACKSPACE	Invokes UNDO. Same as Edit Undo.
DEL	Deletes any contents of the selected range, without cutting them to the clipboard. Be careful—works on data, charts, and drawn objects. Same as Edit Clear Cell contents only.

Index